High Inflation

ARNE RYDE

8 December 1944–1 April 1968

High Inflation

The Arne Ryde Memorial Lectures

Daniel Heymann
and
Axel Leijonhufvud

CLARENDON PRESS · OXFORD
1995

Oxford University Press, Walton Street, Oxford OX2 6DP

Oxford New York
Athens Auckland Bangkok Bombay
Calcutta Cape Town Dar es Salaam Delhi
Florence Hong Kong Istanbul Karachi
Kuala Lumpur Madras Madrid Melbourne
Mexico City Nairobi Paris Singapore
Taipei Tokyo Toronto
and associated companies in
Berlin Ibadan

Oxford is a trade mark of Oxford University Press

Published in the United States
by Oxford University Press Inc., New York

British Library Cataloguing in Publication Data
Data available

Library of Congress Cataloging in Publication Data
Data available
ISBN 0–19–828844–1

1 3 5 7 9 10 8 6 4 2

Set by Hope Services (Abingdon) Ltd.
Printed in Great Britain
on acid-free paper by
Biddles Ltd.
Guildford & King's Lynn

The Arne Ryde Foundation

ARNE RYDE was an exceptionally promising young student on the doctorate programme at the Department of Economics at the University of Lund. He died after an automobile accident in 1968 when only twenty-three years old. In his memory his parents Valborg Ryde and pharmacist Sven Ryde established the Arne Ryde Foundation for the advancement of research at our department. We are most grateful to them. The Foundation has made possible important activities which our ordinary resources could not have afforded.

In agreement with Valborg and Svan Ryde, we have decided to use the funds made available by the Foundation to finance major initiatives. Since 1973 we have arranged a series of symposia in various fields of theoretical and applied economics. In 1990 we published 'Seven Schools of Macroeconomic Thought' by Edmund S. Phelps, the first issue in a series of Arne Ryde Memorial Lectures. Thomas J. Sargent's 'Bounded Rationality in Macroeconomics' followed in 1993. The present book by Professors Daniel Heymann and Axel Leijonhufvud, based on the lectures they held at Snogeholm Castle in Skane in May 1989, is the third issue in this series. We are very glad and grateful that Professor Heymann and Professor Leijonhufvud agreed to come to Lund to give their Arne Ryde Memorial lectures.

Bjørn Thalberg

Acknowledgments

This book originated as the 1989 Arne Ryde Memorial Lectures which we gave at Snogeholm Castle that year. We thank Bjørn Thalberg for the invitation to give the lectures and him and his staff for the wonderful hospitality that we enjoyed.

We subsequently decided to expand on the lectures in the hope of making the book more useful and the argument stronger. One result has been a long delay in completing the work as other duties kept us occupied in Buenos Aires and Los Angeles, respectively. We should thank Professor Thalberg also for his patience in this connection.

The list of people whose ideas, comments and help have contributed to this book has lengthened in the interim. DH has borrowed extensively from joint work with Fernando Navajas, Alfredo Canavese, and Pablo Sanguinetti, and benefited much from conversations with them. Thanks are also due to Alberto Fracchia, José Fanelli, Roberto Frenkel and José Luis Machinea for frequent discussions of the inflation problem in general and the 'Argentine syndrome' in particular. Part of the material has been presented in seminars and lectures: the present version owes much to the feedback from commentators and students. Thus, Sebastián Galiani contributed useful comments on Chapter 2 and the Appendix while doing graduate work at the Instituto Torcuato Di Tella. The Office of CEPAL in Buenos Aires provided DH with a stimulating environment, which greatly facilitated the task of working on the book 'after hours'. CEPAL colleagues and in particular the present and former members of the Macro team—Ricardo Martínez, Esteban Vesperoni, Aníbal Aller, Sebastián Scheimberg, Paul Nicholson and Fabiana Ibáñez—gave much encouragement and support. Of course, CEPAL is not to be held responsible for the views and opinions expressed in this book.

On a more personal note, DH would like to express his gratitude to Cristina F. Bramuglia for her continued help and interest in the work. Federico and Nicolás while growing up during these years also raised his spirits.

AL wishes especially to thank Spiro Latsis for his support of the UCLA Center for Computable Economics and Robert W. Clower and Kumaraswamy 'Vela' Velupillai for countless conversations over the years as well as for specific comments on this book. Peter Howitt, Seonghwan Oh, Christof Rühl, Federico Sturzenegger, and Mariano Tommasi gave detailed comments that were of great help in the final stages of the work. Caroline Shin provided cheerful assistance with the checking of references and the production of successive drafts.

AL's debt of gratitude to Earlene Craver goes far beyond the extensive comments and stylistic suggestions that she contributed to this book.

The usual disavowal is very much in order: the friends and colleagues mentioned above are not responsible for our opinions or errors.

UN Economic Commission for Latin America (CEPAL)
Buenos Aires

Center for Computable Economics
University of California, Los Angeles

Contents

1
Introduction

Deep depressions and high inflations are the two extremes of monetary instability. This book will concentrate on very high inflations. We intend to analyse these processes in some detail, using received theory as we find it helpful. But we also believe that some important aspects of them are not captured by standard theory. Its assumptions about individual decision-making abilities and systemic co-ordination do not allow a good representation of these turbulent economic processes.

This book distinguishes between 'moderate', 'high' and hyperinflations. We consider an inflation to be in the 'moderate' range as long as people who live through it generally remain content to quote the inflation rate in per cent per year. In 'high inflations', people measure inflation in per cent per month, and consider annual figures meaningless except for historical purposes. When the effective horizon for useful forecasts of prices falls below one month, we consider the economy to be in hyperinflation. The conventional criterion for hyperinflation since Philip Cagan's now classic study has been a rate of price rise of 50 per cent per month. This appears to be in rough accord with our behavioural definition. Those who prefer having approximate numerical boundaries for 'high inflations' might think of them as in the range between, say, 5 per cent per month and Cagan's 50 per cent. But the behavioural definition is worth bearing in mind since it carries the reminder that high inflations are invariably associated with short planning horizons.[1]

Twentieth-century history shows several 'epidemics' of high inflation. The inflations that Argentina, Bolivia, Brazil, Israel,

[1] We are used to measuring an acceleration of inflation in terms of the percentage change in the rate of price increases over some conventionally defined time span. But it is often useful to think of it instead in terms of the shrinkage of the time period over which a given percentage change in prices is realized.

Mexico, and Peru suffered through during the 1980s, and that most of the republics of the former Soviet Union are undergoing today, exemplify the type of inflation that is our subject. Although we are not concerned with describing particular country experiences, our material derives mostly from the Latin American cases (especially that of Argentina), and from the European episodes of the 1920s.

To a contemporary Western European or North American audience, these may seem somewhat distant and exotic phenomena. Why devote the Ryde Lectures to such 'special cases'? Arguments for so doing can be made at three distinct levels of discourse.

At the level of *applied macroeconomics*, the subject is obviously of critical importance to the countries affected. In production and distribution, efficiency suffers. The financial structure is impaired and capital accumulation is reduced. To people who have to live through them, these high inflations become a source of highly costly, constant disruptions of their daily lives in the present and, for most of them, an obstacle to a better life in the future. Consequently, these inflations become the dominant, daily political concern of governments.

Until fairly recently, hyperinflations have received more attention from economists than the 'merely' high ones. The high inflations, however, can be sustained for years, but hyperinflations cannot. We need a better understanding than we now have of the economic costs and the social and political consequences of this type of monetary instability. Once mired in high inflation, a country finds it exceedingly hard to extricate itself even though the costs have become apparent to everyone. A better grasp of the process would be helpful also in the design of stabilization strategies.

At the level of *general macrotheory*, observational 'outliers' should be of particular interest in a non-experimental field. The study of pathological system-states can draw our attention to aspects of 'healthy' states the importance of which we might otherwise not realize. It will suggest what features of the normally functioning economy are the most and the least resilient, and what happens when they are absent. The extremes of monetary instability can give us a clearer picture of the purposes that money and financial institutions serve under more normal circumstances and thus deepen our understanding of the benefits of monetary stability.

To call high inflations 'pathological' is, of course, to prejudge the nature of these processes. It needs to be said from the outset, however, that we so regard them (although our reasons for so doing will have to come later). This is not a view generally shared in the theoretical literature. At the other extreme of monetary instability, in contrast, deep depressions are so regarded. The Great Depression remains an anomaly that is acknowledged as a large and important unsolved puzzle also in the most recent literature. In our view, important aspects of these high inflations should also be recognized as anomalies that challenge our theoretical understanding.

At the level of *analytical approach*, finally, our choice of subject matter heightens the tension inherent in so much of present-day macroeconomics between a traditional concern with 'disordered' states of the world and a modern commitment to optimization and equilibrium methods. The issues concerning the most appropriate analytical representation of high inflation processes are difficult and contentious. But they should be secondary. If the method of representation is made primary, there is always a danger that ill-fitting aspects of the subject matter will be overlooked and ignored. The primary objective is to understand the high inflation processes themselves better. Economies in high inflations do not function well. We want to know in what respects they function badly, and we want to try to understand why.

OVERVIEW

Chapter 2 draws entirely on the existing literature on our subject. It is not, however, intended as a comprehensive survey of inflation theory. We neglect that very large part of it which is concerned mainly with moderate inflations in order to focus on that which deals specifically with high inflations. Even here we

are selective (and subjective). Two models, each representative
of a distinct theoretical tradition, are discussed and some minor
variations on each considered. Our objective is to give the
reader an overview of the main ideas of the two lines of analysis and to give our own assessment of their strengths and weaknesses. From an applied standpoint, both help us understand
the conditions that have to be fulfilled and some of the difficulties that have to be overcome for monetary stabilization to be
possible. Thus, these are undeniably useful theories. At the
same time, however, they are remarkably uninformative about
the consequences of inflation. They tell us very little about how
high inflation affects economic performance and, even less, how
it may affect social and political conditions. These limitations
of applied inflation theory suggest to us that the underlying
(more or less 'pure') monetary theory is in an unsatisfactory
state. But our reflections on those matters will have to wait until
the last chapter.

Chapter 3 does, however, take a first step in that direction. It
asks how received inflation theory needs to be changed in order
for it at all to accommodate the various effects on the functioning of the economy which the two following chapters
describe and analyse. It proceeds to argue that steady-state
models in particular assume that the reciprocal interaction
between the public and the private sector is both simple and
transparent to both sides and that the inflation rate outcome of
it, therefore, is fairly predictable to everyone involved. This, we
believe, misrepresents not only the extent but also the nature of
the uncertainty that decision-makers face in high inflation conditions. The complexity of the dynamic interaction of policy-
makers and private sector agents is such as to fashion a high
inflation monetary regime in which all parties have abnormal
difficulties in calculating the future outcomes of present actions.

The following three chapters deal respectively with the financial problems that governments typically have to wrestle with in
a high inflation (Chapter 4), with the private sector's various
adaptations to high inflation conditions (Chapter 5), and with
the difficulties of finding a policy strategy that can be sustained
through disinflation to lasting stabilization (Chapter 6). These

chapters seek above all to describe how a high inflation economy differs in various respects from an economy operating under conditions of relative monetary stability, and to explain how these differences arise from the attempts by public and private decision-makers to adapt as best they can to an unstable environment.

A high inflation is typically a symptom of a deep-seated crisis in the public finances. The general picture is one of governments unable to gain control over fiscal policies. Under strong pressures to spend, they lack the corresponding capacity to tax or to borrow. This high inflation fiscal syndrome is a vicious circle: high inflation results from the political inability to put the public finances on a sound and regular basis; at the same time, it makes rational fiscal management all but impossible by disrupting the budgeting of expenditures, by wrecking the tax collection system, and by ruining the government's credit.

Chapter 4 sketches a simple model of inflationary taxation which differs from standard models in making the discrepancy between the 'desired' level of spending and attainable tax revenues, rather than the actually recorded deficit, the fiscal impulse driving the inflation. The pressure on the government to attempt to command more resources than regular taxes will allow is taken to be the outcome of an underlying political game. The higher the pressure to maximize spending in the short run, the higher is the corresponding stable steady-state inflation rate. The deficit, on the other hand, is endogenous in this model and need not be monotonically related to either the 'fiscal inconsistency' or inflation. Chapter 4 proceeds to discuss problems of debt management, of tax administration, and of expenditure budgeting under high inflation. Unresolved distributional conflicts between social groups block agreement on an effective tax system. Meanwhile, the inflation itself erodes real tax revenues. It also makes budget projections for periods as long as a fiscal year practically impossible. Consequently, the demands on the budget by various sectors and interest groups can not be settled for the coming year in one comprehensive political negotiation. Instead, the government ends up dealing with these groups bilaterally and sequentially—a process which tends to perpetuate excessive reliance on the inflation tax. These characteristics of the 'fiscal game' mean that both the volume and composition of government receipts and disbursements vary erratically. The market for public debt, however, is apt to be so thin that the monetary authorities are largely unable to smooth these high-frequency variations in the cash-deficit. High inflation fiscal regimes, therefore, are inherently volatile.

The behaviour of markets under conditions of high and hyperinflation is the subject of Chapter 5. This begins with an analysis of inflation tax distortions, focusing on the effects of anticipated price increases on transaction costs. However, these effects of inflation, even if non-trivial, are overshadowed by the consequences of the instability of the economic environment. Although people use more time and effort to gather and process information, their ability to make reasonably precise forecasts greatly deteriorates. Among the various responses to such conditions, the disappearance of long-term financial markets is the most notable. Although new types of instruments incorporating sundry adjustment clauses emerge, the economy finds no good substitute for the nominal contracting which prevails in all stable monetary regimes. Moreover, the unwillingness of agents to make irreversible commitments over medium-to-long horizons manifests itself also in reluctance to sink resources in physical investments.

In 'mere' high inflations, ordinary day-to-day trades are not significantly disrupted. But as information about past prices loses relevance for judging future market conditions, consumers find it harder to engage in comparison shopping. Spot markets become more segmented and local prices more sensitive to specific shocks and to idiosyncratic expectations. The overall picture is that of a system which is less well co-ordinated both across space and over time. The limit is reached in 'proper' hyperinflations where even routine exchanges become problematic. When sellers are placed in a setting where they cannot reliably predict even the most immediate outcome of doing business, they react by simply limiting trades to a minimum.

Although the national money has become costly as a medium of exchange and unreliable as a unit of account, no equally useful alternative to these functions of money emerges. Foreign moneys replace domestic money as stores of value and real money balances held in dollars may often far exceed those held in domestic currency. But while 'dollarization' of some prices and transactions is observed, it does not provide a stable standard for price-setting, and currency substitution does not become at all general in the execution of ordinary transactions.

Disinflating can be done quickly, but stabilizing takes longer. The inflation rate may be brought down very abruptly, but lasting stabilization demands that people both in and out of government modify patterns of behaviour that have become ingrained through prolonged experience with inflation. Chapter 6 discusses the design and management of stabilization programmes, based on the historical experiences considered throughout the book. The chapter starts with a brief analysis of the stages that programmes must pass through from initial disinflation to eventual stabilization. Historically, most programmes included measures and announcements—especially on the fiscal and monetary fronts—which signalled a clear break with the inflationary past. But their execution was not a mere unfolding of a completely pre-specified plan. Although private expectations may respond positively to initial policy announcements, the private sector will not act in anticipation of success before actual experience gives tangible indications of the programme's effectiveness. The evidence suggests, therefore, that concrete governmental commitments must be combined with a good deal of adaptive management 'along the way'.

Stabilizations have to obey certain general principles, but they are also historically contingent. Fiscal policies must necessarily be brought under control but no two countries will start from the same situation or choose exactly the same mix of specific measures. The chapter briefly reviews various types of policy actions and their usefulness in the disinflation phase and beyond. These include both measures of a transitory nature, such as those intended to break the initial inflationary inertia, and reforms designed to modify the policy regime over the longer run. We pay particular attention to some of the conflicts

between components of a programme that may have to be faced
as it runs its course.

Finally, Chapter 6 considers the changes in macroeconomic
behaviour that can be expected to occur along the stabilization
path. Sudden disinflations are likely to produce recoveries in
real output and significant shifts in relative prices. Stabilization
will increase wealth in the aggregate, but agents will find it difficult to form accurate wealth perceptions in the new environment. This difficulty may induce cyclical movements in
spending and output. In more general terms, successful
stabilization will noticeably improve the performance of the
economy; by the same token, it will change the type of macro-
analysis most relevant to the economy in question.

One simple analytical theme runs like an undertone through
these chapters and it is helpful to keep track of it. We sometimes interpret observed behaviour as adapting to events after
the fact, sometimes as responding in pre-calculated fashion to
foreseen contingencies. Modern theory obviously maximizes its
reliance on the latter mode but must still make room for learning from experience. We may think of economic models as
arrayed on a spectrum of behaviour representations. At the
'adaptive' extreme of this spectrum lie models of behaviour governed exclusively by feedback. Behaviour is backward-looking
and, in the simplest case, reacts only to immediate past experience. At the 'pre-calculating' extreme we find the infinite horizon dynamic programming models of recent vintage. Infinite
foresight makes them basically teleological, whereas the adaptive ones are causal.

Both extremes have properties that caricature, more than represent, actual economic systems. Infinite horizon intertemporal
optimization models present a world of 'efficient' markets pricing nothing but 'fundamentals' where bubbles and the effects of
disturbances are smoothed (not to say smothered) by rational
agents who take the infinitely long view. Feedback governed
models, on the other hand, almost always contain nonlinear
response functions and produce complex dynamics much too
easily, with agents stubbornly sticking to short-sighted rules of
behaviour that they could easily change to their own advantage.

A market in which price adapts in response to excess demand while output adapts to marginal profit will tend to 'hog-cycle', for example.

The real world has its being somewhere between these two extremes. Economies that manage to maintain a fairly high degree of monetary stability provide an environment that enables people to plan far ahead and provide for a fairly distant future. Consequently, a rich and 'deep' financial structure gradually evolves such that, for a great many analytical purposes, the complete intertemporal markets model peopled by optimizing agents, although still a caricature, becomes a useful approximation. In high inflation economies, on the other hand, planning horizons become very short, long-term commitments are shunned and, as a result, most of the financial institutions and intertemporal markets characteristic of stable industrialized economies wither away. While people spend more time and effort trying to divine what the future will bring, the high inflation environment is such as to shift their behaviour away from the pre-calculated, intertemporal optimizing behavioural mode towards the reactive, feedback governed mode. This, moreover, is as true of those responsible for government policy as it is for decision-makers in the private sector. This turn towards short-sighted adaptive behaviour tends to eliminate stabilizing speculation and the various shock-absorbers that normally dampen the dynamics of economic variables. The result is the complex dynamics revealed, for example, in the turbulence of relative prices that is so characteristic of all high inflations.

But, if this generalization is sound, there is something seriously amiss with contemporary monetary theory. Modern economic theory is routinely constructed in purely non-monetary terms, leaving the theorist with a choice of devices, none of them very satisfactory, whereby money may be appended to the resulting 'real' systems so that money prices can be determined. This is the procedure also in modern finance theory. In these constructions, money may affect real magnitudes through the so-called inflation tax. But the mere lack of 'super-neutrality', that such inflation tax effects imply, will not change virtually all aspects of 'real behaviour' in the pervasive manner sketched above. The non-neutrality of money must run deeper than present-day recipes for integrating monetary and value theory would suggest.

Chapter 7 explores this issue at some length and eventually proposes a different perspective from which to approach the core issues of monetary theory. Rather than theorizing about a system whose structure is simple relative to the cognitive capabilities of 'rational economic man', we might better focus on the institutions that have evolved to make possible a 'division of labour' in society that is far too complex for typical human beings fully to comprehend and control. 'Money' belongs among these institutions. By simplifying economic calculation, communication, and co-ordination, money reduces the demands made on the cognitive abilities of boundedly rational agents and allows them to develop patterns of co-operation of a complexity that would not be feasible in a non-monetary economy. High inflation severely impairs this basic function of monetary institutions. In so doing, it creates an environment where the rational calculation and co-ordination of long-term strategies becomes too difficult for people to handle. It is in this way, we believe, that monetary disorder forces people away from pre-calculated long-horizon optimization towards the shorter-term, feedback-governed adaptive behaviour that generates the phenomena characteristic of economies in the grip of high inflation.

2
Models of High Inflation

What is the cause of inflation? This seems a straightforward question and a likely place to begin. Yet it is one of those questions to which no one's answer commands universal assent and over which contentious debate goes on without an end in sight. This suggests that the question itself is less straightforward than it looks at first.

Inflation is the observable outcome of a complex process of political and economic interaction in society. In such a context, 'cause-and-effect' language easily becomes misleading. Behind the rise in a general price index lies the pricing decisions of innumerable firms and individuals. In a non-trivial sense, those actions are the most direct 'cause' of inflation. But, of course, the decisions to revise prices are motivated by market and policy signals. And these, in turn, are at the end of other chains of causation. Each asserted cause brings into view one or more prior causes of which it may be the effect—and some of these causal chains loop back on themselves, effects at one stage becoming causes at another. Building a complete model of these economic and 'extra-economic' interactions is an impossible task. Of necessity, the economist must begin by deciding which links between variables he will concentrate on and how far he should try to go in the quest for a 'deep enough' explanation. How these decisions should be made is never obvious. In the absence of a comprehensive inflation theory, alternative models coexist. Each of them has its strengths and its weaknesses.

A rise in money prices is the 'effect' that has to be explained. The most immediate reasons for the rise in prices are presumably to be found by studying pricing behaviour in product markets. But economists in fact know rather little about pricing decisions, being more fond of explaining how people choose quantities when prices are given than of explaining how they set prices. So there is not much definite knowledge at this level of proximate causation. Many of the existing models either assume that prices continuously clear markets along an inflationary path, or postulate some simple pricing rule, like a constant mark-up. Such modelling devices do not provide a description of how prices are formed in actual market settings. This state of the art may be unsatisfactory, but this is not to say that it is easily remedied. Inquiry into pricing behaviour is likely to lead back to 'rising costs', which may be somewhat informative but does not tell much about the underlying factors driving the inflationary process. To concentrate on the immediate determinants of the price level also tends to divert attention away from money, since the aggregate money stock is not a good candidate for inclusion in structural equations explaining the prices of particular commodities.

'Inflation is always and everywhere a monetary phenomenon', insists Milton Friedman. Indeed, a theory meant to explain the ongoing decline in the purchasing power of money can hardly avoid dealing with the supply and demand for money. It is a truly well-documented empirical regularity that all persistent inflations are accompanied by a rising stock of nominal money (although recent advances in theory have deprived us of the understanding as to why this should necessarily be so (cf. Hahn 1983, pp. 13, 71)). Yet the channels which transform monetary impulses into price changes are neither simple nor direct. Moreover, it is clear that money is in no sense an ultimate cause of inflation. Even the most determined monetarist, who would insist that money causes prices and never the reverse, can hardly avoid the further question: Why do governments choose to let the money stock increase at an inflationary rate?

In high inflations, the money supply is typically driven by the financing requirements of the government. But the fiscal deficit itself can be considered an endogenous variable. Thus, the causal chain that dominates attention in the high inflation literature traces back from (i) prices to (ii) money to (iii) fiscal deficits to (iv) the political factors influencing the behaviour of governments. At this point, the move to endogenize what at a previous level of discourse was taken as exogenous requires the economist to enlarge his system in ways that often take him into unfamiliar territory. The attempts to explain government behaviour are apt to lead away from the theoretically general into the historical and political particulars of various times and places, or else to generate models which, in fact, are applicable only to a limited number of episodes.

This does not mean, however, that one can rest content with a theory that disregards the analysis of how government policies are determined. As the Lucas critique makes clear—and expectations need not be perfectly 'rational' for the critique to be germane—agents will respond differently to given impulses depending on the process that generates them. There is no escape, therefore, from the need to consider the policy regime within which the inflation is occurring and the various ways in which agents adapt to it.

The literature on high inflation does in fact reflect the regime dependence of behaviour. In this chapter we shall look at the logic and qualitative implications of two distinct 'families' of simple high inflation models. (A more formal exposition is contained in the Appendix.) Both groups of models incorporate features which are specific to high inflation regimes and which clearly distinguish them from inflation models of an earlier generation.[1] Thus, models of a quantity theory lineage typically assume that the central bank passively accommodates fiscal demands, while the 'non-monetary' models of structuralist ancestry concentrate on the effects of price or wage-setting practices based on backward-looking indexation. This selective sampling of the existing literature is meant as an introduction to our more detailed discussion of government policies, pricing

---

[1] Surveys of inflation theory of different 'generations' can be found in Bronfenbrenner and Holzman (1963), Laidler and Parkin (1975), Lipsey (1981) and Frisch (1983). All of these are almost exclusively concerned with moderate inflations. There is a growing recent literature on high inflations: see, for example, Heymann (1986), Dornbusch *et al.* (1990).

behaviour, and portfolio choices in high inflation which follows in Chapters 3 through 6.

THE INFLATION TAX

The government's budget constraint

The link between fiscal deficits and money growth may be tight or loose.[2] The willingness of the public to absorb government debt sets limits on the cumulative deficits that can be sustained without borrowing from the central bank (cf. McCallum 1984). But within those limits, in countries with well developed financial markets where prospective lenders retain confidence in the State's solvency, current deficits and current changes in the money stock need not correspond at all. The central bank retains the ability to choose the amount of government paper in its portfolio and can also vary its credit to the banking system. In such circumstances—with all due regard to intertemporal constraints—the traditional sharp distinction between monetary and fiscal policies continues to hold.

That is not the case in unstable economies, even as a first approximation. Here, governments usually do not have much access to capital markets, yet cannot abstain from borrowing. At the margin, the central bank becomes the only ready taker of government bonds in significant amounts, so that deficits are routinely monetized. Central banks lack the instruments to offset for more than very short periods the monetary expansion they produce through their loans to the government. Moreover, the central banks commonly generate large 'quasi-fiscal' deficits themselves, through the interest on their own liabilities held by the banks, through sales of foreign exchange at multiple rates, or through the granting of rediscounts where repayment is not seriously expected. Thus, the typical picture is one where no

---

[2] We will not discuss the problems involved in defining and measuring the government deficit. The issues currently being debated include how to deal with capital gains and losses, how to treat contingent claims, and how to account for the activities of decentralized agencies (including the Central Bank). See for example Buiter (1983), Eisner (1984), Eisner and Pieper (1984), Tanzi, Blejer and Teijeiro (1987), and Blejer and Cheasty (1991).

clear line can be drawn between fiscal and monetary policies. Not only do the central banks accommodate the demands from government treasuries, they also serve as 'off-budget' channels for the transfer of resources to various groups.

These stylized facts suggest a strategic simplification for the modelling of the government's budget constraint (cf. section A1 in the Appendix). Simple monetary-fiscal models of high inflation assume that the government borrows only from the central bank and, conversely, that the central bank engages in no other transactions than the financing of the government through the issue of money. Consequently, deficits[3] automatically increase the stock of base money and are also the only source of money creation. These models often take the real deficit as an exogenously determined quantity; causality, therefore, runs from the deficit to the rate of money growth. As a consequence, money is 'passive' not only with respect to changes in fiscal policies but also with respect to changes in the price level (Sargent and Wallace 1973*a*; Sargent 1977).

The condition that determines the money supply can then be summarized very simply: at every moment, the real value of the nominal increase in the monetary base (seigniorage) must match the excess of government real spending over receipts. In a continuous time representation, this means (cf. section A1 of the Appendix):

$$(1) \qquad d_t = \frac{D_t}{P_t} = \frac{\dot{M}_t}{P_t}$$

where D and d measure the nominal and real deficit, respectively, and $\dot{M}$ is the time derivative of the stock of base money. Equivalently:

$$(2) \ (A6)^4 \qquad d_t = \dot{m}_t + m_t \pi_t = \mu_t m_t$$

---

[3] In analyzing the intertemporal budget constraint of the government, one must distinguish between the total and the 'primary' (net of interest) deficit. Since by hypothesis the public holds no government debt, this distinction is immaterial in the present context.

[4] Here, and in what follows, the second label of an equation refers to the corresponding formula in the Appendix. Some derivations and extensions are included there.

where m indicates the real stock of base money ($\dot{m}$ is its time derivative), π denotes the inflation rate and μ the proportional rate of increase of the nominal quantity of base money.

Thus, the rate of base money growth equals the ratio of the real deficit to the real money stock.[5] The total seigniorage may be decomposed into the change in the real volume of base money and the loss of purchasing power on the existing stock due to price inflation. This last component of seigniorage has the interpretation of an 'inflation tax': the holders of non-interest bearing debt (base money) suffer a capital loss when prices rise; if the real money stock is to remain constant, agents must 'purchase' from the central bank nominal money for the same real value; they thus surrender command over real resources, which is transferred to the government. In the monetary-fiscal analysis of high inflation, price increases stem from the government's need to collect this inflation tax.

Closing the model: from money to prices

The simplest and best-known models of inflation start from the premise that the natural approach to explaining the decline in the value of money is to focus on the supply and demand for money. Their main elements, consequently, are the following (cf. the Appendix, section A2):

(i)   a *money supply function.* This is assumed to reflect policy decisions, summarized here in the value of the fiscal deficit.

(ii)   a *money demand function*, relating the desired volume of real cash balances to real income and the nominal interest rate.[6] Assuming that the 'average state of expectations' relevant for

[5] This is true when the flows are measured in continuous time; the discrete time representation is slightly different. This difference need not detain us here: it remains the case that money growth depends on fiscal policies and the economy's 'degree of monetization'.

[6] In the simplest formulation, 'M' is defined as base money, and its demand assimilated to a standard money demand function. The behaviour of banks as a factor in high inflations is then neglected. In some historical instances, reserve requirements on demand deposits have been so high that 'M' could be approximated by M_1. Brock (1989) discusses the use of reserve requirements as instruments to collect the inflation tax and presents evidence suggesting that the legal reserve ratio usually grows with inflation.

money demand decisions can be unambiguously defined and that the Fisher equation holds, the nominal interest rate is decomposed into the perceived real rate of interest and the corresponding inflation rate expected to prevail until the next revision of plans. That is:

$$(3) \, (A7) \qquad m_t^d = y_t f(r_t + \pi_t^e)$$

where y and r are real income and the *ex ante* real interest rate, while π_t^e indicates the expected rate of price inflation.

(iii)   a *portfolio balance equation*, expressing the condition that the economy will be in such a state that the money stock is willingly held.

The portfolio balance condition does not by itself close the system. To derive a price level sequence some additional assumptions have to be made. Equations (1) to (3) are sometimes appended to a growth model, which determines real income and the interest rate from purely 'real' factors, independently of the behaviour of nominal variables. The result is a 'dichotomy': the model provides a relationship between money and prices in which the real quantities enter simply as parameters.

In this class of models, therefore, money is not only 'neutral' but 'superneutral', i.e., the steady-state inflation rate does not affect steady-state real income or the return to capital. This, of course, disregards the possibility (much emphasized in similar contexts in the 1960s) that inflation might induce subsitution away from money into real capital. To our knowledge, this 'Tobin effect' has not been empirically confirmed, however, and it has played no role in the discussion of high inflations.[7]

In dealing with high inflations, the nominal–real dichotomy is often rationalized less formally by arguing that movements in real income and the real interest rate are of second order magnitude compared to the changes in the level and rate of change of prices (cf. Cagan 1956). This seems reasonable enough if the

---

[7] Orphanides and Solow (1990, p. 225) comment: 'We know of no study of hyperinflations that mentions the Tobin effect! If the money and growth literature is relevant to anything, this must be where it fits in.' We could not agree more.

only thing we want from inflation theory is a first approximation of the time-path of nominal prices over periods of some
length. But models of the Cagan type are too simple to do at
all well in explaining short-run price level movements. And, if
we are interested also in the real consequences of high inflation,
then this mode of reasoning assumes away the entire problem.

Price expectations and money demand dynamics

One element is still missing before one can identify the set of
price level sequences consistent with a given fiscal policy. The
rate of inflation that generates enough seigniorage revenue to
finance the deficit depends on money demand which, in turn,
varies with inflationary expectations. Although the fiscal deficit
is the only exogenous driving variable of the system, the price
level path will depend on how forecasts are formed.[8]

Money demand and inflationary steady states

We do not have compelling reasons to assert that agents form
their expectations in a particular way, independently of the current context and of the economy's history. Yet, 'reasonable'
expectations ought to satisfy some minimal consistency conditions. One such condition is that, if the economy has settled into
a (deterministic) steady state, the anticipated values of the relevant variables coincide with actual values. Both rational and
adaptive expectations have this property. Once the condition is
met, the characteristics of the steady states do not depend on
the specific expectational scheme.

For inflation to be in steady state, the amount of real balances demanded at the inflation rate in question has to be such
as to yield an inflation tax equal to the (fixed) government
deficit. That is:

---

[8] Note that the only expectations that matter in this class of models are
those that feed into the system via money demand. Taking real income as parametric means that direct expectations effects on prices are assumed away. The
model has no price/quantity dynamics arising from expectational 'errors'. This
becomes a somewhat incongruous feature in versions of the basic model that
assume expectations to be adaptive.

(4) $$d = m(\pi)\pi$$

Current theory does not specify strong restrictions on the shape of the money demand function.[9] For many specifications of the money demand function, (4) will imply multiple steady states. Since the 'base' of the inflation tax, m, declines with the rate of inflation, it may be that a particular revenue stream can be secured at different constant inflation rates. It is possible, therefore, that an economy may get caught in an 'inflationary trap' with an inflation rate that is higher, and probably much higher, than the minimum one that would suffice to finance the same deficit.

Knowing that money demand is a decreasing function of (expected) inflation does not suffice to tell us the number of local maxima and minima of the inflation–tax–revenue function or, therefore, the number of alternative steady states. The money demand functions usually found in the literature imply a single maximum of the inflation tax function. Corresponding to any fiscal deficit smaller than the maximum inflation tax that could be collected, there will consequently be two possible steady states, one on each branch of a 'Laffer curve'. Among the money demand functions that give this result, the most popular is the one proposed years ago by Cagan, which shows real balances to decay exponentially with inflation.

This function has seen much use in empirical work done on various countries and time periods. Still, empirical confirmation is not so strong as to justify 'deducing' the Laffer curve from it. In particular, doubts have arisen about its validity at very high inflation rates where it seems to overestimate the decline in money demand (cf. Easterly and Schmidt-Hebbel 1991; Ahumada 1991). It is, however, very difficult to extract clear evidence on what behaviour to expect in a hypothetical steady state from actual sequences of high inflation observations.

---

[9] Some models derive money demand, for example, from a representative consumer's optimization based on a utility function which includes as an argument the level of real cash balances. Such a procedure, however, does not precisely specify the form of the demand function, beyond the requirement that desired money holdings vary positively with income (or wealth) and negatively with the nominal interest rate.

Some empirical studies find a Laffer-curve pattern in the inflation tax data (e.g. Edwards and Tabellini 1991). In others the picture is less clear. Savastano (1990) reports that in several high inflation countries in Latin America the observed inflation tax curves drift downward over time; controlling for that effect, it becomes harder to identify a definite maximum in the curves. In each case, the successive curves look quite flat at extremely high inflation rates. Heymann (1991) and Ahumada *et al.* (1992) find similar behaviour for Argentina.[10] This time-trend effect is strong enough that one cannot assert that the late 1980s' observations are on the 'bad side' of the Laffer curve.

The present situation appears to be that most economists have a fairly strong *a priori* belief in the Laffer-curve property, but that it is far from clear whether the actual record of high inflations and hyperinflations lets us glimpse the 'far side' of the thing.[11]

Expectational dynamics

In steady-state analysis of the sort we have just been through, the formation of expectations is ignored. How expectations are formed becomes crucial once we turn to genuinely dynamic questions and ask, for instance, whether the system will converge to a steady state and, if so, to which one and by what path. These are not esoteric issues. Actual high inflation economies do not just 'snap' from one steady-state path to

---

[10] To illustrate the point, the Agentine government could collect 5 per cent of GDP through seigniorage with a 4 to 5 per cent monthly inflation in the early 1970s; by the late 1980s, it required a monthly inflation rate of between 15 to 20 per cent to produce the same yield. Yet the data also show that the schedule relating money demand to the inflation rate shifted downwards over this period, so that the measurements are not taken from a single, fixed curve.

[11] Cagan (1956) suggests that in the European hyperinflations of the 1920s the revenue-maximizing steady-state inflation rate was indeed surpassed. Sargent (1977) remarks that the result is made uncertain by large errors in the estimates of the elasticity of money demand.

Note that high inflation typically erodes real government revenues from other sources (Olivera 1967; Tanzi 1977). Consequently, the real volume of government spending that can be financed through inflation reaches a peak before the maximum of the inflation tax.

another. Dynamic questions, such as what will be the likely response of prices to government policy announcements, arise all the time.

It is useful to begin from a distinction between 'forward-looking' and 'backward-looking' expectational schemes. If agents have forecasts of the first type (which may or may not be 'model consistent'),[12] changes in the anticipated sequence of future deficits are immediately incorporated into inflationary expectations. If the interest elasticity of money demand is high, the effect on current prices will be strong. With backward-looking expectations, in contrast, anticipated inflation is calculated as a stable function of past data (which in the particular case of adaptive schemes includes only the values of the inflation rate itself). In this case, a change in the policy regime gets reflected in money demand only with some delay, after it has produced an actual effect on observable variables.

But the manner in which inflationary expectations are formed can generate quite complicated price level dynamics even within a given policy regime. Inflation tax models generally admit a multiplicity of price paths compatible with a constant real deficit. Their solutions—which result from a differential equation like (2)—depend on 'initial conditions' that are not specified within the model itself. The stability properties of systems with two inflationary steady states have been much analysed and discussed in the recent literature. They are found to differ depending on the assumptions made about how agents form their price forecasts. For adaptive expectations, the inflation rate converges locally to the low (and preferred) steady state if coefficients of adaptation and interest elasticity of money demand are sufficiently small. Perfect foresight, on the other hand, implies that the 'bad' steady state will attract an infinite number of paths, while the 'good' one is an unstable point (cf. the Appendix, sections A2.1 and A2.2).

However, stability analysis in perfect foresight models is a slippery subject. In a world of backward-looking expectations, initial conditions are determined by the system's history; when

---

[12] For the concept of model consistent or 'model theoretic' expectations, cf. Phelps (1983) and Di Tata (1983).

solving the model, one knows where the economy starts. No such thing can be assumed with perfect foresight. Instead, the solution will depend on how agents co-ordinate their expectations on one among the possible paths. That choice is timeless: in the logic of the argument, the economy has always been and will always remain on the given path (which is why exercises 'disturbing' perfect foresight solutions are in fact self-contradictory). A definite criterion for choosing a particular solution from within the set of admissible ones is lacking. Nor can one assert that all these solutions are exchangeable. In our particular example, the 'unstable' low-inflation steady state could be considered either as the 'natural' solution, uniquely determining the price level path for a given deficit or as just one member of an infinite set of equally possible outcomes each one of which would have zero probability of being observed. The value of these indeterminate models for interpreting the motion of actual economies appears itself indeterminate.[13]

Moreover, the dynamic solutions turn out to be quite sensitive to the exact specification of the models in matters such as the speed of adjustment of money demand to its 'desired' value, the degree of price flexibility, the strength of fiscal lag effects, and the precise nature of the link between monetary and fiscal policies (cf. for example Sargent and Wallace 1973*b*; Evans and Yarrow 1981; Bruno 1989; Bruno and Fischer 1990; Kiguel 1989; Canavese and Heymann 1989, 1991; Escudé 1989).

Consider, for instance, once more the instability of the low inflation equilibrium in the simple perfect foresight case. It hinges, rather paradoxically, on an assumption that monetary policies cannot or will not be used to expand the money supply beyond fiscal requirements. At the low steady state, inflation tax revenue increases with the rate of inflation, while it decreases at the 'bad' stationary solution. If the initial condition happens to be in the region between those two points, the divergence from

---

[13] Note that invoking learning to resolve indeterminacy problems necessarily reintroduces history: among the initial conditions will be initial beliefs (themselves derived from past experience). Many models of this type generate outcomes which qualitatively resemble those obtained under adaptive expectations (cf. Sargent 1993).

the low steady state means that real money demand 'must' fall to compensate for an excess of the inflation tax over the given deficit (in order to satisfy equation (2)). Inflation would accelerate not because the government collects insufficient revenue from the inflation tax, but because it gets too much. The preferred stationary point would be stable if the Central Bank were running a more expansionary monetary policy (e.g. by buying private assets) so that total seigniorage was larger than the deficit.[14] The dynamics of these models depend, of course, just as much on what is assumed about the government's behaviour as on what is assumed about the public's. That the authorities would insist through thick and thin (i) to keep the deficit absolutely constant, neither more nor less, and (ii) to monetize exactly that deficit, neither more nor less, is hardly the most plausible policy strategy imaginable.

Thus, monetary-fiscal models of this family embody the view that the monetization of deficits drives high inflations, but they do not imply any unique period-by-period correspondence between the inflation rate and the value of the deficit. Given that there are multiple inflationary paths on which seigniorage revenues might match a given budget deficit, and that for every such path the sequence of monetary injections is different, we may regain an independent role for monetary policy. Even when constrained to finance an exogenous deficit, monetary policy could serve to set the economy on the preferred equilibrium path (cf. Bruno and Fischer 1990). If, to take the case in point, the government were to announce the sequence of monetary injections that is consistent only with the low inflation steady state, private sector agents endowed with perfect foresight would have no choice but to produce the low inflation equilibrium. The trouble is that, in order to use a monetary rule to anchor expectations, the government must be able to precommit its policies. Once mired in the high inflation syndrome, this is virtually impossible for the government to do.

---

[14] The Appendix demonstrates this point. We are not arguing, of course, that such policies would be found adequate in any actual situation, but only that the result follows from the logic of the model.

The inflation tax and regular taxes

It is instructive to look at inflation as a tax on money balances. Every time prices rise, the real value of the money held by the public falls. The right to issue money without backing does allow the government to appropriate real resources. But the metaphor should not be stretched too far. The 'inflation tax' differs from other sources of government revenue in important respects. These differences are built into the conceptual experiment underlying inflation models. In the case of regular taxes, one usually deals with a revenue function that has the tax rate as the independent variable. The authorities pre-set the rate and collect whatever revenue results from the endogenously varying tax base. Monetary-fiscal models of inflation have it the other way around: the inflation rate is endogenous, while the volume of seigniorage revenues is taken to be exogenous.

As a matter of logic, this is not the only form that a tax on money balances could take. Consider, for example, the case of a government that issues Gesell-money, i.e. dated currency whose nominal value falls over time at a predetermined rate. In this experiment, the tax is explicit, and its rate is legislated just as with any other tax. If the government had a fixed (and feasible) revenue target for the tax, it could control the rate so as to obtain that income while staying on the 'good' branch of the Laffer curve. In this hypothetical setting, the authorities would act as 'leaders' for private expectations and the tax base would be determined on the basis of knowledge of the announced rate. By contrast, models of inflation typically assume that monetary policies 'follow' the public's choice of how much real money balances to hold. If, for instance, agents anticipate an inflation rate on the 'far side' on the Laffer curve, the authorities will supposedly produce the money growth that will accommodate those expectations.[15]

---

[15] In this section, we continue to take the fiscal deficit as an exogenous variable. It may be the case, however, that governments perceive an incentive to generate 'surprise inflation' in an attempt to raise seigniorage revenues in the short-run (cf. Calvo 1978; Barro 1983; Grossman and Van Huyck 1986). We defer a discussion of such time-inconsistency problems until Chapter 4. See also the Appendix, section A6.

High inflations have not been uncommon in this century. But explicit taxes on money are indeed uncommon. In fact, we do not observe them at all. Yet, one would not expect governments systematically to choose inflation over this alternative, if the choice to draw revenue from money was part of a calculated and deliberate decision on an overall budget. Inflation taxes are in fact not decided upon in the same deliberate manner or in the same forum as regular taxes; they do not have the same consequences either. The age-old image of inflation as an 'emergency' form of government finance fits the unstable, high inflation economies well. These economies are not necessarily distinguished by their high government deficits. What does characterize them are the politically strong pressures on the budget from every direction and the inability of governments to stick to a consistent fiscal policy in the face of the sundry demands that hit them from one moment to the next. Monetary financing suits those conditions because it is a particularly flexible way of raising revenue. Inflation allows governments to cope after a fashion with sudden changes in regular revenues, in the claims on the public purse, or in the demand for public debt. Seigniorage is the residual source of revenue; reliance on it will reflect the underlying fiscal instability.

From an analytical perspective, this has several implications. In high inflation economies, monetary policy is indeed passive. The monetary authorities are not capable of anchoring private sector expectations. Consequently, dramatic expectations-driven price movements are far more likely than in stable monetary regimes. Models that calculate steady-state inflation paths as stemming from predictable budget deficits do not provide an inflation theory that can be relied on in such a context. They may perhaps offer a useful tool for analysing some aspects of the inflationary process, but they should not be taken literally. They are particularly misleading when it comes to understanding the consequences of inflation.

Government debts and the unpleasant arithmetic

The basic monetary-fiscal model can be extended in a number of ways. One of these is to readmit some debt financing of

government deficits but with an upper limit to how much public debt the market will absorb (as in Sargent and Wallace
1981). The fact that inflation tax revenue has an upper bound
can be used to rationalize the existence of this limit to government borrowing. If, namely, the current deficit is near the maximum steady-state inflation tax revenue and is not expected to
decline in the future, the public would refuse to purchase additional bond issues, since any further increases in debt would
spell insolvency for the government. This may be one of the reasons why the market for government debt is generally so small
in high inflation economies (cf. Chapter 4 below). Note the
implication: governments who find themselves close to the limit
of what revenue the inflation tax can produce will also find that
no other sources of financing are open to them.

The result of this ceiling to what the market will absorb is a
trade-off between present and future monetary expansion. As
long as the stock of bonds outstanding remains below the ceiling, the current fiscal deficit does not constrain the central bank.
It has freedom to decide how much of that deficit it will monetize. A lax fiscal policy can then coexist for some time with a
tight monetary policy. But while borrowing today delays monetization, it does so at the cost of increasing the public debt on
which interest will have to be paid. When the debt hits the ceiling, the central bank will have no choice but to buy the bonds
that the market will no longer absorb. At this point, not only
the primary deficit, but also the additional interest burden will
have to be financed by seigniorage.

The permanent inflation rate associated with the given primary deficit will then increase because the central bank ends up
creating more money than if it had simply financed the primary
deficit in every period.[16] Moreover, when the government proceeds to borrow with no realistic prospect of a future correction
in fiscal policies, money demand will fall so as to create inflationary pressures on prices even *before* the actual monetization
of deficits begins to take place.[17] This once more highlights the

---

[16] Here we are assuming that the economy remains on the 'good side' of the
Laffer curve.

[17] It is even possible in some cases to obtain the spectacular result that a

proposition that, with forward-looking expectations, the current price level depends on the whole expected sequence of monetary policies. Thus, anticipated shifts in the fiscal deficit may have effects beforehand (cf. Flood and Garber 1980; Bental and Eckstein 1988), and the stock of government bonds can have either a strong or a negligible influence on prices depending on whether the public expects the government to service the debt by future monetization or by raising taxes (cf. Aiyagari and Gertler 1985).

When the closed economy model is 'opened up', we find new unpleasant uses for the monetarist arithmetic. A sale of foreign reserves by the central bank is equivalent to a contractionary open market operation; the limit to such policies is set by the available stock of assets which can be supplied to the market. Consider the case where the authorities at one and the same time peg the exchange rate and, finding no market for bonds, monetize the deficit. A slowly sliding peg can keep inflation low for some time. But, if central bank loans to the government make domestic credit rise faster than nominal money demand, foreign reserves will fall. At some point, the contradictory combination of policies becomes impossible to maintain, the exchange rate has to be let go, and inflation will then accelerate.

The unpleasant conclusion in this case is that the government must raise enough seigniorage on average to cover its average deficit. Exchange rate management can provide some flexibility with respect to the timing of the inflation tax but it cannot[18] modify its 'permanent' value (cf. Rodriguez 1978). This line of analysis can be pushed further by allowing forward-looking agents to unleash 'speculative attacks' on official reserves and thus to precipitate the collapse of an unsustainable peg (e.g. Krugman 1979; Flood and Garber 1984). Yet other extensions have spread the unpleasantness to models with dual equilibria (Savastano 1992), and to models of multiple exchange rate systems (Lizondo 1987; Kharas and Pinto 1989).

policy of tight money could bring about a higher current price level than a policy of accommodation. See Drazen (1985) and the Appendix, section A3.

[18] Here we are disregarding the possibility of multiple equilibria.

In summary, the introduction of some limited autonomy for monetary policy does not much affect the interpretation of the inflationary process as fiscal in origin, but it does weaken the link between the inflation rate and the budget deficit in the short run. Monetary-fiscal models that try to capture the dynamics of money supply and demand produced by the interaction of government policies with private expectations turn out to be quite complicated, and the specific results about the period-by-period movements in the inflation rate depend on the assumptions of the particular model. The same basic approach can generate a great variety of outcomes. The proposition that the fiscal deficit drives the price level through its effect on money supply does not establish what inflation rate will result from given fiscal policies.

At the same time, these models, as a class, are categorical in ignoring the possibility of price movements that do not stem from changes either in the money supply or in inflationary expectations acting through the demand for money. 'Non-monetary' influences on inflation are explored by another group of models.

PRICE INERTIA, RELATIVE PRICE CHANGES, AND INFLATION

The theories of inflation that do not have the causal chain from fiscal deficit to money supply to price level as their analytical backbone form a less coherent category than those of the orthodox approach. But they have a long tradition and continue to be influential, in part because they deal with aspects of the inflationary process on which purely monetary theories are mute.

These alternative models focus directly on the pricing of goods and factors of production. In contrast to the monetary-fiscal approach, the implicit strategy is to 'move backwards' from the proximate determinants of prices to the driving impulses of inflation. The style of analysis is also different: pricing behaviour is represented as obeying certain 'reasonable'

rules which the models impute to agents on the basis of phenomenological regularities.[19]

Fix-prices and flex-prices

The distinction between flex-price and fix-price markets is crucial here. Flex-prices are assumed to be determined as on a commodity exchange while fix-prices are set by producers (cf. Hicks
1965, 1989; Okun 1981; Gordon 1981, 1990). The usual hypothesis is that administered prices are calculated by adding a more
or less fixed mark-up to average variable costs.

The older 'structuralist' analysis assumed that fix-prices generally were inflexible downward but not upward. This asymme-
try of price responses was seen to result in creeping inflation: if
a real disturbance were to require a reduction in the relative
price of some fix-price goods, markets would not equilibrate
unless the aggregate price level increased, so as to keep constant
the nominal price of the goods whose real values had declined.[20]
The analysis suggests, therefore, that whenever a shock induces
a change in relative prices, the price system will be governed by
the fix-price good whose relative price falls the most, since its
nominal price will stay unchanged. This resembles the
'Scandinavian model' (Aukrust 1977) where, in a fixed exchange
rate economy, the rate of inflation will exceed that of trading
partners if there is an upward drift in the relative price of its
non-traded goods. In the Aukrust model, the exchange rate
regime makes the money supply endogenous. Olivera's formulation of the structuralist model similarly assumes money to
behave 'passively' (cf. Olivera 1964, 1970; also Canavese 1982).
A structural inflation of the Olivera type, therefore, is not just
the outcome of the pricing practices of agents. It is, rather, the

---

[19] However, some recent papers on optimal pricing under conditions of
monopolistic competition should be mentioned here. Cf. Blanchard (1987),
Blanchard and Kiyotaki (1987), and Ball and Romer (1989, 1991).
[20] A disturbance causing real flex-prices to fall might occasionally make the
price level decline but, on average, it would drift up.

joint result of fix-prices that are sticky downwards and of a
monetary regime that will accommodate price increases.[21]

Obviously, these models raise the question whether the downward rigidity of prices is some sort of behavioural constant or
a learned response to monetary accommodation. But this issue
need not detain us here. For the analysis of high inflations, the
postulate that nominal prices cannot fall can hardly be a
binding restriction. The operative assumptions of the 'non-
monetary' models of high inflation are instead that administered prices are formed by using a simple mark-up rule, while
wages are adjusted based on backward-looking indexation.

Indexation, inflationary inertia, and the transmission of real shocks

In some countries, indexation has been established by law or,
somewhat less formally, by government-dictated wage adjustment procedures applying either to the economy as a whole or
to large segments of the labour force, such as public employees
or workers earning the minimum wage (cf. Dornbusch and
Simonsen 1983; Williamson 1985). But indexing tends to emerge
also without government intervention. These practices evolve in
that intermediate range of inflation where the instability of
prices is high enough to require a substitute for nominal contracting but not so high that past inflation rates lose all relevance for current pricing.

Backward-looking indexation is a rough and ready price
adjustment scheme. So, for that matter, is nominal pricing and
contracting. Neither is easy to rationalize except by common-
sense argument. In certain markets, such as those for labour
and housing rentals, search and adjustment costs are such that
trading relationships have to be maintained over periods of
some length. But to establish and maintain those durable
'matches' becomes difficult, or at least costly, if the price has to
be re-negotiated frequently. The parties have an incentive,
therefore, to agree in advance upon a routine procedure for

---

[21] Other versions of the structuralist approach, however, de-emphasize the
role of money. For an overview of the structuralist literature, see Baer and
Kerstenetzky (1964) and Sunkel *et al.* (1973).

revising the terms of their transactions. This procedure had better be simple, and based on 'objective' data observable by both parties and subject to manipulation by neither. In moderate inflations, fixing the nominal price on the basis of a forecast of inflation over the contract period may do quite well. At higher, but not too erratic, rates of inflation, indexing to an aggregate price variable such as the CPI becomes a likely norm for adjusting payments. But indices summarize information about past prices, and do so only with a delay. Payments are thus made contingent on new information, but this is lagged rather than contemporaneous.[22] Thus wages and rentals may end up being revised through a more or less mechanical, backward-looking procedure.

Consider now the rate of change of a price index, defined as a weighted average of the growth rate of flex- and fix-prices (cf. the Appendix, section A4):

(5) (A16) $$\pi_t = \alpha \pi_t^F + (1 - \alpha)\pi_t^A$$

One can decompose the rate of increase of fix-prices, π^A, into a linear combination of the proportional change of input prices (say, wages and public sector prices),[23] with an additional term which allows for changes in mark-ups:

(6) (A17) $$\pi_t^A = \lambda_1 W_t + \lambda_2 S_t + K_t^*$$

The rate of wage change can in turn be written as an indexation term, equal to the lagged inflation rate,[24] plus a wage-push term:

(7) (A18) $$W_t = \pi_{t-1} + W_t^*$$

---

[22] Frenkel (1984, 1990), Bacha (1986, 1988), Lopes (1984, 1986), Bresser Pereira and Nakano (1987) deal with the effects of backward-looking indexation. Adjustments based on the current price level have been discussed among others by Gray (1976), Fischer (1977), Cukierman (1980).

[23] We are sketching here a closed economy model. An open economy analysis would of course include the exchange rate (or, more generally, the prices of internationally traded inputs).

[24] The case described here has all wage adjustments synchronous as well as price revisions simultaneous with the wage increases. The argument can be extended to account for staggered setting of prices and wages à la Taylor (1980).

Such operations are purely definitional. As in the case of the equation of exchange in monetary theory, they suggest a 'way of looking' at price determination.

Starting from the decomposition above, the inflation rate can be expressed in a straightforward fashion as the sum of: (i) a persistence term, given by the past inflation rate whose weight in determining the current inflation rate depends on the share of fix-price goods in the output or consumption basket and the share of labour in the cost of producing these goods; (ii) a number of terms representing changes in the relative prices, e.g. those of flex-price commodities and public sector goods, and (iii) a term which combines the change in wages in excess of straight indexing[25] and any change of mark-ups in the fix-price sector:

$$\pi_t = \pi_{t-1} + \frac{\alpha}{(1-\alpha)\lambda_1}(\pi_t^F - \pi_t) + \frac{\lambda_2}{\lambda_1}(S_t - \pi_t) + \left(W_t + \frac{K_t^*}{\lambda_1}\right)$$

(8) (A19)

Turning now to the properties of the model, we begin with the case where wages are fully indexed and mark-ups stay unchanged. The lagged indexation of wages will impart *inertia* to the inflation rate, so that whenever changes in the rate occur they will be propagated forward and tend to persist.[26] The central property of the model is the reciprocal interaction between relative and nominal prices. If relative prices do not change, neither will the inflation rate. If relative prices do change, the inflation rate must change and, conversely, if inflation changes, the structure of relative prices must change. The reason is simple. Suppose, for example, that some shock induces an increase in the real value of flex-price goods. This requires that wages fall relative to consumer goods prices. But, since the rate of change of nominal wages is predetermined by the lagged inflation rate,

[25] Note that forward-looking elements in wage-setting may be incorporated through this term. Some models describe wage-adjustments as combining backward-looking indexing with an expectation component (e.g. Simonsen 1983).

[26] This conforms with the impression, generally shared in high inflation economies, that major movements in the inflation rate take place in more or less discrete 'jumps'.

this can only happen if inflation accelerates. Furthermore, every rise in the inflation rate implies a decline in real wages and in the relative price of fix-price goods.

Lagged indexation leaves some room for changes in the real wage. Contemporaneous indexing would, if it could be implemented, make relative prices rigid. The non-monetary model alerts us to the implications of the inevitable time-lags in the indexing schemes: relative prices are capable of adjustment but only through accelerations and decelerations in the inflation rate; conversely, every change in the inflation rate will be non-neutral for some time.

But wages need not be strictly indexed, and mark-ups may vary. If wages rise at a rate above that of past inflation, and this is not offset by other factors, the rate of inflation will increase. Such accelerations of inflation are subject to a number of competing interpretations. When wages rise by more than the backward-looking index and mark-ups do not shrink correspondingly, this may reflect a conflict over income shares in the course of which firms and trade unions end up behaving at cross purposes and generating a 'price–wage spiral'. On occasion it could also be due to a temporary inconsistency between the expectations guiding workers in setting their reservation real wages and the sustainable real wage implicit in the pricing policies of firms. Large shifts in the sustainable real wage, as might occur through wide swings in the exchange rate for example, make the occurrence of such inconsistencies fairly likely. Or accelerations of inflations may stem from growth in actual or expected aggregate demand, which would induce agents to depart from mechanical wage-indexing and from constant mark-ups. This is a possible channel through which money can be brought into the model (see below).

The unit time period of these models is implicitly defined by the indexing scheme in force. The higher the inflation, the shorter we expect the period to be (cf. Frenkel 1984; Giambiagi 1987)—until indexation itself breaks down in hyperinflation. The properties of the persistence term depend on the frequency of index-based wage adjustments. If, for example, wages are revised every three months on the basis of the lagged inflation

rate, month-to-month shifts in the inflation rate within a quar-
ter will have no 'permanent' consequences. When, at higher
rates of inflation, indexing periods shorten, the system will
begin to propagate higher frequency disturbances. The inflation
rate then becomes more volatile, relative price variability
increases, and the real value of the indexed earnings themselves
turns more erratic, until, entering into hyperinflations proper,
the price system loses any detectable 'memory' of past prices.

The kind of analysis based on decomposing the price level
index is obviously open-ended. The prototypical monetary-
fiscal model requires strong assumptions about how prices are
determined in order to close the model. The models discussed
in this section are incomplete without further specification of
how workers and firms act when setting wages and prices. Non-
monetary price equations make the inflation rate dependent on
several endogenous variables; one has to track 'backwards' in
the chain of explanations in order to describe how those variables are determined. It is possible in this way to obtain a purely
'non-monetary' model of the movements in the inflation rate.
But this requires denying any effect of money either on flex-
prices, on wages, on mark-ups, or even on the exchange rate. A
more balanced approach would let the various non-monetary
influences on the short-run inflation rate modulate the longer-
run correspondence between the price level and the money
stock.

'Bridge' models

Many macromodels handle short-run price determination by
assuming that, within any given period, nominal wages have a
predetermined component but that prices respond to the level
of output as well. This model property is obtained by a variety
of routes: (i) by taking wages as contractually fixed before the
period, but allowing the average mark-up (or the supply price
of goods) to respond to changes in output; (ii) by assuming that
flex-prices react to aggregate demand, even if 'administered
prices' do not; (iii) by modelling the 'contractual' component of
wages as resulting from previously formed expectations of the

current price level (cf. Fischer 1977; Taylor 1980), or as linked to a backward-looking index (cf. Simonsen 1983; Heymann and Canavese 1989; Dornbusch and Fischer 1991) but assuming that 'wage drift' related to current employment will also be present. When combined, for instance, with a quantity-theory equation for nominal output, such formulations typically imply that, if money grows at a steady rate, the trend of the price level will increase at the same rate. At the same time, monetary disturbances are transitorily non-neutral, and real shocks have nominal consequences. In the indexing case, occasional shifts in relative prices can bring about persistent (albeit not 'permanent') movements in the inflation rate (cf. section A5 of the Appendix).

The distinction between 'contractual' and 'expectational' inertia is difficult to make operational, but models of this class can be classified according to whether they represent wage-setting as backward- or forward-looking. The difference is of considerable policy relevance since, to the extent that expectations adjust to news, forward-looking pricing means less inflationary persistence than mechanical indexing. The issue between the two approaches can hardly be settled on *a priori* grounds, or by appeal to general principles. True, agents have an incentive to adapt to new circumstances. But they must also face the costs of complicating their decision rules and, perhaps, of breaking explicit or implicit contracts.

The point underscores a matter that is commonly raised when discussing this type of model. Simple price adjustment procedures basically lack 'microfoundations' within the standard optimization framework. The absence of a definite behavioural basis for these models is troublesome, not so much for methodological reasons—after all, the hypothesis that markets automatically clear is equally questionable—but because it makes it difficult to define the conditions under which the assumptions built into the analysis would be valid or not. In particular, it is hard to tell precisely what determines whether agents adopt or abandon indexation as a widespread practice.

Despite these shortcomings, 'bridge models' address questions which are not handled well by the more one-sided theories. Whatever the judgement about their analytical rigour, these models direct attention to various channels that link money and the price level, and also to the implications of short-run price-setting behaviour. Neither aspect of inflation should be ignored.

A brief overview

Rapid inflations are associated with high rates of monetary growth. The cross-country evidence does not show inflation to be strongly correlated with the size of public sector deficits. In high inflation economies, however, increases in the money supply do as a rule originate in the governments' need for funds. Central bank operations intended to influence credit or exchange markets or to support real activity may be important on occasion but in general play a secondary role.

There is no dispute over the proposition that high inflations are a symptom of great difficulties in financing the government. But there is no one-to-one correspondence between inflation and the numerical value of the deficit. With regard to how period-by-period movements of the price level are to be explained, theoretical opinions diverge—as they do also with regard to the forces that are ultimately to be held responsible for high inflation. These uncertainties and disagreements among economists at both ends of the causal chain have their counterparts in the problems faced by agents who have to live with high inflation. Even if they have a broadly defined 'model' on which to base their decisions, they can only make very rough predictions about future prices or about the course that policies will follow over time, and they will be ever conscious that their views are not universally shared.

The proposition that behavioural rules are regime-dependent is a familiar rational expectations result, consistent also with other views of how people process information. Regime-dependence is already implicit in the assumptions of the simplest models. In the analysis of stable economies, one does not depict the government as unable to borrow, or assume an ever-present risk of a drastic drop in money demand induced by expectations of accelerating inflation, or worry that episodic shifts in relative prices might generate persistent movements in the aggregate inflation rate. Generally, models of high inflation differ from their more traditional counterparts in allowing for speedier and stronger reactions to impulses: deficits are quickly monetized; expectations are likely to be volatile; prices are adjusted with high frequency. The economy is portrayed as lacking 'shock absorbers' to dampen the effects of shocks. The shocks are themselves likely to be larger than in stable economies. Consequently, prices and other macroeconomic variables are apt to fluctuate widely and agents will have a correspondingly hard time keeping track of the state of the economy and finding out what to expect in the future. Economies in high inflation are also volatile: although models that focus on steady-state outcomes may be analytically convenient, they leave out essential characteristics of high inflation regimes. The following chapters try to describe in some detail the behaviour patterns of governments and private agents in such regimes.

3

Monetary Regimes and Inflation

INFLATION AND ECONOMIC PERFORMANCE

Models of perfectly anticipated inflation suggest that high inflation rates have little or no effect on the real performance of the
economy. An 'as-if-legislated' inflation tax will indeed distort
individual choices on some margins. But so do the regular taxes
that are the relevant alternatives. When these models are taken
literally, they yield no presumption as to whether second-best
policy ought to produce no inflation, low inflation, or high
inflation. These models are influential. They shape the ways
in which most economists perceive inflation and its costs to
society.

But the presumption that inflation does not affect economic
performance is unfounded. In particular, the assumption that it
has no effect on economic growth does not fit the facts. The evidence indicates that countries suffering macroeconomic instability in general, and high inflation in particular, perform less
well than would be the case under more stable conditions
(Harberger and Edwards 1980; Harberger 1988; Kormendi and
Meguire 1985; Rodrik 1990).

True, external shocks may indeed complicate the picture.
And countries that inflate also tend to have other policies inim-
ical to growth.[1] Their inferior growth performance, therefore, is
not attributable purely to inflation. At this point, however, we
are less interested in isolating the direct effects of inflation than
in coming to grips with the high inflation syndrome as a whole.

[1] For example, Harberger (1988) finds that 'small countries selected by a criterion of inflation (taken as suggesting the absence of a full and disciplined
control over the instruments of policy) have growth performances that are inferior to those of their less inflationary counterparts. At the same time, they
reveal other signs (reduced exports and private sector credit, increased financing of the government through the banking system) of policy weakness.'

That syndrome, as we shall see later, causes the performance of governments to deteriorate in various ways just as it does that of the private sector.

To begin to understand why and how inflation has economic consequences that go deeper than the waste involved in efforts to avoid today's inflation tax, we first consider the interaction of the monetary authorities with the private sector. The concept of 'monetary regime' will be useful for the purpose.

MONETARY REGIMES

By a policy regime, we mean, on the one hand, a system of expectations on the part of the public that governs their decisions and, on the other, that pattern of behaviour on the part of the policy-making authorities that sustains these expectations. The monetary regime forms a crucial part of the environment in which both the public and the authorities have to make their decisions. This is obviously enough in the case of private agents; the regime shapes their expectations of how nominal prices and interest rates will evolve and influences their decisions correspondingly. In the case of the monetary authorities, the same applies at one remove, as it were. The expectations held by the public will determine the actual effects of particular policy actions. Given one state of expectations, monetary stimulus may increase output and employment with very little effect on the price level. With a different state of expectations, the result may be a dramatic inflationary acceleration with no significant, predictable effect on employment.

Old controversies over the 'causes' of inflation are defused if put in the regime context, and if the regime in question is appropriately defined so as to bring the reciprocal interaction between the private and public sectors clearly into focus. The issue of 'cost-push versus demand-pull', for instance, should become moot once an analytically satisfactory characterization of the relevant regime is achieved. Similarly, it should be feasible to provide regime descriptions that incorporate the legitimate insights of structuralists and monetarists at the same time. It is not logically necessary, after all, to deny the role of money stock growth in inflation in order to give pricing practices their due—or, vice versa, to be wilfully obtuse about political and social factors in order to give money its due.

The 'regime' concept postulates that the actual behaviour of the authorities matches the expectations of the public. In cases where the public is assumed to have complete knowledge of the policy strategy of the government (including the distribution of the irreducible random component), this becomes a rational expectations concept in the strict sense most common in the literature. For reasons that will become apparent, however, the study of high inflations cannot be restricted to such cases. We want also to consider situations in which people do not all make the same inferences about the policy rules generating the observed behaviour of governments and of private sector agents and where, consequently, they do not have identical expectations, but where, instead, the collective state of expectations is in some degree incoherent.

In thus backing away somewhat from the standard rational expectations concept, we do not intend to depart from the assumption of purposeful, calculating behaviour as it is commonly understood. The regime concept used here presupposes that individuals understand 'how the government works' in general terms and have identified simple regularities of behaviour. In relatively simple environments, this may allow expectations about policies to be 'rationally' formed. It can mean, but it need not mean, that people all arrive at the same inferences in a given situation or have the same confidence in the inferences they do draw.

Learning what behaviour to expect from the government is more akin to pattern recognition than it is to sampling from some distribution the type of which is known. IQ tests often contain questions that ask the respondent to fill in the next few numbers in some numerical sequence: 1,2,3, 1,2,3, 1, x, y, . . . Mathematicians often express irritation over questions of this type because they do not have uniquely correct answers to be deduced. The next number could be any number, since the simple and obvious pattern might be a component of a more complex one or be a random occurrence within a larger whole that shows no pattern at all. The psychologists have a point none the less: the ability to recognize patterns is an essential aspect of human intelligence. It is essential, moreover, exactly because it allows the agent to make sense of incomplete information where no uniquely correct inference is to be drawn.

Agents may identify simple regularities in the behaviour of the government only to see them 'violated' the next time around. The knowledge that information relevant to the pattern is always incomplete means that individuals always have less than complete confidence in the inferences they have drawn and recognize the limitations of their ability to predict future policy action. When an observation is drawn that does not 'fit' the pre-viously inferred pattern, the actual pattern is seen to be more complex than anticipated—how much more complex is not to be known. This in turn means that whatever the length of the 'string' of past observations happens to be, the individual comes to realize that it is less informative than he had thought. Moreover, people do not all have the same set of observations; nor do they necessarily put the same construction on the 'facts' to begin with.[2] The more complex the behaviour pattern, there-fore, the more likely it is that people will form different 'mod-els' that they use to forecast policy and market variables. We know that this is true of economists. To assume that it may be true of people in general seems a fair extrapolation. In complex regimes, individual expectations are thus more likely to be inconsistent with one another and agents may, in particular situations, act on quite different presumptions about what course policies are likely to take and what effects they will have.

---

[2] 'The' inflation-rate itself is a construct of statisticians that may have little behavioural relevance to individuals all of whom are buying baskets of goods that differ from the CPI basket. Jonung (1981) found systematic sex and age differences not only in people's inflation expectations but also in their memo-ries of past inflation.

RELIABILITY

We will be much concerned, therefore, about the *reliability* of inflationary regimes. We use this concept in the sense of Heiner's 1983 theory of reliable interactions. The general problem is how well agents are able to predict the consequences of their own actions in a particular setting. One of the main contentions of these lectures is that monetary regimes differ very considerably in this regard. High inflation regimes, in particular, make the eventual real outcomes of entire categories of actions so unpredictable that people largely cease to engage in them.

In any social context, the outcome of action depends on the (conditional) behaviour of others. In the present context, we are considering the interaction of private and public sector agents. To the monetary authorities, the outcome of action depends on the expectations of the public. But expectational variables are on the whole not directly observable, so policy-makers must infer their values. The public, on its side, forms expectations (of the inflation rate in prospect, for instance) on the basis of inferences about the policy strategies of the authorities.

In this interaction, the reliability of the inferences made by one party will depend indirectly on the reliability of those made by the other. The public may, for instance, not be able to make unique inferences with regard to the policy strategy of the government if, over some period of time, monetary policy has not been sufficiently systematic. (Perhaps they are faced with policy-makers who believe that *unanticipated* action is the essence of effective policy!) Private agents may then form a variety of 'theories' about the government's likely behaviour. The collective state of nominal expectations is then incoherent and, since people know their expectations to be unreliable, it is also likely to be volatile and to change in ways that policy-makers will not be able to make reliable inferences about. Not knowing the state of expectations, they will on occasion be badly surprised by the consequences of their own actions and have to reverse course. But the public cannot be sure what policy actions were due to miscalculations and which ones not, so this makes the 'basic' policy strategy of the authorities still more opaque to the public—and so on. By an 'unreliable regime', we mean a vicious circle of this kind.

Many institutional arrangements in society exist in order to ensure the reliability of interactions. They accomplish this function by imposing *rules* that set bounds on permissible behaviour. The task of calculating the probable outcome of action conditional on the behaviour of others becomes less complex the more rule-bound are those other people. In recent years,[3] the debate over Rules versus Discretion in monetary policy has been almost exclusively concerned with opportunistic behaviour on the part of the monetary authorities. In this literature, it is presumed that governments have ever-present incentives to create inflationary 'surprises', and that what is at issue in the Rules versus Discretion debate is whether reputational considerations are likely to outweigh such malincentives or whether rules need to be imposed (cf. especially Barro and Gordon 1983*a*, 1983*b*).

These hypotheses have become somewhat of a cornerstone of the new, game-theoretically oriented political economy. Whether this body of work comes to grips with the core of the Rules versus Discretion issue is none the less somewhat doubtful. In models of the Barro–Gordon type, the policy-makers are assumed to have an incentive to break any rule they might announce in order to create surprise inflation and, thereby, an increase in employment. Unanticipated inflation makes the consumer work more than he would like to if he knew what was going on. But why should the representative consumer, in his role as the representative voter, reward the policy-maker for swindling him into working too much? (The policy-maker expects to be rewarded and, in these models, this has to be a rational expectation.) We are asked, in fact, to consider a world in which inflation is to be somewhat deplored but unanticipated inflation encouraged. But why should rational agents dislike anticipated and like unanticipated inflation in a world where the first is basically neutral while the second fools them into

---

[3] The analytical issue is not of recent origin, however. It is not obvious that the recent literature improves on Lindahl (1924).

behaviour inoptimally? The answer to this question that has been proposed is that the representative voter has already made the mistake of imposing an income tax on himself (obviously having forgotten his rational preference for lump-sum taxation); the income tax has induced him to goof off, so that he is actually grateful to be fooled into working more. In the end, however, it turns out to be impossible to devise a monetary regime that will satisfy the representative person's rational desire to be fooled into not working less than he truly wants! (Cf. Leijonhufvud 1986*a*.)

The issue that has been overshadowed in this discussion is precisely the problem of reliability in the sense we use it here. Monetary policies may well be subject to malincentives of the sort emphasized in recent work. But, whatever their cause, volatile policies create a very difficult environment for decision-makers in the private sector. Rule-bound monetary policy reduces the conjectural complexity that they have to face. The recipe for breaking out of a vicious circle of unreliable interaction, therefore, is to reduce the complexity of policy strategies and define more transparent decision rules. (It is not always a simple recipe to follow, however—as we shall soon see.)

A simple analogy may be helpful at this point. Consider the game of basketball (any other team sport will do as well). Play of the game is constrained by a complex set of rules, adding up to a small book. Some of these rules are intended to prevent intentional injuries. Their function is analogous to the way in which the criminal law constrains economic activities, and may be ignored in the present context. Consider all the remaining rules, however, and suppose that we could watch a game in progress as the rules governing that game are relaxed step-by-step. Imagine, for instance, that starting from the back of the rule book, we proceed by tearing out the pages one by one. How would this be reflected in the game? Probably, there would be little visible change at first, but then play would get more and more 'sloppy'. Unintentional injuries would start to happen, and long before we get to the pages toward the front of the book, whose removal makes it impossible for the players to know what game it is they are playing, the whole thing will no longer be worth watching.

One might also imagine constraining the game further by adding rules to make it more predictable. In the end, we might make it resemble some sort of religious ceremony in which the two teams take turns marching in slow and stately procession down the floor to deposit the ball as an offering in the basket! The point, of course, is that fast and exciting play requires a well-designed mix of 'Rules *and* Discretion'. Presumably, 'Rules versus Discretion' is a false choice in the design of economic policy regimes as well.

It should be obvious, finally, that if we assume no bounds on the knowledge and cognitive abilities of agents, reliability might not be an issue.[4] Unboundedly rational actors participating in all the relevant markets could make contracts conditional also on future (possibly state-contingent) government policies and, consequently, achieve the perfectly pre-co-ordinated equilibrium paths for all possible futures that constitute the standard theoretical bench-mark. The performance of a system of this kind cannot, of course, be improved by one set of agents restricting themselves to a subspace of available strategies, since it does not matter to other agents how complex their strategies are. The inhabitants of these models share the mindset of their creators, who concern themselves only with correct *deductions* from 'known' premises and never face the problems of *induction* from incomplete data. To abandon this conception of the human predicament goes against the grain of the leading contemporary research programme in monetary theory which seeks to build on strictly optimizing foundations. But while it may be necessary to confess our departure from this conception, it is hardly necessary to debate it at length at this point.

---

[4] On the other hand, it might well be: if some actors face undecidable choices or uncomputable allocation problems, even complete knowledge and the information processing capability of a universal Turing machine on everyone's part will not eliminate the problem (cf. Rustem and Velupillai (1990). But we will not venture into those deep waters here!

ANTICIPATED INFLATION

The distinction between anticipated and unanticipated inflation has been central to modern inflation debates. But it is trickier than it seems. An inflation, the reasoning goes, is either anticipated or unanticipated. Anticipated inflation has basically no real effects (except for the inflation tax distortions).[5] Unanticipated inflation stimulates output and employment. If it is one, it does not hurt, and if it is the other, it helps. Down this road lies the previously mentioned hypothesis that all governments normally have an incentive to create inflationary surprises—and beyond it the riddle of why people persist in disliking inflation so much when economic theorists have not provided them with much of a reason for so doing.[6]

Something has gone awry here, and rather seriously so. The concept of anticipated inflation is worth a closer look. In theory, anticipated inflation differs from monetary stability only in the one respect that real balances depreciate at a predictable rate. The *regime* is supposed to be the same, only the *rate* of this depreciation differs. For moderate inflation rates, at least, the welfare costs of such inflation would be trivial—on the order of the distortions attributable to sundry excise taxes or subsidies.

In order to see how limiting is the regime concept implicit in models of anticipated inflation, it is instructive to contrast two methods for eliminating such an inflation (cf. Leijonhufvud 1984). Imagine an initial situation of a constant inflation rate to which the economy has had time to adjust completely, so that

---

[5] If it is not anticipated far enough in advance, of course, it will also have distribution effects through those still outstanding contracts that antedate the anticipation.

[6] Cf. the (1976) survey by Barro and Fischer where the authors indicated their own dissatisfaction with the then accepted theory of the welfare costs of inflation: 'An urgent order of business remains clarification of the reason for the public's dislike of inflation: if it is merely unanticipated inflation that is objected to, is the public under some illusion, or are economists under some illusion?' Many economists have become disillusioned since that time, but it must be said that this has occurred without much progress in clarifying the welfare costs of inflation.

all outstanding contracts have been entered into in the shared belief that the inflation will continue indefinitely at this same rate. Let the inflation be a moderate one—15 per cent per annum, for example.

The slow and painful way of getting rid of this inflation is by conventional *disinflation*. If in some given year the rate of money supply growth is forced down by 15 percentage points, the likely outcome is a great depression. By assumption, nobody expects such a deflationary shock. It violates firm and universally shared expectations and will, therefore, bring about the worst possible contraction of output and employment. Unanticipated deflation will dictate a massive transfer of wealth from debtors to creditors. But it is unlikely that all of this wealth transfer could actually be effectuated. Instead, widespread bankruptcies are bound to occur, and could bring about a general financial collapse.

Note that this analysis of disinflation from a firmly anticipated inflation verges on self-contradiction. One poses a hypothetical inflationary process that has minimal social cost because it is fully anticipated; one juxtaposes a mode of ending the inflation that incurs maximal social cost because it is totally unanticipated. Less starkly drawn, this contrast has often been painted to suggest that disinflation is always too costly and that it is preferable to make permanent whatever inflation rate has happened to develop. But one should not assume that people who live in a regime where a 15 per cent monetary deceleration might happen at any time are going to plan quite confidently on the continuation of inflation at a constant rate. If, however, they know that large changes in the rate may happen, they will prepare for such eventualities, for example, by not entering into long-term nominal contracts. But the thinning out or disappearance of the markets for such contracts is not predicted by the theory of anticipated inflation. Yet, it presumably entails social costs. If people do not have quite extraordinary (and warranted) confidence in their anticipations of the inflation rate, therefore, the whole matter of its welfare costs needs to be re-examined.

The quick and painless method to end a hypothetical

anticipated inflation is by way of a particular type of currency reform, the 'blueback' scheme. Under the assumed conditions, 'greenback' dollars depreciate in purchasing power at a rate of 15 per cent per year. The government might then create a new blueback currency and make it, by law, appreciate relative to greenbacks at 15 per cent per year. On the initial day of the reform, the two monies exchange one for one, but from that day onward bluebacks grow constantly in their legal capacity to extinguish debts contracted in greenbacks. One year later, 85 blueback cents will pay off a 1-dollar greenback debt; 2 years later, it takes about 71 blueback cents; 10 years later, 19 cents.[7]

If the original confident anticipation of a constant 15 per cent greenback inflation of indefinite duration was indeed warranted, the blueback reform would ensure perfect price level stability ever after. Bluebacking would have two advantages over disinflation under the assumed conditions. The first advantage it shares with the theoretical case of a perfectly credible disinflation,[8] namely, that employment and output is entirely unaffected. Thus it is not necessary to suffer through a recession to get back to a stable price level. The second is an advantage *over* the perfectly credible disinflation, namely, that no one is swindled in the process. The real terms of contracts remain to be fulfilled as originally envisaged. Creditors who after 10 years receive 19 blue cents instead of 1 green dollar are getting exactly what they expected to get in real purchasing power.

Both of these advantages of bluebacking over disinflation stem from the fact that *nothing is really done* about the pre-existing greenback inflation. The rate of that inflation is not reduced at all; it is merely made subject to an arithmetical conversion. Under the conditions assumed in the anticipated inflation case, it would be completely irrational and destructive to force a change in the green inflation rate. The theory assumes

[7] Note that the rate of depreciation of green money in terms of blue is fixed and predetermined here. This differs from the idea advanced by Arida and Lara Resende (1985) of introducing a new and 'fully backed' money against which the old currency would be left to float.

[8] Note however that to assume an initial situation of 'fully anticipated' inflation that is followed by a 'perfectly credible' disinflation is inconsistent for reasons previously sketched.

that we start from a quite stable *monetary standard*, which happens to have the peculiar property that money depreciates in real purchasing power at a perfectly foreseen rate. The public firmly expects this regime to continue. To disinflate is to adopt a policy that is inconsistent with this system of expectations. It would break the prevailing regime and consequently wreak havoc. The blueback scheme, in contrast, merely removes the peculiar property of this otherwise stable regime.

From a public finance perspective, however, that peculiar property is the inflation tax on greenbacks. This tax can no longer be collected. On the first day of the reform, people have their choice of two moneys, one taxed, the other not. The green money will quickly be abandoned and with it goes the 'tax base'.[9] To shift the tax to the blue money would amount to a doubling of the pre-existing green inflation rate, and thus to violating the firmly held anticipations and breaking the green regime in a different way. The blueback scheme requires, therefore, that other taxes be raised or else that expenditures be reduced to compensate for the loss of inflationary seigniorage.[10]

To do so might not be difficult under the kind of conditions consistent with the anticipated inflation model. Under what conditions would the firm anticipation of a constant inflation rate (or some other pattern known in advance) be a *rational expectation*? Clearly, the model presupposes a believable pre-commitment, extending into the indefinite future, on part of the government to inflate at exactly the anticipated rate. Only an utterly reliable commitment of this sort (and the recognized ability to fine tune inflation rates) could sustain the expectations assumed. Rational agents will surely not anticipate a rate of inflation that no one is even trying to bring about. The behaviour of policy-makers may be predictable either because their beliefs and objectives are utterly transparent to the public or because they are made to operate under a very restrictive

---

[9] The government gets a measure of compensation in that it gets to issue more blue money than it retires green since the demand for real cash balances will increase once they are no longer taxed. But this one-time gain will not compensate for the hitherto permanent stream of green inflation taxes.

[10] The 'real world' use of currency reform as part of a stabilization package will be discussed in Chapter 6 below.

monetary constitution. Whether we suppose that the authorities have relinquished or been deprived of short-run discretion, the model asks us to contemplate an economy where policy is in effect made by an automaton. This, in turn, presupposes that the fiscal side is also well in hand: expenditures are under control, taxes are collected, and the constitutionally allowed inflationary seigniorage balances the budget. In as tidy a system as this, we must imagine, the inflation tax is imposed with the consent of the governed.[11] If the governed, or their representatives, find reason to shift that tax to another base, they can then resort to the blueback scheme to eliminate the inflation while preserving the monetary constitution.

The blueback exercise teaches us that, within a regime that allows the inflation rate to be firmly anticipated, whatever the *rate* of inflation might be, it can be brought to zero very quickly and at no social cost. The conclusions to be drawn are straightforward: (i) The problem on which inflation theory should focus is *not the rate but the regime*. (ii) The predictable 'constitutional' regime of the anticipated inflation case may be a neat model but it is bad theory. It is irrelevant—or worse, misleading—when the object is to try to understand actual inflations.

RANDOM WALK MONETARY STANDARDS

To get one step closer to actual inflationary regimes, we should relinquish the governmental precommitment assumption implicit in the anticipated inflation model. A simple alternative is to assume that the monetary authorities make a sequence of short-term decisions on whether to accelerate, keep constant, or decelerate the growth of the (outside) money stock. In each

---

[11] Strive as we might, it seems impossible to make the anticipated inflation story completely self-consistent: even if we assume that the money supply is a suitable taxation object, the polity makes a mistake in choosing to pay these taxes through inflation. Instead, the tax ought to be handled in the way discussed in the previous chapter, that is, it should be levied on bank deposits and an equal tax put on currency (through the use of dated notes *á la* Silvio Gesell). This would avoid the 'menu costs' associated with inflation and thus be preferable.

instance, only current economic conditions and immediate political pressures enter into the step taken. Policy follows no particular predetermined trajectory, nor is it constrained by concern over what price levels will result in the more distant future. Regimes governed by short-term discretion in this manner we will call *random walk monetary standards* (RWMS).[12]

The RWMS model highlights an important feature of inconvertible fiat standard inflations, namely, that the uncertainty attaching to forecasts of future price levels grows exponentially with distance from the present.[13] This property is not necessarily shared by all monetary standards. In regimes where the monetary authorities have to manage reserves so as to maintain convertibility into either a monetary metal or some key currency, the future path of nominal prices may still be subject to considerable uncertainty, but its policy-generated component will have to have the property or reverting to the trend determined by the demand and supply of the reserve medium.

This tendency for the uncertainty about the price level to increase with distance from the present can be weak or strong, of course, depending on the frequency and size of the random walk 'steps'. When it is sufficiently weak, people will still measure inflation in per cent per year. When it is strong, they will think in terms of per cent per month, and when it is extremely strong, they will give up on the monthly measure. Thus, it is this property of random walk monetary regimes, and not the average rate of inflation, that gives us the behavioural definitions of 'moderate', 'high', and 'hyper' inflations introduced in Chapter 1. The stronger is this random walk property, the more

---

[12] The term should be construed broadly to include random walk with drift. Any actual inflation process will have drift in its past; reasonable people will have to suppose that this was 'not for the last time'. The discussion of the inflation tax in the previous chapter suggests that regimes characterized by a high average rate of money growth will also show a high degree of policy volatility. This theme will be developed further in Chapters 4 and 5 below.

[13] Benjamin Klein drew attention to the significance of the regime shift from mean-reverting to (what are here called) random walk standards already some 20 years ago. Cf. especially his (1976) demonstration that the negative autocorrelation of US inflation rates in the nineteenth century had turned positive in the post-World War II period.

pronounced is the foreshortening of planning horizons that it induces.

The rise in the ratio of long-term to short-term nominal uncertainty means that the uncertainty about what the price level will be at some given future date diminishes more rapidly with the passage of time. The risk in real terms of any nominal contract will be smaller the closer to its maturity date the commitment is made. The random walk inflationary process induces increased flexibility preference.[14] One aspect of this is the increased willingness to forgo a higher yield for the privilege of short placements. Random walk inflation, therefore, may tend to reduce real short-term rates of interest. Persistently low *ex post* real rates should not be interpreted as due necessarily to *ex ante* underestimation of the inflation rate. Increased flexibility preference in the face of a random walk inflation may even make the market tolerate persistently negative real rates in the short end.

But in high inflation, the long end of the term structure tends simply to vanish. An aspect of this phenomenon of *corto-placismo*, as it is known in Latin America, is the substitution of two or more successive short-term contracts for one long-term one. When this becomes general, markets for long-term contracts calling for payment in domestic money will thin out and some will disappear. Both sides to such a contract would like to be compensated for the price level risk, but cannot, obviously, expect risk premia from each other. The result is clearly seen even in quite moderate inflations. Thus, for instance, the markets for 30-year bonds and for 30-year fixed rate mortgages basically disappeared in the US inflation of the 1970s. In high inflations, 'long term' may come to mean, not 30 years, but 3 months and it is 90-day trade credit that is vanishing.

Financing is an essential part of any intertemporal production plan. Investment will suffer, therefore, when normal methods for financing it wither away. This is one channel, therefore,

---

[14] The concept of 'flexibility preference' goes back to A. G. Hart (1942), was revived by John Hicks (1974), and given its modern development in R. Jones and J. Ostroy (1984).

through which we would expect economic growth to be adversely affected. But not the only one.

The simplest model of a RWMS would be a purely probabilistic one. If accelerations and decelerations of the nominal impulse were actually drawn from some Urn of Nature (kept from public sight in the meeting room of the Open Market Committee), we might imagine that most agents would with experience come to learn the moments of this unchanging probability distribution. The system would settle down to a coherent state of nominal expectations. But of course no one believes that the policy-making authorities are just playing dice or roulette. Policy is made with more purpose than that. The problem is to know who will be in charge when, what they will be trying to accomplish, what conditions they will face—and what economic theory they might believe in. In systems where policy is not fairly tightly constrained, these things are impossible to know very far in advance. Hence, the long-term uncertainty. Economic agents will strive to make sense of the near-term future by drawing on their experience to form their own theories about how policy evolves. But 'strings' of observations, that are never very long in this context, can be rationalized in more ways than one. So a variety of monetarist, structuralist, and political business cycle theories comes to flourish among economists and a more abundant flora, we can be sure, to bloom among the public at large.

Consequently, people differ in their inflationary expectations. When they fail to converge to a coherent state of expectations, the result is that capital will be inefficiently allocated throughout the economy. Any two transactors, who face the same nominal interest rate but who differ in the rate of inflation they expect, will calculate with different real rates in their intertemporal allocation decisions. When, in addition, those markets disappear in which long-term nominal interest rates are normally determined, the economy comes to lack any mechanism that might bring about consistency in the allocation of capital.[15]

---

[15] To the extent that credit markets disappear so that take-overs cannot be financed, this mechanism for correcting inefficiencies will not be operative either.

So economies on a RWMS not only accumulate capital less rapidly, they also allocate it badly.

The ability to predict the frequent turnarounds in monetary policy, and the ability to hedge against them when they cannot be predicted, becomes paramount to the success and survival of firms under this kind of regime. Efficiency in production, in quality control, and in marketing and distribution becomes less important. The random walk standard changes the rules that govern the 'natural selection' of people for success within corporations and in the system generally. Financial experts, accountants, lawyers, and people with political connections are among the species favoured. Engineers, product designers, and production managers do less well. Ambitious people will reallocate their efforts and their ingenuity accordingly, which is to say, in directions that may be privately rewarding but are not socially productive.

The unsteady course of policy characteristic of the regime is most likely the outcome of monetary discretion exercised under strong and shifting political pressures. But this kind of inflation also tends by itself to create a highly politicized environment. When inflation cannot be forecast with any accuracy, private contractual agreements become less effective, less reliable as instruments for reducing business risks to manageable proportions.[16] Alternative strategies will be political. Random walk monetary mismanagement will induce all sorts of influence peddlers and pressure groups to seek to obtain by public compulsion what private co-operation will no longer deliver.

---

[16] Cf. Leijonhufvud (1977). For a discussion of the reasons why indexing will not provide a perfect solution to this problem, see below, Chapter 5.

4
The Finances of the Government

If high inflations are virulent processes, with large social and economic costs, the obvious question is why any sane government would allow the malady to fester. Outright policy mistakes do occur but surely cannot provide a complete explanation. Similarly, erratic inflation makes it difficult to conduct policy in a coherent manner. But governments do not end up with high inflations merely because they adapt to an unstable environment. In a manner of speaking, they 'choose' the policies that result in high inflation, albeit a choice made under political duress and in difficult circumstances.

The problem of financing the public sector lies at the very core of high inflations. The sources and uses of public revenue vary considerably from country to country and from period to period. Moreover, fiscal policies emerge through processes of political bargaining, carried out within particular institutions that also differ between countries. Thus, each high inflation episode has its own history which explains the demands on the government budget, the alternatives under debate, and the play among the relevant actors. For these histories of descent into the maelstrom, not much in the way of a 'general theory' can be provided. Still, the various cases have in common the persistent failure of a polity to reach a fiscal compromise that allows the government to operate within its means.

The perception of inflation as the outcome of an unresolved distributive struggle has been shared by a number of influential writers (cf. Hirschman 1963, 1970, 1980; Prebisch 1982; Mallon and Sourrouille 1975; Canitrot 1975; Hirsch and Goldthorpe 1978). The argument has resurfaced in different guise in recent models of policy games. It is particularly persuasive for high inflations. Underneath the disorder in public finances one typically does find a political system unable to resolve conflicts that are at bottom struggles over the distribution of income.

FISCAL INCONSISTENCIES AND RELIANCE ON THE INFLATION TAX

Money creation is a significant source of government revenue in only a few countries (cf. King and Plosser 1985; Easterly and Schmidt-Hebbel 1991; Cukierman *et al.* 1992). In low inflation countries, governments do not generally consider it a relevant option to finance expenditures by money creation. Strong external constraints are not needed to prevent them from inflating. Although most countries experience fiscal difficulties from time to time, governments in stable economies are expected to manage eventually to live within their means, matching their projected spending to their actual or potential taxing capacity. Fiscal authorities do not maximize seigniorage and the public does not calculate with the possibility of inflationary surprises taxing their money balances.

In high inflation economies, in contrast, seigniorage revenues are generally a non-negligible proportion of GDP. In some of them the inflation tax ranks among the largest sources of government income. Still, their fiscal policies are not adequately described just by the amount of resources derived from the inflation tax. What distinguishes these economies, rather, is the spectacle of governments urgently pressed into expenditures which they lack the capacity to finance by ordinary taxes. Moreover, the incentive for the government to produce revenue by inflationary accelerations is ever-present and a problem that the public cannot ignore.

How are these obvious contrasts between low- and high-inflation countries to be understood? The recent literature emphasizes the time inconsistency problems associated with reliance on the inflation tax as a possible explanation of the nature of high inflations. It is shown, for example, that a government which maximizes revenue in the short run but does not precommit to a particular inflation rate will have an incentive to create inflationary surprises (Auernheimer 1974; Calvo 1978; Lucas and Stokey 1983). In such circumstances, the interplay between the government's incentives and the expectations of private agents generates an equilibrium where the inflation rate has no upper bound while (if money demand responds sufficiently to anticipated inflation) seigniorage revenues tend to zero. Less extreme outcomes result if a not-too-myopic government engages in a 'reputation game' with the private sector (Grossman and Van Huyck 1986), or else if its revenue motive is tempered by dislike of inflation (Bruno 1990).[1]

Still, attributing the differences in inflationary performance among countries to diverse policy 'preferences' only begs the question. We prefer to see the short-sighted policies and apparent tolerance of price instability of high inflation governments as the results of their grappling with a dilemma they are unable to resolve. A simple steady-state model[2] makes the argument clear.

Define the 'fiscal pressure' that the government has to contend with as the discrepancy between the 'target' level of spending that it would find most politically expedient to deliver and its capacity to collect taxes. Both the target level of expenditures and the taxing capacity are treated as exogenous.[3] (Some aspects of the distributional games that might determine their values will be considered later on.) The target is, of course, unobservable and need not bear a monotonic relation to realized spending. None the less, it is often possible to judge

[1] This type of reputational argument raises the question of how the multitude of private agents co-ordinate their expectations in order to play a 'punishment strategy' against the government (e.g. Rogoff 1989). However, in models where fiscal policies are endogenous, the way in which agents form expectations can influence not only the dynamic path but also the stationary state of the price level. If private sector expectations were to be backward-looking, for example, governments have to contemplate the consequences of their current actions for future outcomes. Although this is no part of agents' intentions, the nature of their expectations generate what amounts to a reputational game.

[2] The model, drawn from Heymann and Sanguinetti (1994), is summarized in the Appendix, section A6. A steady-state construction will suffice for our argument at this point, although it obviously neglects essential aspects of high inflations.

[3] The maximum attainable zero-inflation tax revenue is assumed to be given. It is subject to erosion through the fiscal lag effect, but cannot be augmented by marginal policy actions. There is a sizeable literature, to which we make reference later, which treats the level of taxation as a choice variable subject to smoothly increasing collection or distortion costs.

qualitatively how large are the claims on the budget. If actual spending falls short of target, the government is assumed to incur a cost; in practice, this cost is imposed by disappointed interest groups or results from more widespread dissatisfaction with the provision of public services. But high inflation is also politically costly to the government.[4] Suppose, finally, that the government is unable to borrow so that the deficit must be financed through the central bank.

As is common in much of the recent literature, we assume that policy-makers in effect 'choose' the inflation rate each period by weighing the costs of inflation against the costs of spending less than is politically desirable. We can now contrast the consequences of low and of high 'fiscal pressure'.

In the case where the potential revenue from regular taxes exceeds the expenditure target, there is no trade-off between policy goals. The government is able to tax 'below capacity' and still run a zero deficit. It has no fiscal motive to inflate. Moreover, if private agents for some reason came to expect inflation and reduced their demand for real balances accordingly, the authorities would see no reason to validate those expectations. Consequently, the only possible steady-state equilibrium is one with zero 'fiscal' inflation (cf. section A6 of the Appendix). The result remains similar as long as fiscal pressures are slight. The government might then collect some seigniorage revenue, but it would do so at a low inflation rate.

While the inflation tax may have the Laffer-curve property, states on the 'far side' of the curve do *not* qualify as stationary points in this low-pressure case. Stationarity on the far side is simply not consistent with the incentives of a solvent government. The government will not elect to run the constant deficit that would stabilize the system at such points since that would incur the costs of a high inflation. Economies with reasonably solid fiscal systems will not wander into high inflation traps.

---

[4] That high inflation makes governments unpopular is a readily observable fact. But it is mainly the unpredictability of volatile prices that causes opposition to the government to mount. To assume a sizeable inflation cost in a steady-state argument therefore borders on contradiction. Our model must not be taken altogether literally!

At the other extreme, very strong fiscal pressures make the government desperate to appropriate as much resources as possible as soon as possible. Now, the low inflation states are not sustainable (cf. the Appendix) since the correspondingly large inflation tax base offers the opportunity temporarily to satisfy the demands for higher spending by inflating faster than expected. Only at very high (actual and expected) inflation rates would the government cease its attempts to profit from inflationary surprises. Thus, once again, there is only a single steady state. But this one is likely to lie beyond the peak of the inflation tax curve.[5] Once there, the government loses 'at both ends'. It bears the political costs of high inflation and it fails to satisfy the demands for more expenditures. Thus, the government is hurt both by the 'voice' of the various interest groups—and by that of the general public who suffer from inflation and may prefer a larger supply of government services—and by the 'exit' of agents who cut their holdings of domestic currency.

In this model, the variable driving the inflation rate is the fiscal inconsistency (i.e. the difference between 'target' expenditures and the taxing capacity) rather than the actual deficit. This eliminates the counter-intuitive properties of the Laffer-curve models reviewed in Chapter 2. Here the deficit is an endogenous variable rather than a parameter and the same measured deficit can be an outcome of two utterly different situations. In the first one, the government is close to its target for expenditures and does not truly want to increase its deficit. In the other one, the authorities manage as best they can in a state of 'repressed

---

[5] For some values of the 'preference' parameters and a Cagan money demand curve, the model would allow for multiple steady states. However, these appear at intermediate values of fiscal pressures, not for low or very large ones (see the Appendix). Analytically this means that one may find 'catastrophic' changes in the steady-state inflation rate as the difference between the spending target and the taxing capacity varies. The equilibrium inflation rate may then also be path-dependent. Numerical simulations with the model generate high inflation outcomes for 'reasonable' values of the parameters but will not generate solutions in the hypcrinflation range—say, above 50% per month—except for extremely large fiscal pressures or exceedingly low values of the 'inflation cost' parameter. These simulation results suggest that steady-state constructions may be inappropriate in seeking to rationalize 'true' hyperinflations. See the Appendix and Heymann and Sanguinetti (1994).

spending'. The revenue constraint prevents the deficit from being larger, since (for given expectations) larger seigniorage revenues can be extracted only by pushing inflation to intolerable levels. In this latter case, the government must first regain control over fiscal policies in order to bring the inflation down. But finding ways to resist the pressures to spend or else to reform the tax system is not just a matter of will-power and good intentions.

The argument also suggests that the dependence of behaviour on the fiscal regime extends to other policy experiments. For example, if taxes are subject to inflationary erosion, tax indexing under moderate fiscal pressures allows the government to gain at the margin of both of its objectives: it can increase spending while reducing its dependence on the inflation tax. By contrast, if the underlying fiscal inconsistency is large, indexing of taxes removes a disincentive against producing surprise inflation.[6] If it is so perceived by the public, the demand for money will fall and the government will see the inflation tax base erode.

The argument of this model obviously invites the further question of what determines the fiscal pressures themselves. At this point, we will not venture back along this particular chain of causation. Instead, we should turn to the consequences of the government's inability to contain the pressures and control the overall fiscal situation.

THE FISCAL MAZE

Once the economy is mired in high inflation, the government's economic policy-makers will become absorbed in the day-to-day management of the situation, devoting much time and energy to adjusting public sector prices, to manipulating the exchange rate, and to exploiting whatever degrees of freedom may remain for monetary policy. Yet their actions lack any

---

[6] The last possibility has been pointed out by Fischer and Summers (1989). There is an analogy between the incentive effects of having different exposures of taxes to inflation and that of having differently denominated government liabilities; on this, see the following section.

overall design. Instead, policy results from the accumulation of short-run decisions as the authorities lurch from one emergency to another without any control of the process. Many of the characteristics of high inflation stem from this loss of control.

High inflation fiscal regimes may be characterized by the following 'stylized facts' (as that all too useful evasion goes):

(i) Revenues cannot easily be augmented by legislating higher rates on existing taxes. There may be several reasons for this: an already high level of taxation, deficiencies in the design of the tax system, or ineffective methods of collection.

(ii) A systematic and comprehensive budget process to allocate planned expenditures and control the actual ones is lacking. Government departments, state industries and other organizations operate in effect under 'soft budgets'. Interest groups negotiate directly with the government or with particular agencies instead of competing with one another for a share in the overall budget. Moreover, the budget may be burdened with large extraordinary expenditures for wars, reparations, or foreign debt service.

(iii) New debt can be floated only with great difficulty. Bonds can be placed in the domestic market only at yields which incorporate sizeable default premia that rise steeply with the size of the debt. The government is for all practical purposes unable to attract new 'voluntary' lending from abroad. In extreme cases, it simply cannot find a market where its paper can be sold.

Several strands of causation run from the underlying inconsistency of fiscal policies to the resulting high and erratic inflation (see Figure 4.1). The perception that the government is unable either to increase taxes or systematically to curb spending reduces the public's demand for government bonds. The absence of immediate means of financing makes it exceedingly difficult for the government to take the 'long view' and choose a course of action, such as tax reform, that may incur short-run costs for long-run benefits. If it can neither make ends meet nor issue debt, monetary financing becomes the only remaining option. The central bank ends up covering not only the 'permanent' deficit, but also transitory disturbances to the

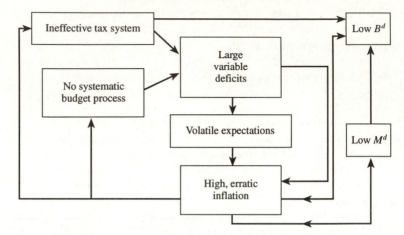

Fig. 4.1. High inflation fiscal regimes

treasury's cash flow. The public comes to anticipate fiscal and monetary instability and adapts its money demand and pricing practices to it. Consequently, the base of the inflation tax erodes (so that the government's ability to repay debt by issuing money is itself put into question) even as high and variable rates of money growth get more quickly transmitted to prices. High and variable inflation, in turn, reduces real tax revenues and makes them more erratic. Moreover, volatile inflation disrupts credit transactions, including those which involve the government itself, and makes budgeting much more difficult.

High inflation feeds on itself by further complicating fiscal management. It does so through a number of feedback loops. Figure 4.1 also conveys an implicit policy message, namely, that no single policy change is likely to bring stability. If the high inflation syndrome is to be broken, it has to be attacked at several points simultaneously.

DEBT MANAGEMENT AND ITS PROBLEMS

Public debt in high inflations

In most cases, governments of high inflation economies have accumulated large debts in the past and face tight credit constraints in the present. The inability either to service or to refinance the public debt in an orderly fashion played a major role both in the European hyperinflations of the 1920s and in the more recent high and hyperinflations in Latin America. Although these debt burdens explain an important part of the fiscal problems in those high inflation episodes, they do not explain all: a number of countries have managed with debts larger, say, than those of the Latin American cases (around or below 100 per cent of GDP) without ending up with extreme price level instability.

The role of government liabilities in high inflations is a complicated subject. In the post-World War I episodes, much of the debt consisted of long-run nominal bonds issued in a more stable past. When a country already has a history of monetary instability, however, its entire domestically denominated debt will be of short maturity, with rates of return embodying the expectation of a high rate of inflation. The government may also have a sizeable foreign debt. In several Latin American cases, such foreign debts were at least in part the result of the public sector having assumed liabilities originally incurred by the private sector on subsidized terms. Often, the status of this foreign debt is highly ambiguous: the government accumulates arrears on the service of it, but does not openly declare an intention to default; the terms of repayment are continuously being re-negotiated, while the interest accruals on the outstanding debt bear a significant 'risk premium' spread, and the country receives little or no new 'voluntary' lending from abroad.

At the same time, the government will try to float some domestic debt, by offering a variety of short-maturity bonds either at high nominal interest rates or with sundry adjustment clauses. Generally, such issues are sold at yields that exceed those that prime private sector borrowers have to pay.[7] Since the authorities find it very difficult to sell bonds in the open market, they are likely to borrow indirectly, by setting high reserve requirements on bank deposits. When this is done also with savings and time deposits, the central bank will be forced to pay interest on reserves if it wants to avoid very large spreads between the borrowing and lending rates of banks. Such policies reduce the volume of bank-intermediated credit going to the private sector. In some instances, the central bank may also hold significant claims on the banks, usually in the form of rediscounts, but it is then often doubtful whether these will prove recoverable. If the government is in truly desperate straits, it will engage in various unconventional borrowing operations such as delaying payments to suppliers or, in extreme cases, even to state employees.

The various instruments of government debt differ, not only in their contractual specification of yield and maturity, but also in their prospects for repayment. This is true also for its implicit financial commitments, such as payment arrears. Once the government is in default on part of its outstanding debt, the 'ranking' of liabilities in the queue for repayment is hardly a matter of systematic design, but depends very much on the circumstances of the moment and on the pressures that the several categories of bond holders can exercise. The traditional image of government bonds as 'safe' assets obviously does not apply—even though it would be all but impossible to specify with any precision the nature of all the risks that attach to them. In a similar fashion, the government's own various claims on the private sector are likely to become the subject of case by case negotiations and thus be of equally uncertain value.

---

[7] Private sector borrowers do, of course, have to pay the same anticipated inflation premia as the government. When the market demands an additional risk premium from the government, it is because it has learned from experience that governments have ways to default that ordinary borrowers do not have. Forced roll-overs of maturing debt at interest rates below market rates is an example.

Debt and government incentives

The incentive problems associated with debt management have received much attention in the recent literature. If taxes are raised at a net social cost—because of the distortions they induce or because of the resources required to collect them—a government that maximizes the welfare of the 'representative agent' would choose to smooth out the burden over time, by running deficits in periods of high public spending or low real income. The 'optimal debt contract' would generally make service payments contingent on the future state of the economy (Lucas and Stokey 1983; Lucas 1986). But, when the time comes to service the debt, the best course for the government will be either to default outright or, if the debt is nominal, to do so by provoking a jump in the price level. According to this line of analysis, default would be the best course in the sense that it substitutes a lump-sum tax on bond holders for distortionary taxes. But the common knowledge that such incentives are present would eliminate the demand for public debt. Thus, this argument turns the puzzle around. Instead of asking under what conditions a government would default, one asks what makes governments ever repay their debts and what induces people to hold government bonds at all?

From a historical perspective, this way of putting the question is a useful one. The dealings between the 'sovereign' and its lenders have long been recognized as fraught with special complications, and the record shows a long list of governments which either lost or never established their creditworthiness (cf. Hicks 1969, chap. 6; Parker 1974). Still, the experience of modern organized states shows that governments can in general rely on obtaining credit at 'normal' interest rates in order to cover transitory deficits and are thus able to buy time to reach a political solution, if their finances threaten to get out of order. A large public debt does not always cause fears that it will be repudiated or inflated away.

A government that defaults does face non-trivial costs which, however, are easier to identify qualitatively than to quantify. First, even if the government can avoid coming into conflict with its own legal system, breaking a contractual obligation can result in a general loss of confidence in the word of the authorities. This, in turn, may have repercussions that go beyond the future refusal of the public to lend. But such a threat need not be much of a restraining influence if the government is short-sighted or if, in order to service the debt, it has to renege on other promises made beforehand. It is sometimes possible for default to be credibly presented as a one-time event due to an extraordinary emergency. What combination of circumstances will persuade the public that such default will not recur is, however, a question hardly capable of a general answer.[8] Second, bond holders, whether foreign or domestic, most often constitute groups with considerable capacity to make their 'voice' effective.

Clearly, then, default should not be thought of as a strategy in a game between the government and a representative agent. It always has serious redistributive implications and, consequently, has the potential to become the subject of fierce political conflict.

The incentives to default may depend on the terms on which lenders supply credit. Several models of debt servicing emphasizing this property have appeared recently. In Calvo (1988*a*), the government would opt for servicing the debt in full if it could borrow without paying a 'default premium'. When forced to borrow at a very high interest rate, however, it will choose to validate the expectations of default, since the debt burden would otherwise exceed its willingness to tax. Similarly, when the debt is fixed in nominal terms, the government would pick a different inflation rate depending on whether the market sets

---

[8] The argument extends to capital taxation in various forms. The issue of whether the government could make a convincing case for non-recurrence was central to the discussion of 'capital levies' in a number of historical episodes. Eichengreen (1990), for example, suggests that the proposal to apply a capital tax in Britain in the 1920s was abandoned because of the fear that the public would come to expect similar measures to be taken in the future. Even countries with much deeper fiscal crises refrained from imposing explicit levies during that period (cf. Keynes 1923). However, there have also been historical cases of default or forced refinancings of debts which did not cause large or lasting costs to the governments in question.

the nominal interest rate high or low. Multiple equilibria can also arise when the debt is of short maturity. The expectation that the government cannot raise taxes sufficiently to redeem its bonds on demand may produce a run, analogous to a banking panic; in that case, the government would default, while it would not do so if its creditors decided to refinance the debt (Alesina, Prati, and Tabellini 1990).

These models are not far-fetched. However, in stable economies, debt default is an alternative the authorities and the public appear to leave out of consideration without so much as thinking through prospective costs and benefits. Under normal, stable conditions, one does not expect the public to precipitate default by demanding a steep interest premium or by creating a funding crisis merely through an unprovoked turn of mood. But governments which are perceived to have lost control over their policies may indeed be vulnerable to sudden shifts in expectations.

Debt management under conditions of strong fiscal pressures

Very high inflations stem from the inability of governments to reconcile the demands for public spending with the public's willingness to pay taxes. Desperately short of revenues, the authorities may be driven to consider measures that would reduce the resources going to debt service. Triggering unanticipated inflation will do.

To make the argument a bit more precise, suppose that a certain amount of nominal debt must contractually be repaid in the present period but that outright default will incur a sizeable cost. A simple extension of the analysis of the previous section suggests that the presence of the nominal debt has two consequences. First, like any other claim on the budget, it reduces the level of operational expenditures that can be financed; this would make the government more willing at the margin to tolerate the loss of support due to higher inflation if by so doing it can bring actual spending closer to desired. Second, nominal bonds increase the base of the inflation tax and, consequently, make 'jumps' in the price level more attractive from the government's point of view. On both accounts, the debt raises the equilibrium inflation rate. When fiscal pressures are strong, therefore, we expect the nominal interest rate to increase steeply with the size of the debt. But this lowers money demand. So, while trying to reduce debt service by accelerating the inflation may be tempting as a temporary expendient, in the end the costs to the government may be of much the same magnitude as those of outright default.

In this context, indexing of the debt would signal to the private sector that 'inflationary surprises' have been made less tempting to the government. This might make the demand for real balances recover to some degree.[9] But indexing is not always a credible guarantee. Ultimately, it is the government's inability to provide a backing for its debt that limits its ability to borrow. Clearly, there cannot be steady states in which the real deficit, including the interest burden, exceeds the maximum revenues from the inflation tax. The size of the debt that the public will be willing to absorb may well reach a ceiling before that condition holds. In the limit, if the authorities try to issue index bonds in a more or less desperate fiscal situation, where the sources of additional revenue, including inflation, are already exhausted, they are not likely to find lenders willing to buy that paper.[10] Under less extreme conditions, the government may have some degree of freedom to operate in the mar-

[9] Cf. Calvo (1988*b*), Calvo and Guidotti (1990). It has been argued (Persson *et al.* 1987) that the government could induce a decline in inflationary expectations—and escape the bad inflationary equilibria on the far side of the Laffer curve—by issuing indexed debt to an amount larger than its net liabilities and, at the same time, invest in nominal liabilities of the private sector. However, in order for this to be effective, it must be expected that the authorities will in fact enforce repayment of their claims against the private sector. But this is not much different from assuming that the government can in fact collect taxes, which is its problem in the first place. In high inflation economies, government loans to the private sector are typically regarded simply as subsidies.

[10] Note that it is in practice impossible to link payments to the contemporaneous price level. The indexing lag means that a possibility to expropriate bond holders by surprise inflation remains—but that a very much larger acceleration of the price level is now required for the government to gain a given amount of resources this way. It is possible, therefore, that the introduction of indexation could actually have a destabilizing expectational effect.

ket, but high inflations generally do not leave much manœuvering room for financial management.

Strong fiscal pressures threaten the government's solvency. The demand for public debt accordingly shrinks (although it may not vanish totally), and interest rates, nominal and real, become very sensitive to the size of the debt. Moreover, shifts in the public's perceptions of the government's fiscal intentions can effect the market dramatically. Outright repudiation of debt has costly repercussions, so it is not an action to be taken lightly. But interest rates will reflect the expectation that repayment cannot be taken for granted. Thus, the authorities do not so much engage in debt management as muddle through from one period to the next as best they can.

In relatively stable economies, variations in the national debt are used to dampen the immediate effect of disturbances to the budget and to spread them over time. In high inflation economies, the debt is more often an additional source of instability.

INEFFECTIVE TAX SYSTEMS

Government expenditures in high inflation economies are not necessarily all that large.[11] But their tax systems are often

[11] The Israeli syndrome differed from the Latin American one on both the expenditure and the tax side. In the Latin American cases of high inflation during the 1980s, total spending (including all levels of government and the capital expenditures of public enterprises) ranged between 25% and 40% of GDP, well below, say, European standards (cf. CEPAL 1991). On the other hand, the Latin American data show no simple pattern in the evolution of government spending during the period of high inflation. But in 'proper' hyperinflations, expenditures do fall. For example, in Argentina, public spending in 1989 was 7 points of GDP below the peak of the decade; in Peru, the drop was even more dramatic, from 35% of GDP in 1983 (when inflation was around 125% a year) to 13% of GDP in 1989, when the economy was approaching hyperinflation.

Compare also the figures for government consumption from 1980 to 1990 for Argentina, Peru, Venezuela, and Mexico reported in Labán and Sturzenegger (1992), table 1, which show a 'clear pattern' of accelerations of inflation being accompanied by sizeable reductions in government consumption.

strikingly deficient in both design and operation. The broad general taxes (such as the income tax or the VAT) tend to be full of loopholes and to be widely evaded besides. A significant proportion of government revenues derives from sundry excise taxes that are frequently imposed at such high rates that they cause costly allocational distortions even while producing little revenue. The upshot is a system that not only generates little income, but is also quite 'inelastic' in the sense that realized receipts do not increase significantly if tax rates are raised.

Once more, the same anomaly: it does not seem 'optimal'. How do we explain it? It is convenient to begin with certain features which are endogenous consequences of inflation itself and that high inflation countries, therefore, tend to have in common.

First, high rates of inflation do, of course, reduce real tax revenues, due to the lag between tax accrual and actual payment. This Olivera–Tanzi effect can be quite sizeable. Taxpayers would rather reverse the old adage 'Better late than never'. But in a high inflation, late is almost as good as never. For a variety of technical reasons, accruals and payments cannot be perfectly synchronized. A truly 'pay as you go' system is simply not feasible. Nor can the problem be eliminated by indexation. The time-lags built into the adjustment clauses are unavoidable.

Second, the administration of tax collection is likely to be erratic and inefficient. It may happen, for instance, that for years on end practically no new names are added to the tax rolls, so that no one gets taxed today who was not paying taxes already years ago. The economic disorder that characterizes high inflations tends to undermine the performance of the public sector and it does not spare tax agencies. Wide fluctuations in real salaries and ill-fated 'rationalizations' cause many of the best people to leave public service and demoralize those who stay.

The 'pure' Olivera–Tanzi effect is reversed when the inflation rate is brought down. Indeed, the rise in real tax collections that occurs in this way can contribute much to getting the deficit under control. But the other effects are not easily reversed. In particular, taxes that may have been 'on the books' but have not been systematically collected for a long time lose their legitimacy, and any sudden resolve by the government to start collecting them is apt to encounter strong resistance. Stabilization may ultimately require recreating a politically legitimized tax structure more or less from scratch.

High inflations are negative sum games for society as a whole. A weak and ineffective tax system will make the country more or less ungovernable whatever the party or coalition in power. So why is it not in 'everyone's interest' (or, more realistically, in the interest of most groups), to make a 'New Deal' for a tax structure that will restore the solvency of the State? It is not that the point is not understood. The history of high inflations and hyperinflations shows both governments and the general public obsessed with the State's financial predicaments. Each case history is a story of repeated attempts to cut the deficit. But in most cases it is as if a succession of failed attempts is necessary before a coalition can finally be formed to put into place a realistic stabilization package.[12] The commonly shared recognition that systematic taxation is collectively preferable to continued inflation does not by itself produce agreement on the concrete steps that could stabilize the public finances.

The main reason, of course, is that both inflation and fiscal stabilization have distributive consequences. Inflation is a strong negative externality that individuals and groups impose on one another. Most agents may realize this, but they must still find a path to a negotiated solution and this is not easy. For a variety of reasons, it is likely that the conflict will have to be 'played out' before an agreement can be reached. In the meantime, all bear the costs of inflation.

An effective tax system is an instrument of power. Building such an organization is a long-term investment that will provide command over resources for a long time to come. This potential power may well be seen as a danger in a society that

---

[12] Cf. Alesina (1988), Eichengreen (1990), Maier (1975) on the European episodes in the 1920s; Carciofi (1990), Cardoso (1991), Dornbusch and De Pablo (1989), Heymann (1986, 1991), Machinea (1989), Modiano (1988), Morales (1991), Sachs (1987) on recent Latin American cases.

is politically unstable and polarized. Various groups might well refuse to support the creation of a workable revenue-raising machinery that could fall under the control of others in the future and become the instrument of a 'predatory State' (cf. Heymann *et al.* 1991*a*; Cukierman *et al.* 1992). Furthermore, the distribution of the costs and benefits of a comprehensive fiscal reform cannot be accurately foreseen; such instrument uncertainty adds to the risks that groups perceive in the move toward tax reform (cf. Dornbusch 1991; Labán and Sturzenegger 1991; Fernandez and Rodrik 1990). Moreover, the parties to a political negotiation are not only trying to determine the distributive results of alternative proposals, they are also engaging in a contest in which they measure their strength (cf. Alesina and Drazen 1991). Thus, the inflation drags on while the groups learn from the ongoing political struggle (and from how the economy itself is faring in the process) what they can hope to obtain.

Many high inflations were triggered by a major shock, such as a lost war, a big political change, or a debt crisis, which disrupts the distributive status quo and may bring new powerful actors into the game. Such shocks may cause existing coalitions to dissolve and may modify the power structure also in other ways that are not immediately apparent. In such fluid conditions, a new sustainable distributive configuration is not likely to be established quickly.

High inflations have eventful political histories. The distributive struggle is not only waged by groups exercising their 'voice'. It is also influenced by individuals exercising their option to 'exit'. When, for example, in a hyperinflation, asset holders individually move their funds out of a country, they collectively change the conditions of the game so as to make low income groups more predisposed in bargaining over taxes or over wages to make concessions that might encourage capital to return.[13]

---

[13] The point has been emphasized by Labán and Sturzenegger (1991). This type of exit behaviour—driven by individual decisions, but none the less politically influential—extends beyond the portfolio shift away from domestic assets. Another example is the refusal during hyperinflations of retailers to sell (cf. Chapter 5 below). This also imposes high costs on people with low incomes.

EXPENDITURES: LACK OF STRUCTURED BUDGETING PROCEDURES

Conflicting demands on the public purse are not a peculiarity of unstable economies. Pressure groups compete, by various means, for a bigger slice of the pie everywhere. Even authoritarian regimes will have competing ministries—or, if nothing else, competing armed services—whose demands have to be in some manner reconciled. This reconciliation may be arrived at in several ways, not all of them equally rational.

Fiscal stability requires that such conflicts over distribution or allocation be settled *in advance*, consistently with the resources available, and that there be means to enforce the resulting agreement. Ideally, of course, a number of other conditions should be fulfilled as well. The costs and benefits to various groups of alternative allocations should be appropriately taken into account at all margins, and so on.

Most countries have developed standard budget procedures for these purposes. Usually, major categories of expenditures and receipts as well as the total deficit or surplus are planned or proposed by the government. The overall budget then becomes the subject of a major political discussion in and out of parliament in the course of which it is revised. Once legislated, the budget becomes a binding constraint on what the executive branch may do.

Procedures of this type ensure that all groups with representation confront one another in a simultaneous negotiation. The respective claims have to be put on the table at the same time— and the total cut down to the resources that will be appropriated. This reduces the costs of gathering information about the demands of various sections of the public, and also reduces the trouble of organizing coalitions of those most likely to pay the bill when a particular interest is benefited. The binding nature of the budget, once passed, makes it more difficult for groups to get from the government by the back door what they were not able to achieve out in front.

Comprehensive budget negotiations do not, of course,

guarantee a consistent fiscal policy. They will not do so, for instance, if numerous and large items are kept 'off budget'. More importantly, it is entirely possible that the process will not arrive at a solution which is securely based on a reasonably stable, underlying political equilibrium. But a comprehensive budget, if not sufficient, does seem a necessary condition.

High and erratic inflation makes budget projections for periods as long as a fiscal year a futile exercise not just for the private sector, but for the government and its departments and agencies as well. When consistent financial projections can only be made over very short horizons, the consequences are in some respects worse for government than for private budgeting. Private budgets can at least be revised with a frequency that the legislative process will not allow, particularly since such revisions may invite the reopening of the political agreements previously reached. Since there is no way of avoiding frequent revisions of the government budget anyway, these are often done in a piecemeal fashion and without the benefit of parliamentary legitimation.

In the absence of an explicit budget that could possibly be enforced, the fiscal authorities will find themselves involved in a series of bilateral negotiations with interest groups in and out of the public sector. The overall budget emerges piecemeal from their attempts to deal with the demands of these groups one by one. In this process, the pressure groups are not able to trade concessions with each other. Instead, each one will come to the table with no incentive to limit its demands on the government but thoroughly intent on applying all its leverage to maximize transfers in its favour. Since the bargaining takes place outside those regular political forums where effective counter-coalitions are normally formed, each group is also less likely to face the countervailing pressure of those who eventually are to foot the bill. Hence all the pressure from all the groups is exerted in the same direction—towards a bigger deficit.

One may of course imagine cases where a government is able to face down each group in succession and keep the process under reasonable control. But this requires an uncommon power of resistance on the part of government—a power that may not even be desirable. It seems hardly a coincidence that so many of the high inflations on record have been associated either with the emergence of new democratic regimes that have yet to develop well-functioning fiscal institutions or with the decline of authoritarian governments. But high inflation, once underway, will weaken the authority of any government, and also make it all but certain that each successive group or government bureau bringing its demands to the fiscal authorities will be able to invoke an obvious injustice or a serious emergency.

The fiscal deficit that results from this process of one-by-one negotiations with pressure groups is likely to be 'suboptimally' high; indeed, it it quite possible that every major group ends up worse off, playing the negative sum game of high inflation (cf. Heymann and Navajas 1991*a*; Heymann *et al*. 1991*b*). But it is not a simple matter to organize the collectively improving 'moves' that must exist, for the deficits that emerge from ill-co-ordinated budget procedures feed the inflation that makes impossible the more rational budgeting of stable countries. To make matters worse, the process tends to undermine trust, not only in the intentions of the government presently presiding over the inflation, but in the good faith of other groups running the distributive race. It is in the nature of such vicious circles that they offer no easy escape.

SOFT BUDGETS

Even if budget plans could have been drawn up in a systematic manner, the central government is often unable effectively to enforce budget constraints on its own departments, on provincial and local governments, or on public utilities and nationalized industries. These subordinate units are themselves not able to project money expenditures and receipts forward for more than some months at best, and they can with considerable reason hold the central government responsible for the erosion and unpredictable variations in their real revenues. State and local governments (to use North American terminology) collect their own tax revenues with a lag and see their real value, therefore, as prey to the level and variability of the inflation rate. To the extent, moreover, that they depend on 'federal' revenue sharing, the real purchasing power of what they receive will vary similarly—when it is not suddenly curtailed in the course of some intermittent stabilization attempt by the national government. Public utilities and nationalized industries are often subject to price control and thus unable to manage the relationships between their costs and the prices they are allowed to charge.

In such circumstances, these units do in effect violate their budget constraints—and get away with it. Claiming *force majeure*, they demand and receive supplementary appropriations from the national governments.[14] These requests often come with short notice and many of them are of such nature that they can hardly be refused: '... or the hospitals will be without nurses on Monday.' The private sector quickly learns to play the same game. This inability to control budgets means that there is much uncertainty within the government itself about the future course of money creation, and thus of inflation, even in the short term.

Economic behaviour in contexts where budget constraints are not strictly binding has been discussed by János Kornai in a series of contributions (Kornai 1980, ch. 13; 1986). Although Kornai stresses the applicability of his analysis to a variety of areas, such as defence procurement, where fiscal discipline may be lacking in capitalist or mixed economies, the original context was the centrally planned systems of the erstwhile East Bloc. The 'soft budget constraint' is a key concept in Kornai's 'Economics of Shortage', i.e., his explanation of how economic systems function in conditions of chronic excess demand. It is of interest here for two related reasons: first, Kornai's analysis of the inefficiencies typically associated with 'soft budgets' in

---

[14] Sometimes, this behaviour takes the form of delaying, or not executing, payments due to other agencies in the public sector. When such a chain of 'multiple defaults' between government entities has taken shape, it becomes exceedingly difficult to establish precisely where the aggregate deficit does in fact originate. The inter-enterprise arrears in Russia in 1992–3 exemplified this problem on a fantastic scale.

socialist regimes helps us spot similar symptoms in high inflation economies; second, it offers a conceptual bridge that may be travelled also in the other direction, i.e., towards understanding the high inflation dangers that threaten the liberalization of the previously planned systems.

In conventional models of exchange, each agent is assumed to contemplate only such trading plans as have zero net present value. *Ex ante* this constraint could only be self-imposed by the decision-maker, but we imagine that he does so in the rational expectation that, *ex post*, society will not let you get away with violating it. This familiar construct Kornai terms the 'hard budget constraint'. The hardest of the hard would be the version we find in the competitive model where prices are parametric and cannot be influenced by the agent. But, while a monopolist has the market power to choose his terms of trade, he must still plan to finance his purchases from the proceeds of his sales. Persons who acquire goods from others by deceit or coercion, on the other hand, obviously do not obey the constraint. Neither do philanthropists. Theft, robbery and gift-giving are among the social interactions excluded from the pure theory of exchange.[15]

In socialist economies, household behaviour was budget constrained in the usual 'hard' way. But enterprise behaviour was not. In principle, legal regulations required state-owned firms in socialist economies to balance their budgets. In practice, however, enterprises chronically planned uses of funds in excess of assured sources of funds. They did so, of course, because they did not anticipate any drastic 'hard' consequences of so doing. In particular, they did not anticipate going bankrupt or being forced out of business. Instead, the rational expectation governing their financial planning was that emerging deficits would be negotiable with higher authorities.

This 'softness' of the financial constraint changes enterprise behaviour. Socialist firms normally had an incentive to maximize output. With soft budgets, it was not the relationship between marginal sales receipts and marginal monetary costs that limited output in the short-run. Instead, it would typically

[15] This is the 'Say's Principle' statement of the budget constraint of Clower and Leijonhufvud (1975).

be some bottle-neck or other—that is, physical rather than financial constraints determined activity levels. As a direct consequence, socialist enterprises showed relatively little responsiveness to prices; price-elasticities of supply and of demand for inputs were low. Prices, therefore, would be relatively ineffective regulators for the purpose of co-ordinating activities within socialist systems. Use of the price mechanism, moreover, could not have assured that resources would move consistently into their highest valued uses. Decentralization without the imposition of financial discipline will not produce allocational efficiency, since there is no assurance that soft-budgeting firms will calculate with equal shadow-prices for the same inputs. Since, finally, socialist firms were not constrained eventually to pay out of sales proceeds for resources used, their input demand tended to be 'almost insatiable'. Capacity utilization was chronically very high and registered unemployment very low in the typical socialist economy. Markets operated in a constant state of excess demand.

Clearly, this analysis will not carry over without modification to high inflation market economies or even to their government sectors. In particular, Kornai's output maximizing postulate will not apply; firms are not generally constrained by physical bottle-necks, nor are markets in a chronic state of 'shortage'. Yet, in some other respects, the picture fits: the incentives for public sector agencies and enterprises to respond to price changes are much attenuated;[16] inconsistencies in the valuation of resources within the public sector will worsen as a result.

Many economists are apt to rebel at the notion of a 'soft constraint'. From the standpoint of standard decision theory, it might seem, this could only mean that the constraints have been incompletely specified.[17] If so, the very term would be an invi-

---

[16] This will be true also for some entities outside the public sector proper but with a history of enjoying government subsidies. Once the shared expectations have been established that losses will be covered by a renegotiation of subsidies, soft budgets reign here too.

[17] Since Kornai's analysis originally concerned the economics of chronic shortages, the soft budget constraint theme is often thought to belong only in 'fix-price disequilibrium' contexts. Kornai himself has been intent on dispelling this interpretation (cf., e.g., Kornai 1986, p. 10).

tation to soft-headed analysis. To avoid such misunderstanding, it is preferable to stress 'soft *budgets*'. From the standpoint of our concerns here at least, the deeper relevance of Kornai's theory concerns co-ordination of activities in systems *where the ability to pay (or promise) money is not the sole legitimate way in which resources may be rightfully appropriated*. The socialist firm could continue to appropriate inputs, although financially 'bankrupt', because fulfilling the plan made it legitimate to do so. The socialist economy could not dispense with a monetary circulation system as long as the consumption of each individual household was not also going to be centrally planned. But the physical and the monetary control systems were inconsistent under central planning. Where the two clashed, the plan took precedence and the rules of monetary/financial control were— had to be—broken.

High inflation makes strict financial control of the public and quasi-public sectors impossible. But there are many socially legitimate objectives that are met by politically allocating budgets to the relevant agencies and that still have to be (more or less) met when budgets cannot reasonably be enforced. For instance, the government will be held responsible for keeping the schools and hospitals running and, of course, it must keep the police on and the army off the streets.

But once public agencies and enterprises begin to operate on the understanding that they will not be held to pre-specified budgets as long as 'legitimate' reasons can be adduced for running in the red, the soft-budget syndrome is established. It, in turn, feeds back on the finances of the central government, making the latter's deficit, the rate of money creation, and the inflation increasingly difficult to control and to predict.

There is, we feel, a lesson for monetary theory in this. Our standard theory of resource allocation and income distribution is developed entirely in non-monetary terms. The 'hard' budget constraints are specified as if they were, in effect, 'barter' constraints. The unit of account is taken to be arbitrary and is left unspecified. The stability and efficiency properties of general competitive equilibria are obtained within such non-monetary structures. Money is then introduced as an afterthought, found to be neutral—and we end up with the familiar problems of understanding how inflation matters.

One of the lessons of high inflation is that money *as unit of account* matters. In relation to the existing literature this is a surprise. Somewhat less surprisingly, the unit of account matters for *accounting* and for *accountability*. Here we have seen how, in the public sector, monetary budgeting is part and parcel of the mechanisms by which activity levels are controlled.[18] When money fails as an instrument for calculating plans and for enforcing accountability, the immediate consequences are not hard barter budgets but soft money budgets and the ultimate results are the co-ordination failures and inefficiencies just described. Now, inefficiencies in the public sector seldom surprise economists and they will not automatically infer that the profit-motivated private sector is similarly affected. But large private firms, for instance, have a variety of internal principal-agent relationships, similar to those in the public sector, in the monitoring of which monetary accountability may play a crucial role. The 'softening' of accountability means that cost control, for example, is weakened here as well.[19]

Firms encounter great difficulties in adapting their accounting procedures to the high inflation environment. Good substitutes for a stable money as a unit of account are not easily developed. Some large Brazilian multinationals have developed cost-accounting systems wherein the (private) unit of account is an index of their own input-prices. It may be impossible to know whether or not a particular division is making a profit from accounts kept in cruzeiros—or even in dollars, if the exchange rate is volatile—but it may be possible to determine whether its sales revenues would command a greater number of input baskets than was used in producing the output sold. The procedure will not ensure that costs are minimized and is not

[18] Our standpoint is more closely akin to Martin Shubik's than to that of the money-in-general-equilibrium literature. Shubik has long insisted on regarding the monetary-financial system as a *necessary* control mechanism for a market economy. Cf., for example, Shubik (1990).

[19] That inflation distorts conventional accounting procedures and thereby the basis for business decision-making has been stressed particularly by Howitt (1990).

likely to be of much help in calculating optimal output rates. But in a highly unstable nominal environment, the ability to find out whether one is breaking even or not is an important asset. Such sophisticated accounting will be beyond smaller firms and will not spread through the economy in general.[20]

The point goes farther. One of the puzzles of high inflations is that markets in equities do about as badly as do markets in money-denominated securities. If nominal instability makes people shun nominal assets, we expect them to flock to 'real' assets—and theoretical convention treats equities as such. But the unit of account has a role to play here as well. When monetary accounting produces 'meaningless numbers', corporate reports lose all transparency. Lacking reasonably reliable information on 'real' net earnings, market analysts become unable to evaluate corporate performance. Without the requisite, properly encoded information, the stock market cannot function.

The external, market relationships between profit-maximizing firms are a different matter, particularly if both sides are also disciplined by competition. Nevertheless, in high inflations, the contracts normally governing customer–supplier relationships also become less effective in regulating the outcomes to the parties involved. Monetary theory should not take it for granted that equally effective substitute control mechanisms will come into operation when money 'gets out of order'.[21]

INFLATION AND THE LIBERALIZATION OF PLAN-ECONOMIES

The picture we have given of government finances in high inflation economies of the Latin American type should make clear why the attempt to liberalize in communist countries unleashes strong inflationary pressures. The former Soviet republics and the countries of Eastern Europe also lack thick markets for government debt and functioning tax systems capable of producing

---

[20] Sophisticated as it may seem, however, its similarities to Soviet-style 'physical indicator' planning are worth noting.
[21] The reference is to John Stuart Mill. Cf. Ch. 7 below.

revenues commensurate with the share of GNP that the state seeks to appropriate or direct. The planning bureaucracy that has been built up to 'command' the allocation of physical resources is not easily converted into a budget administration and an accounting office capable of planning and controlling the moneys spent by departments and agencies held to hard budgets. Hard budgets cannot be instituted at once in a system that lacks credit markets, moreover. If the government were actually to succeed in suddenly imposing hard budget constraints, innumerable enterprises will be without the funds required to sustain normal production. To both eliminate subsidies and raise taxes on a population that has already seen their nominal assets consumed by inflation would pose a somewhat rough welcome to the market economy.

The Latin American economies with a history of high inflation have a big advantage over the countries of the former Soviet bloc in that the legal structures of a private enterprise economy, with a long evolutionary history to guarantee their consistency, are still more or less intact despite the high inflation turmoil. If monetary stabilization can be achieved, markets start to work again. Admittedly, the inherited distribution of wealth can be far from universally accepted and the underlying distributional conflicts make lasting stabilization difficult to bring about. But the formerly communist countries are in far more troublesome straits. Property rights are more unclear and politically conditional than in the unstable economies in the West. The legal framework of a market economy has to be created or recreated—not a task to be completed overnight. Beyond that, a broadly acceptable distribution of wealth has to be established *de novo*. This is surely a more difficult endeavour than that of modifying an inherited distribution that no longer has sufficiently firm support in the populace at large. Furthermore, cautious liberalization, starting from severely inconsistent prices, will offer easy arbitrage profits of enormous magnitude to those able to trade at those prices, while the population as a whole bears the costs of the transition. This all too easily exacerbates distributive social tensions.

High inflation overtook the Russian economy before a modern tax system and administration could be put in place and before much in the way of market reform had been accomplished. Accustomed to the command economy, the former Soviet leaders had to get used to a system where the government rules not by the power to command but by the power of the purse. They found it all but impossible to govern without the printing press but were slow to realize the near impossibility of governing by means of the printing press. In this brave new world, the power to control events vanishes when inflation mounts. When the money in the purse is worth no more than the paper it is printed on, the ability to govern is gone.

5

Living with High Inflation

Living with high inflation forces people to adapt every aspect of their economic activities to this peculiarly unstable and unpredictable environment. Even the most routine day-to-day transactions have to be organized differently. In some respects, the survival of relatively normal forms of economic behaviour is striking. The economy does not collapse—at least, not short of actual hyperinflation. But the capacity of individuals and of the economic system as a whole to cope with high inflation should not be exaggerated. Price instability greatly complicates the planning and co-ordination of economic activities. It wastes resources. In the extreme, it wastes them on a grand scale.

THE EFFECTS OF ANTICIPATED INFLATION

It seems appropriate to begin with the effects predicted by the simplest models. Setting the perfect foresight, market-clearing model 'in search of reality', what do we find?

Inflation tax distortions

An inflation running at a constant, predictable rate acts mainly as a tax on money balances, and thus creates incentives to reduce real money holdings. The 'liquidity services' that the inflationary society forgoes in this way can be produced at virtually zero social cost, since the assets that yield them are simply pieces of paper acceptable as media of exchange. The social loss due to the inflation tax can be identified, therefore, with the 'triangle' under the money demand function (cf. Bailey 1956; Friedman 1969). True, if the alternative to the inflation tax is another distortionary tax, the logic of the argument suggests that, in this second best context, the costs should be compared with one another (Phelps 1973).[1] However, while empirical estimates of money demand functions for relatively stable economies suggest that the welfare loss from anticipated inflation is quite small, they also suggest that the costs are none the less higher than the ones deriving from regular taxes (e.g. Fischer 1981*a*). Even at low levels, inflation appears to be an inefficient form of taxation. And, for high inflations, the welfare loss stemming from the reduction in money balances becomes quite significant, on the same order of magnitude as the revenue the government obtains from inflation, or perhaps even larger (cf., for example, Barro 1972; Driffill *et al.* 1990).

Even a perfectly anticipated inflation would have far from trivial costs, therefore. Still, so saying does not convey an intuitive grasp of the behavioural adaptations that correspond to the lost welfare triangle. Money is not a refrigerator. The picture of money as a service-producing asset is incomplete without a look at transactions practices. 'What money is' and 'what money does' are age-old, still debated, questions. What, then, are the concrete and specific inefficiencies that result from inflation tax avoidance?

The Baumol–Tobin (and Allais) theory of the demand for money directs attention to the transactions costs of moving in and out of money substitutes. The 'shoe-leather' metaphor—the real costs of too many trips to the bank or broker—stems directly from it. This is a narrow view of inflationary distortions, but it serves to point out that the movement out of money will start at the long end. People will not keep money for long periods, since the inflation tax varies in proportion to the holding period while the transactions costs do not. So the 'store of value' function of money is the first to give way. As the inflation rate rises, 'velocity' increases. This accords with the evidence from even quite moderate inflations.

----

[1] This comparison can produce quite different results depending on how the demand for money is rationalized. Some models would support a positive rate of inflationary taxation in the presence of distortionary taxes, while others maintain the 'optimal currency' position that society should be saturated with the costlessly produced money balances also in that case (cf. Woodford 1990).

A glimpse of cash-balance management in Brazil illustrates, moreover, how high are the shoe-leather costs incurred by agents in high inflations:[2]

'That's all I do in the morning,' says 25-year-old Maria Claudia Gebaili, a secretary at a Sao Paulo newspaper. 'When I come in, the first thing I do is call the bank. Usually it's busy because everybody else is trying to do the same thing. So I have to go over and wait in line to talk to the manager and ask him to take money out of my boss's short-term funds and put some in the checking account to cover the checks he wrote overnight. On Fridays, I always have to make sure that my boss's checking account is emptied because the money left there would be devalued over the weekend. But on Monday morning, some of the checks he wrote over the weekend have already appeared at the bank. So I have to race over to make sure he doesn't get over-drawn. It wears you down.'

In high inflations, people will make great efforts to synchronize payments and receipts. But other payment practices customarily used to economize on money holdings are also eroded by inflation. Trade credit,[3] in particular, becomes harder to negotiate and, like other nominal contracts, is granted on very short term (7 days, for example, when 90 days would have been normal under price stability). This is not an effect of anticipated inflation itself, but it suggests that, as inflation rises, the set of 'credit goods'[4] tends to shrink and cash requirements consequently rise. However, other adaptations work in the expected direction. Firms may enter into arrangements with one another

---

[2] The quote is taken from an article in the *Wall Street Journal*, 29 January 1990 ('Daily Inflation Struggle Obsesses Brazil', by Thomas Kamm). At the time, Brazil was experiencing very high inflation. Keynes (1923) and Bresciani-Turroni (1937) present vivid examples of the lengths to which people went in order to economize on cash balances in the German and other European hyperinflations of the 1920s. While people may not go to quite the same extremes, all the same economic strategems are observable also in high inflations.

[3] Ferris (1981) notes that the typical firm is simultaneously both a borrower and a lender, on basically identical terms, of trade credit. His model explains how trade credit arrangements permit networks of firms to pre-plan the timing of cash settlements so as to reduce money balances.

[4] Credit goods as opposed to 'cash goods'. The terminology is that of Lucas and Stokey (1983).

in order to get rid of unwanted surpluses of money when their cash flows are systematically out of phase (as, for example, if they pay wages on different days).

In other markets, transactions are often 'dollarized'. This is especially likely to happen in the markets for real estate and consumer durables. None the less, purchases of everyday consumer goods continue to be settled in domestic currency. The result is that the economy operates in effect with two currencies (or perhaps more), with each one used in different types of transactions. Wages are paid in domestic money, and the payment period generally does not change unless the inflation rate gets extremely high. Households adapt by building up inventories of consumer goods on paydays and the more well-to-do among them will quickly place the rest of their current earnings in short-term deposits or convert them into foreign currencies.

Some of these strategies to reduce real money balances are simply a matter of individual choice; others, such as switching to another currency of settlement, require a large number of transactors to co-ordinate their actions. In either case, such adaptations often involve investments, either in physical form, such as the introduction of automatic tellers by banks, or in working out new practices and arrangements. Once made, these investments allow agents to manage with lower money holdings more or less permanently. To that extent the inflation-induced drop in money demand becomes irreversible, thus reducing the base of the inflation tax in the long run. This 'hysteresis' effect has been studied empirically in both Argentina and Israel (cf. Ahumada 1988; Piterman 1988).

People will incur large transaction costs to elude a high inflation tax. These costs exist because substitute arrangements to the use of money are not easily found, except in special cases. Money retains its property as a medium of exchange even when taxed at exorbitant rates. Economic theory hardly prepares us for this fact. Why do high and foreseen inflations not lead to the disappearance of the taxed money? Why do they not lead to the smooth evolution of exchanges with other media, if needed, throughout the economy? The 'foundations' of monetary theory are in an unsatisfactory state.

This lack of secure foundations is commonly taken to be a problem that is as arcane as it is intractable and, therefore, one suitably left to the patient attention of ivory-tower specialists in pure theory. But it is anything but an academic problem in extremely high inflations. In the hyperinflationary limit, it becomes critical to know, for instance, whether the demand for transactions balances has a minimum below which it will not go, or whether it will converge asymptotically to zero as inflation rises, or whether at some point it will drop in a sudden catastrophe as people decide to switch altogether to another means of payment. The question of how long and to what extent domestic money may 'hang in there' becomes an intensely practical, highly urgent one—to which theory, pure or otherwise, gives hardly a hint of an answer.

Incidence of the inflation tax

The focus on transactions costs has the merit of drawing attention to how unevenly the ability to elude the inflation tax is distributed. High inflation certainly forces the average individual to become more financially sophisticated and also induces banks and other intermediaries to offer new money substitutes (if central banks so allow) and to increase the number of their branches and other facilities.[5] But it is well-informed people of means who have ease of access to financial instruments. Just moving about the city for the purpose is a trivial matter for the well-to-do, but not so for the poor. Minimum size requirements for bank deposits and foreign exchange transactions are fixed costs which bar the entrance of low-income people into those markets. The well-to-do, moreover, tend to have both the discretionary income and the complementary resources (such as

---

[5] It is a common observation that the 'physical' size of the banking sector tended to grow in the Latin American high inflations; Bresciani-Turroni (1937) noticed the same tendency in the German episode of the 1920s. This diversion of resources into financial activities does not mean, however, that the real value of the intermediated funds increases, since erratic inflation discourages the holding of domestic assets in general (see below) and since banks are typically forced to immobilize a large proportion of deposits in the form of required reserves at the central bank.

cars and freezers) that will allow them to bunch purchases early in the month when prices are 'low', whereas the poor are more or less constrained to carry a larger proportion of their income to the end of the pay period. Although a precise measure of tax incidence may be hard to get, there are thus a number of reasons to believe that the inflation tax is distributionally regressive (cf. Ahumada *et al.* 1993; Sturzenegger 1992*a*, 1992*b*). The point is worth stressing because the notion that anti-inflationary policy measures are regressive is so deeply ingrained in much of the literature.

Liquidity constraints

'Too much money chasing too few goods'—so runs the popular cliché about inflation. But whereas nominal balances keep increasing, real balances shrink. If money is an institution to facilitate exchange, one would expect lower real balances to be associated with fewer trades. Such effects can be modelled in relatively simple ways, albeit for highly stylized environments. Consider, for instance, an exchange economy where two types of transactors have inversely correlated endowment flows, so that the consumption streams of both can be smoothed by engaging in periodically reversing exchanges. Suppose further that the social contrivance of money is the vehicle for effecting these transfers; agents of type A accumulate real balances in high A-income periods to augment their consumption in low A-income periods by purchases from type B agents. A tax on real balances will clearly cause this trade to be curtailed.[6]

How much relevance can one attribute to such highly stylized models? In moderate inflations, the effects on everyday trade opportunities of the tax on money balances are unlikely to be of much significance. Even in high inflations, as long as they fall short of hyperinflation, the commodity trades of households are probably not all that much affected. Where the cash constraint will bite for most people is, first, in the ability to exploit more

---

[6] The example is due to Michael Woodford, who in discussion of these problems sketched a formal version of it based on the model by Bewley (1980). See also Casella and Feinstein (1990).

or less randomly occurring 'bargains'. This requires ready cash, for opportunities of this sort evaporate quickly and have to be grasped on the spot. A second effect occurs because people try to get along with virtually no precautionary balances. In bunching their purchases as far as possible early in the earnings period, they choose an illiquid position and thus take a bet on the contingencies that may happen before next payday. An unexpected medical expenditure, for instance, can easily unbalance the household budget and force a deep cut in consumption subsequently. This kind of risk seems to contribute much to the distaste that people, and especially low-income workers, feel for price instability. The fear of not 'getting to the end of the month' is a typical complaint often voiced in high inflations.

Other effects

Theory suggests that inflation should induce a change in the composition of portfolios. The effect most often adduced, in the technical literature as well as in popular discussion, is a shift from financial assets into real capital. Financial assets, the argument goes, will at least in part be subject to the inflation tax, whereas real capital is presumed to be a 'hedge against inflation'. One should not quarrel with the logic of this hypothesis in the context of the models used to derive it. But the proposition that high inflation promotes capital accumulation is utterly misleading. The very opposite is true. The various ways in which inflation disturbs economic growth will have to be considered further below, out of the context of anticipated inflation models.

A number of phenomena can be rationalized, albeit in somewhat *ad hoc* manner, under the assumption that the rise in the general price level is fully anticipated. For example, the commonly found association between inflation and relative price variability can be explained, after a fashion, by postulating costs of changing money prices and lack of synchronization in price revisions (Sheshinski and Weiss 1977; Danziger 1987). More variability in relative prices, furthermore, should induce more customer search (Bénabou 1988), although there are other, and probably stronger effects acting in the opposite direction (see below).

The conception of inflation as just a predictable rate of depreciation of money permits one to build simple, tractable models that yield definite results. So it pays in simplicity to stay as close as possible to this conception. But these extensions of models of a frictionless, predictable economy are of limited use. The presupposition that only menu costs prevent price setters from tracking the inflation rate perfectly constitutes a refusal by theorists to take the pricing problems of sellers seriously. Moreover, when prices lose their residual stickiness in hyperinflation, the noise in relative prices does not die away—if anything, it gets louder.[7]

Having set the model of a perfectly anticipated inflation in search of a reality to fit we will not attempt to stretch it to take in further ground. In the end, some quite crucial aspects of high inflations, from the way they originate to their economic consequences, are in any case going to be left out. It is time to turn to the 'reality (still) in search of models'.

INFORMATION AND THE SHORTENING OF PLANNING HORIZONS

Ask a chosen-at-random citizen of a low inflation country what last month's increase in the CPI was and he or she will most probably decline to answer. This monthly figure, although regularly published and easily available, is of no interest to him or her except maybe in very special circumstances. The average transactor in such an economy does not make decisions based on such high frequency observations. Some people will keep an eye on the price trend as described by annualized data, but that will be the extent of their interest in inflation. If the need arises,

[7] This is not an altogether uncontroversial assertion. As long as many consumer goods continue to be priced in terms of the domestic unit of account, relative price variability seems to vary monotonically with inflation. It may be that in the very last stage of hyperinflation virtually all goods get 'dollarized', and that relative price variability collapses at that point. The issue is discussed further in the next section and again in Chapter 7.

prices can be predicted one month or one year ahead with some precision; even the most naive forecasts will have errors no larger than a few percentage points.

Next repeat the experiment in a high inflation economy. Here the subject will be unable to recall the inflation figure for the past 12-month period, not because the number is large, but because it is irrelevant. Price changes over so long a period do not provide information of any use for current plans. Shift the question to the monthly CPI and the agent is not only likely to know the figure, but he may comment on the behaviour of the index component by component and offer personal reflections on the chances, say, that current policies will finally bring about 'single digit inflation' in the coming month. While he will probably make quite a well-informed impression, he will not even try to risk a projection of the price level beyond one month or two, and his guess over that horizon will in any case have a sizeable margin of error.

Now make the enquiry in a country in the midst of a hyperinflation. The subject might have a recollection of the latest published monthly inflation rate, but will treat this as a matter of historical record. A monthly interval is now perceived as a long run. In this case, weekly or even daily indices are in high demand, and people will focus their attention on variables for which such high frequency observations are available. In hyperinflations, hourly movements in the exchange rate often make front-page news in the papers. But, of course, the news refers to yesterday's events, and may not be informative as to what is happening right now.

This change in time perspective is characteristic of the difference between inflationary regimes. It applies not only to how agents view aggregate price level movements but real variables as well. In high inflations, real and nominal instability are intertwined. The steady high inflation where the real economy evolves undisturbed except for the distortion of the tax on money balances is a theoretical construction without empirical counterpart.

As we have suggested in the previous chapter, reliance on the inflation tax is almost by definition associated with unsteady economic policies. The context in which private sector activities take place, therefore, is one where governments operate without well-defined budgets and are subject to the immediate pressure of numerous urgent demands. Policies are likely to change course as new emergencies become the focal point of public attention, and the authorities use their imagination in dealing with them. If the country is indebted, its actual debt payments will be subject to periodic renegotiations and are consequently not known in advance. Future real exchange rates and real wages and profit rates will depend on the outcome of the bargaining with creditors. Thus, the prospective real returns to specific activities are typically highly uncertain. Policy instability and external shocks complicate private decision-making. Governments, on their side, cannot anticipate with confidence how the economy will respond to their actions.

In those circumstances, people express a strong demand for information, raw and processed. The time and effort spent on keeping informed increase. The diversion of resources by people trying to make sense of where the economy is going is one of the subtle but more important costs of instability (cf. Okun 1975; Leijonhufvud 1977; Dornbusch and De Pablo 1989; Sturzenegger and Tommasi 1991). But the price of knowledge (as it were) rises faster. The joint complexity of the political games and the market reactions becomes such that the models people use to form expectations and decide a course of action become more and more inadequate even as the data requirements increase. Some rough empirical generalizations can be relied upon, of course. People living in high inflation will not miss the connection between deficits, money and prices, for example. However, experience will not dictate a unique way of interpreting the available facts. At any given moment, reasonable people may react differently to the same set of data.

Moreover, incoherent beliefs make learning more difficult. If market behaviour is not only driven by 'fundamental' (as seen through agent A's model, say), but also by expectations (which, from A's point of view are on the whole both unobservable and idiosyncratic), then A will have a hard time distinguishing one effect from the other. Beyond a certain point, therefore, the complexity of the situation becomes self-reinforcing.

The uncertainty that the individual agent confronts increases rapidly with the distance from the present. Over a short time horizon, the individual may be able to guess what group will be most favoured in the next round of the fiscal game, what exchange rate policy will be followed, and so on. These guesses may be inaccurate, but it is still possible to act on them. What is practically impossible to know more than a few steps ahead is what outcomes will be produced by the sequence of moves made by all actors in the economic game. The range of possibilities is simply too wide to sort through. The uncertainty is not that of a game of chance. Instead, people constantly find themselves in situations where they know that tomorrow will bring news that will inform them of what futures are probable beyond tomorrow, but where they cannot guess today what that information may be like.

The end result is that agents, public and private, have to act on the basis of knowledge that is much less reliable than in a stable economy, although they give the superficial impression of being alert and sophisticated in their analysis of events. Not to act, or to postpone action, will then often be the preferred course (cf. Hicks 1974, ch. 2). When one knows that one does not know how to form expectations with confidence, the safest course is usually just to withdraw from the game.

People engage in active 'speculation' on the short-run course of the economy, but they are reluctant to commit resources over long horizons. Their decisions on setting prices, on buying and selling, and on managing portfolios are predicated on opinions about where government policies and aggregate prices are heading. Actions that cannot be reversed for some time will be undertaken only if they promise very high yields. A radical alternative, of course, is just to move whatever assets are moveable out of the country. By their very nature, high inflations are associated with high 'country risk' and, consequently, with capital flight. Long-run positions in financial assets will be held abroad.[8] This has feedback effects. Rapid reactions of capital

---

[8] It should be noted, however, that not all high inflation economies show the same propensity for capital flight. During the high inflation periods of the 1980s, for example, the outflow of private funds from Argentina seems to have been larger in relative terms than from Brazil.

flows to political or other news cause exchange rate and price volatility and, insofar as this in turn restricts growth, it also makes the budget situation worse (cf. Dornbusch 1991).

High inflation tends to reduce investment. It leads firms to require larger anticipated returns and shorter repayment periods; at the same time, it makes projects harder to finance. Instability 'dulls animal spirits', and channels them into political lobbying and short-run gambling in financial markets. The consequences may extend to intangible forms of investment. For reputational considerations to constrain opportunistic behaviour, agents must care about the future. When repeated interaction becomes less probable or when people start to discount delayed payoffs more heavily, 'hit and run' tactics that produce short-run gains will become more common. Unstable environments reduce the scope for co-operative modes of behaviour.

CONTRACTING

Flexibility can be purchased, at a cost, by delaying decisions, by loading portfolios with liquid rather than 'fixed' assets and by reducing specialization in production. Many ventures, however, are such that they cannot take place unless the parties make specific, irreversible investments of one sort or another. When that is the case, they must have some sort of guarantee that the arrangement will last for a certain period on more or less well-specified terms. Contracts are, of course, also essential to make resources flow through financial channels. But, in high inflation environments, individuals are unable to ascertain in what 'real' conditions they and their potential partners will find themselves in the future. The instability of prices also makes it harder to specify a mutually agreeable denominator for future payments. Consequently, simple long-term contracts and especially those specified in nominal terms come to be seen as very risky.

Transactors can adapt at three margins. First, they can write more complicated contracts that make future payments contingent on a larger set of 'states of the world' according to whatever sources of risk they see as salient. Second, they may shorten the maturity of contracts and incur the resulting costs of periodic renegotiation. In this case, they have to accept that they do not know what the exact terms of the next agreement will be and take the chance that next time an agreement might not be reached. Third, they can simply refrain from entering into contracts that inflation has made too risky. In that case fewer transactions are realized, markets become thinner, and some markets are thinned out of existence. The high inflation economy ends up with an impoverished set of markets compared to what one would find in an otherwise similar but stable economy. The qualitative evidence available shows that high inflation induces all three types of adaptation.

As the economy grows more unstable, one might expect to find agents increasingly willing to trade risks among themselves. But complicated contracts are difficult to write and to enforce, and people can shy away from them for fear of being exploited by more knowledgeable transactors—if the other party wants to include an uncommon clause, maybe 'he knows something that I don't'. Although various forms of indexing do emerge,[9] the typical written contract remains simple and relatively standardized. The overall impression of these new index contracts is not that they represent contractual innovations providing 'mutual insurance' of a sort that would enhance the welfare of the parties even were they living under monetary stability. On the contrary, they emerge as attempts to find acceptable substitutes for the nominal standard of stable economies. As such they are only partially successful.

The baskets of goods in terms of which the two parties to a business contract would most prefer to stabilize 'real' payments will often differ. The inputs and intermediate goods that are the

---

[9] In addition to the use of conventional indexing clauses in the German inflation of the 1920s, Bresciani-Turroni (1937, p. 310) refers to a practice of linking payments to the prices of specific goods such as coal, lignite, electricity, and rye. In Argentina, it was common to index public sector contracts by 'polynomial' formulas weighing different indices (e.g. particular components of the CPI or WPI, wages, the exchange rate) as an approximation to the unit cost of the input basket of the supplier. This last type of contract, it may be noted, is not immune to the reporting lag problem (see below).

most important to the two parties in a customer–supplier relationship, for example, will most often be very different. Consequently, the choice of the adjustment formula becomes the cause of sometimes lengthy negotiations. This decentralized search for an acceptable standard of contract is not likely to converge—at least not short of universal 'dollarization'. In Brazil, in 1993, some 30 different indices were said to be in use.[10]

An agreed-upon adjustment formula can still result in completely unintended outcomes when prices are very volatile. The Argentine legal system, for example, evolved a 'doctrine of unforeseeability' (*doctrina de imprevisibilidad*) by which a party to an indexed contract could obtain a revision of the original agreement if its escalator showed large deviations from the aggregate price level. But, in a state of high inflation, a new price swing can easily undo the effects of the legally enforced escape clause.[11] Naturally, such economic and legal complications increase the perceived cost of contracting and consequently reduce people's willingness to make long, binding commitments, especially if the index proposed as an escalator is not a standard one.

Large numbers of contracts end up being indexed to the CPI or some similar 'standard' basket. In some cases, such as Brazil or Israel, CPI-based indexation was promoted by the government which, for instance, established legal adjustment clauses for wages. In other cases, such as that of Argentina, it developed more spontaneously. The CPI does have some attractive

---

[10] *El Cronista* (Buenos Aires), 10 December 1993: 'Industrial firms like Xerox, for example, use up to 11 indices to adjust accounts receivable and payable with customers and suppliers. Exporters typically use the dollar, but a number of sectoral indices are also in use.'

[11] It occurred that a court would grant one party to a contract a change in the adjustment clause of an ongoing contract but the 'winning' party ended worse off than if the contract had been kept in its original form, as the relative price movement subsequently reversed itself. If real wages had fallen, for example, a plaintiff might persuade the court to change the indexing of payments from the CPI to a wage index—only to find that real wages would then start to rise. In a somewhat curious twist, second-generation contracts eventually evolved in which the parties explicitly resigned their right to initiate legal action based on the 'unforeseeability doctrine'.

features as an escalator of payments. The index is available for all individuals at the same time and clearly cannot be manipulated by the parties to a private contract.[12] Its very visibility, furthermore, means that it will come under instant scrutiny should its accuracy become suspect.[13] When this form of contract becomes predominant, linking payments to the CPI avoids bargaining costs. Once the practice becomes widespread, moreover, it will impart inertia to the inflation rate. This inertia in turn tends to limit the variability of the real value of payments even when the information that the index conveys only becomes available with some delay (cf. Chapter 2 above).

The specific characteristics of the arrangements used to escalate payments vary from country to country. For example, at the beginning of 1986, with inflation around 15 per cent per month, wages in Brazil were adjusted every 6 months based on an explicit indexation formula. In early 1985, when inflation ranged between 20 and 30 per cent per month, the Argentinian practice was one of monthly wage adjustments. These wage increases were often made with reference to the rate of growth of the CPI in the previous month, but they were not predetermined by a contractual indexation clause. The German experience of the 1920s shows an interesting example of how wage adjustments evolved as inflation accelerated. At first, the length of nominal contracts shortened, and indexation gradually became common. Later on, at very high rates of inflation, wages were sometimes linked to the exchange rate. When the inflation reached hyperinflationary levels, in August 1923, trade unions and business firms agreed on a system by which wages were adjusted according to the price level expected for the following week; forecast errors were corrected by retroactive

---

[12] But private parties will still find a way to profit. In Brazil, some investment funds maintained their own organizations for sampling consumer prices. This enabled them to predict some days in advance what the next revision in the nominal value of government bonds would be—and to profit handsomely thereby. In a stable monetary regime, financial expertise of this order might be put to better social use!

[13] There may have been cases in which governments manipulated the price indices in order to influence the outcome of private sector contracts. For instance, the Chilean military government may have used this unorthodox tool to de-index wages in the 1970s. Cf. Cortázar (1983).

compensation in the next payment (Bresciani-Turroni 1937). It is not clear how this complicated scheme was applied in practice, since it remained in effect for only a short period.

CPI indexation brings with it problems both for short and for long contracts which become particularly serious when the inflation rate is highly variable. The indices never report truly contemporaneous prices; they are compiled only intermittently; and they are published only with a lag. Indexation, therefore, is necessarily backward-looking. Hence, it makes little sense to index very short contracts, since the adjustment term would either be predetermined (if the contract terminates before the next date the index is scheduled to be published) or else would incorporate mostly price movements that occurred before the start of the contract. Very long indexed contracts, on the other hand, can generate highly variable real payments if the inflation rate is volatile. An indexed sum retains approximately constant purchasing power over the CPI basket only when the inflation rate is of the same order of magnitude in the current period as it was at the start of the contract. This condition is far from always satisfied. In Argentina in the late 1980s, for instance, the monthly growth rate of the CPI ranged between a minimum of 2 per cent and a maximum of almost 200 per cent.

Nominal contracting over long periods is a feature of economies where the price level is expected to remain stable, or at least predictable. Similarly, indexation is useful if the inflation rate is more or less steady. Widespread indexing, therefore, appears to be specific to a certain class of inflationary regimes. It may help to preserve long-run contracting in moderate-to-high inflations, but not when the inflation rate is highly volatile. We conjecture that the longest typical length of indexed contracts will be of the same order of magnitude as the period over which the variance of inflation remains within a certain tolerance limit. Thus, a very erratic inflation would reduce the number of long-indexed contracts and, beyond that limit, make the corresponding markets disappear.

There are alternative indexing arrangements which are not subject to a reporting lag. The simplest ones are those where payments are linked to the movements of the exchange rate or else directly denominated in foreign currencies. However, the link between the exchange rate and the aggregate price level is not one of proportionality, even in hyperinflation (see below). For most people, maintaining constant purchasing power over a basket of foreign goods is of little or no help if, in so doing, their command over the domestic goods that are the stuff of their daily lives is rendered more variable. When some people keep a good portion of their wealth in foreign assets they do not do so because it makes their wealth in terms of domestic goods more predictable, but mainly because they are unwilling to lend to other residents.

Some markets may become dollarized. For a market in houses and apartments to function, sellers must be able to post a price which can be maintained for some time. They do so by quoting in dollars. The alternative wealth-placements for buyers may also be abroad and they are likely to finance purchases out of foreign currency holdings. That real estate and perhaps other durable assets are transacted in a stable currency does not mean that corresponding credit markets will develop. In Argentina, for instance, houses were purchased by paying cash dollars, but there were no suppliers of dollar-linked mortgages.[14]

At the very short end of the maturity spectrum, nominal contracts still survive in high inflations. The demand for short-run interest-bearing assets is fed from two sides as people move away both from money and from long-run portfolios. But, as inflation becomes more and more erratic, they refuse to hold deposits with maturities extending longer than a few days. In the limit, if the economy approaches hyperinflation, only the offer of extremely high yields will induce people to keep funds in the banks at all. In less extreme cases, an active market for short-run nominal credits may survive, but it is not likely that

---

[14] In fact, a market for multi-year dollar loans only began to emerge after the start of the 1991 stabilization programme, which fixed the exchange rate by law. People chose not to make long-term contracts in dollars when the domestic currency was unstable, but began doing so as soon as the exchange rate was fixed at one-for-one.

it will maintain the volume of intermediation[15] as inflation rises. Moreover, many transactions in this market are probably based on differences in inflationary expectations and would not have taken place if both parties had similar beliefs. Although mutually agreeable, such 'speculative' trades on the whole do not serve efficiency in resource allocation.

In sum, economies in high inflation end up operating on a *triple standard* of deferred payments: very short contracts stay nominal; agreements of intermediate term such as housing rentals and wage settlements become indexed; and transactions in real estate and certain durable physical assets are foreign-currency denominated. But markets for long-term contracts are lacking no matter what the standard. Such a triple standard system is shot through with problems and inconsistencies of various kinds. For example, real estate prices may be quoted in dollars, but the purchase or holding of real estate cannot be financed by credit in any currency. When the exchange rate varies, this changes the relative price of dollarized houses and indexed rentals for reasons totally unrelated to the state of the two markets in question. Individual real incomes oscillate as the adjustment formulas of the contracts they depend on fail to track the changes in consumer goods prices. Prospective investors who rely on bank financing have to count on constantly rolling over loans with a maturity of a few weeks at real interest rates that vary between exorbitantly positive and rewardingly negative values. Gamble for gamble, it is not surprising that they often prefer to place their bets day by day in the foreign exchange market.

Productive enterprise is not such a day-to-day affair—and it suffers.

---

[15] For example, interest-yielding bank deposits in Argentina fell from a little above 20% of GDP in 1980 to 12% in 1988. This period does not include any episodes of hyperinflation. Moreover, in both years of comparison, interest rates were unregulated.

CURRENT TRANSACTIONS

Short of hyperinflation, the economy retains some residual stability over limited periods of time and this allows agents to predict roughly what market conditions they will face in the most
immediate future. This residual stability results from the survival of business practices that seek to avoid violent swings in
nominal prices. Even at very high inflation rates, the prices of
currently produced goods still continue to be quoted in domestic money and the interval between revisions of fix-prices never
quite shrinks to zero. None the less, prices become exceedingly
volatile.

Although the empirical findings are still under discussion (cf.
Driffill *et al.* 1990), the evidence indicates a connection between
the level and the variability of the inflation rate, and between
those two variables and relative price variability.[16] In general,
prediction errors for the price level are larger the higher the
average inflation rate. The variance of relative price changes
increases with the inflation rate, both in month-to-month data
and when longer periods with different average levels of inflation are compared. In monthly data, the 'unanticipated' component of inflation has the stronger correlation with relative
price variability, but a distinct effect of the 'anticipated' component remains.[17] Moreover, at higher rates of inflation, it

[16] The literature on this subject is large. See, for example, Glejser (1965),
Vining and Elwertowski (1976), Parks (1978), Blejer and Leiderman (1980),
Logue and Sweeney (1981), Fischer (1981*b*), Sheshinski *et al.* (1981), Blejer
(1983), Pagan *et al.* (1983), Marquez and Vining (1984), Domberger (1987),
Van Hoomissen (1988), Palerm (1990), Tommasi (1992*b*), Weiss (1992) and
Dabús (1993). Palerm surveys the literature in considerable detail.

[17] However, Lach and Tsiddon (1992), working with highly disaggregated
data (prices of 26 food products, each reported by a substantial number of
sales outlets), find the effect of expected inflation to be stronger than that of
unexpected inflation. In 'islands' models, relative price variability depends on
unanticipated inflation; evidence for the role of anticipated inflation is often
taken to favour the 'menu cost' explanation. Whether 'the' rate of inflation
measures the behaviourally relevant variable at the level of any particular individual's decision is questionable, however, and this is even more so with its
anticipated and unanticipated components. Cf., again, Jonung (1981). It is
quite uncertain, therefore, whether regressions on these components can do
much to help us discriminate between the two classes of models.

appears that relative prices of similar goods, and relative prices of the same good at different locations, show increased variability; in addition, at any given moment, the prices quoted by different sellers of the same good show larger dispersion.

The 'noise' in relative prices that characterizes high inflation regimes need not derive from a single source. Frequent policy turnarounds, or external disturbances, are likely to induce swings in the relative prices of broad categories of goods. Large movements in relative prices are commonly observed in connection with devaluations or discrete adjustments in public sector prices, for example. Firms setting prices in a high inflation must in any case act in haste and on the basis of information of very limited reliability. The 'islands model' (cf. Phelps 1970; Lucas 1973; Cukierman 1979, 1982) illustrates the problem of discriminating between aggregate and specific shocks. It suggests that sellers will make their prices respond more elastically to 'local' information as the volatility of the aggregate price level increases. In addition, every individual seller posting a price that will be maintained for some time has to exercise his own judgement about market conditions in the near future; differences in the way agents 'read' the data will be reflected in the prices they set. The dispersion and variability of relative prices due to the use of partial information and to idiosyncratic beliefs gets amplified, rather than tuned down, as prices are revised more frequently (cf. Kaufman 1992). The main problem, it appears, is not that some prices adjust while others 'stick'; it is rather that most prices become excessively volatile (cf. Chapter 7 below).

Segmentation of markets becomes ubiquitous in a high inflation. The 'law of one price' often fails even over short distances. And such price differences are not eliminated through arbitrage. Price instability makes 'comparison shopping' much more difficult. Learning the price of a good in a particular shop does not tell the shopper much if his or her information about prices of similar goods at other places is dated, since those prices have almost certainly changed in the meantime. As a consequence, while price dispersion may induce agents to search more intensively, they will none the less be less informed when deciding on a purchase. Since price competition becomes a less effective way of attracting customers, average mark-ups are very likely to increase (Tommasi 1992a; see also Frenkel 1979).

Firms face a perpetual dilemma in a high inflation. They need not only to make more frequent corrections but also to provide an 'orderly market' for their customers.[18] The pricing practices observed stem from the compromises they make between these requirements. Businesses that keep prices fixed for a certain interval (say, on the order of the average holding period of money) make it possible for their customers to know approximately 'what their money can buy'. This is a valuable service to consumers in that it allows them to do their purchases sequentially out of the cash they carry with them. This is probably one reason why even at extremely high rates of inflation retail markets resist 'dollarizing' prices. While manufacturers are often motivated to dollarize, especially if their products are import-intensive, and may face little or no direct resistance from distributors and wholesalers when they do so, retailers will rebel as long as their customers earn their incomes in domestic money. When all such 'stickiness' of nominal prices disappears, money in effect loses its function as the unit of account for prices of everyday goods, and retail trade is most definitely disrupted.

OVER THE BRINK: 'CLOSED FOR LACK OF PRICES'

Inflation causes the intertemporal structure of markets to shrink, starting at the long end. In moderate inflations, it may be only the markets for 30-year bonds and fixed-rate mortgages

---

[18] Palerm (1990, p. 477) stresses this in interpreting his findings from the Mexican data: 'the discrete price adjustment in the fix-price sector is the product of an optimal policy by market-makers striving to offer stable trading arrangements. The rise in frequency [of price revisions] as inflation rises may well be an indication of the difficulties that market-makers face in maintaining a stable trading environment for their customers under high and unstable inflation. This shattering of market arrangements leads to a greater price variability.' Palerm's work on Mexico offers a rich empirical picture of price behaviour in an inflationary economy. His findings will be further discussed in Chapter 7 below.

that disappear. In high inflations, bank loans and trade credit of a few weeks maturity may be the longest term financial instruments surviving in the private sector. The limit is reached in hyperinflation, when even spot markets threaten to close down.

The movement into hyperinflation tends to come as a sudden phase transition. The onset therefore can often be dated rather precisely. In the German case, for example, the assassination of Rathenau in mid-1922 and the crisis that followed the occupation of the Ruhr in early 1923 were followed by sudden jumps in the already high inflation rate. Argentina burst into hyperinflation in early 1989 and, again in December, following the collapse of disinflation programmes; in both instances, the inflation rate went from single-digit monthly figures to well above 50 per cent in a few weeks. Although the class of events that may trigger this transition is not easy to define, it is clear enough that economies at the high end of the high inflation range walk a tightrope. The shortening of the horizon over which agents are willing to make commitments indicates that they are 'ready to go'. People hold money-denominated assets for only a few days. Virtually any alarming news can precipitate a rush into foreign currencies. Firms change their prices with such frequency that inflationary impulses are swiftly propagated. As the risk of prices suddenly accelerating grows, wage-setting schemes that extrapolate past price trends and therefore impart upward inertia to wages become less and less acceptable to labour. They become prone, therefore, to give way suddenly to forward-looking arrangements. When this anchor lets go, one of the few remaining links between past and current prices is lost.

In hyperinflation, agents must recalculate their plans from day to day, or even from hour to hour. Commonplace activities like selling a product off the shelf now become risky. Uncertain over restocking costs, firms build large precautionary margins into their prices; in the limit, they just stop selling. The signs posted in many shops during Argentinian bouts of hyperinflation, 'Closed for Lack of Prices', reveal in a striking way how some people will simply quit trading when deprived of any and all guideposts to the real outcomes of transactions.[19] Thus, shortages of goods arise spontaneously, without outside intervention. When the economic system has to recompute prices continuously, the result of this ultimate price flexibility is not efficiency but the very opposite.

As the inflation rate reaches levels of several percentage points per day, money demand falls drastically. But the decline is actually less dramatic than estimates of interest-elasticities for periods of less extreme inflation would lead one to predict. The government still conducts its transactions in domestic money and workers typically continue to receive their wages in that currency. This is probably an important reason why money remains acceptable in retail, although payment in foreign currencies becomes more common. In some episodes one finds instances of firms setting different prices according to the medium of exchange they are offered.[20] Since hyperinflations usually last only for short periods, it is hard to establish whether the demand for domestic money can be sustained indefinitely at such high inflation rates, or whether agents would altogether stop accepting it at some point. Be that as it may,

---

[19] The reluctance to engage in trade in moments of great uncertainty during a hyperinflation can be illustrated by the following scene, which took place in Argentina at a period of great turbulence in December 1989. A customer finds a good inside a shop, with a clearly marked price, and decides to buy it. The shopkeeper refuses; he explains that the posted price has no significance, because he cannot be sure that the wholesaler will not double his own price the next day. When asked what he would do if someone offered to pay double the marked price, the shopkeeper answers that he would not sell anyway, for what if the wholesale price tripled before he replaced the good? Such reactions bring to mind the 'no trade' results of Milgrom and Stokey (1982): if the seller comes to believe that the prospective buyer has better information about the inflation in prospect than he has himself, it may become impossible for the prospective buyer to come up with an unconditional bid that will be accepted. Yet, in general the disappearance of markets in very high inflations appears to stem from 'complexity avoidance' rather than from specific informational asymmetries (cf. Chapter 7).

[20] For example, Bresciani-Turroni (1937, p. 124) mentions the case of some German firms in 1923, who offered the following discounts with respect to mark prices: 20% if payment was made in gold-indexed bonds, 30% on sales in dollar bonds, and 45% if payment was made in foreign currency. At about the same time, the Hamburg authorities explicitly allowed shops to apply price surcharges of up to 30% on their sales in paper marks.

money is seen to stay in use as a medium of exchange. When stripped of its precautionary and speculative demand and with transactions balances down to a minimum, the excess demand for money can flicker between positive and negative, depending not only on the quantity that the central bank issues and on expectations, but also on the volume of transactions that are to be settled each day. These high-frequency oscillations are transmitted to the goods and foreign exchange markets very swiftly.[21]

The search for a pricing standard leads to widespread but incomplete 'dollarization' of goods prices. The move is often started by large firms selling internationally traded goods or intermediate commodities, and is transmitted 'downstream' to the markets for final goods; however, it usually does not reach the retail markets for non-durables. That firms post their prices in dollars does not mean that they keep prices constant in that unit: dollar prices too are revised very frequently and by large percentages. Thus, although the exchange rate serves as a common reference for price setting, the real exchange rate and relative prices in general exhibit wide fluctuations none the less.

In hyperinflation, the unit of account for current prices and the means of payment become more and more disassociated and neither function is performed well. The business of firms and consumers is complicated accordingly. Wage earners find it impossible to predict the purchasing power of their periodic income. When managing their monthly purchases, they have to choose between taking the loss from holding on to money for too long and running the risk of being left without enough cash to manage until the next payday. To arrange even routine payments from one firm to another becomes troublesome.[22] In such

---

[21] One consequence is that the exchange rate oscillates widely over very short periods. In hyperinflation, money demand no longer acts as 'shock absorber' for the period-by-period injections of money—with consequences discussed further in Chapter 7.

[22] During the Argentine hyperinflations, it was common for firms to order goods without knowing the price they would pay for them; the price would be communicated when the goods were delivered. Some transactions were settled in the following way. The price was determined as the domestic money equivalent of a dollar price. Upon delivery, the seller received a check for an amount

circumstances, trade credit vanishes completely for all practical purposes and sellers refuse to grant even the simplest forms of credit to consumers. With money on the edge of becoming valueless, people more often find themselves cash-constrained. Sellers are without incentives to supply goods to the market. While the effect that milder forms of high inflation have on output is hard to measure precisely, hyperinflation brings on a depression in real activity.[23]

At the root of hyperinflation lies the inability of the government to provide a monetary instrument that people can confidently use. Good substitutes for working monetary institutions that will permit the private sector 'to go about its business' simply do not emerge spontaneously. At the same time, hyperinflation disrupts the operation of the State itself as all sources of funds for the government dry up. Hyperinflation 'cuts the size of the public sector' in the most destructive way: even the most elementary activities of government are carried out, if at all, with great difficulty. When the government comes to depend on worthless paper to maintain the loyalty of public servants, the State is in great danger.

Hyperinflations therefore cannot be sustained for long. When a society has reached this extreme, the alternatives become stark and simple: Stabilize or else![24]

based on the exchange rate of that moment. When the check was credited, the price was recalculated, taking into account the movement of the exchange rate during the interval; the buyer then issued a check for the difference between that price and his original payment. But his check also took time to clear, which motivated a new round of recalculation and payment. A single transaction could result in several iterations of this type.

[23] Good data on output are lacking for the European episodes of the 1920s. In the German case, it is clear that industrial production reached a well defined trough in the hyperinflation year of 1923, and that in the period of most rapid inflation, unemployment was very high. Contemporary observers debated whether inflation had been detrimental to production until it reached hyperinflation levels, but: 'there is a unanimous opinion that in the final phases of the German inflation, the depreciation of money was, to say the least, a discouragement for productive effort' (Graham 1930, p. 320). The Latin American hyperinflations of the 1980s generally saw aggregate output plunge sharply.

[24] Bernholz (1989) arrives at the same conclusion: 'we have to expect that each hyperinflation leads to attempts at currency reform. Historically this has been true for all hyperinflations until 1985.'

6

Stabilization: Finding a Way Back

Stabilization programmes have to fit the type of inflation they confront. If the inflation is moderate, policy-makers usually rely on a gradual correction of monetary policies to bring about the desired disinflation. This need not involve any major changes in other instruments. One attempts to minimize the disruption of the plans of individual agents. High inflations, in contrast, are attacked with far more comprehensive policy 'packages' that aim to force a sudden change in modes of behaviour that the inflation has induced. These programmes typically announce large-scale policy reforms with significant distributive consequences. They never lack for political drama, therefore.

High inflations are unpopular. Governments have the incentive to bring them to an end and to do it quickly. But motivation must be translated into concrete actions. What makes a serious stabilization effort politically feasible is a question that we are not prepared to tackle. But the basic economic prerequisites for success are reasonably simple—or so they appear from a safe distance at least. First and foremost, the government must gain control over its fiscal policies so as to reduce drastically its dependence on the inflation tax. This is a necessary condition for a disinflation to last. Moreover, when the public recognizes that the government can manage its affairs over time without relying on monetary financing, a rapid disinflation becomes far easier to bring about and to maintain (cf. Sargent 1982).

However, a stabilization process will not just unfold as a predetermined programme wherein the actions of the government and the reactions of the public are constantly well matched. The transition out of high inflation confronts both the authorities and private agents with frequent choices for which they do not have ready-made solutions. Policy-makers find that they cannot accurately discern how the public's expectations and plans will respond to their measures; private individuals find that they are not too sure how policy will evolve in response to political events or market developments. In this game, the authorities and the public must constantly assess the 'state of play' and make a judgement about the next moves of other parties. Policies have to be managed from day to day, no matter what the design of the programme or what precommitments on particular issues it includes. Policy-makers act less as dynamic programmers plotting contingent paths to the eventual desired outcome than as chess players trying to reach a somewhat stronger position a few moves down the road, hoping that the opponent will not always make the strongest move against them—and fighting the temptation to count on that hope.

In each historical episode, the economy's behaviour stems in large part from the perceptions and patterns of response that people have learned from past experience. Thus, the path to success, or to failure, of a stabilization programme depends on the particulars of time and place. Stabilization programmes do have a general logic which should not be obscured. But in their specifics they are also historically contingent.

DISINFLATION AND STABILIZATION

Monetary stability has been achieved when business practices, the portfolios held, and the horizon over which decisions are made conform to the expectation that prices will move slowly and predictably over a reasonably long period. But an economy may show low rates of inflation for some time and still remain in a high inflation regime. Disinflations which are perceived as fragile are vulnerable to shocks or to vacillations in policy that would have little effect in a stable economy. Disinflation does not automatically entail stabilization.

Programmes to stabilize high inflations or hyperinflations have to make a definite break with the policies of an inflationary past. Whether a stabilization strategy will prove sustainable or not depends as much on the public's reactions as on the government's actions. Policy-makers have to think of the elements of their programme not only as *actions* on variables that are the 'fundamentals' of their own model of the economy, but equally as *signals* that will be filtered through the economic models held by various segments of the public. Successful stabilization programmes (and even some which ultimately unravelled) have in fact managed to change expectations with favourable effects on prices and asset demands right from the start (cf. Bernholz 1989).

But the memory of inflation is not to be erased in one fell swoop. However solid its design may seem, a programme must pass the test of performance—both in terms of what the government in fact does and of how markets respond—before expectations will definitively settle down to price stability. Although promises of future moves can help to provide breathing space for a while, the economy will not stabilize until the actual experience of low inflation supports a permanent change in the behaviour of private agents. Even in the best of cases, people will not behave as if they were certain that the government's actions will correspond to its announcements—which is to say, they will not do so even when the programme is seen to have strong support and when the authorities are thought to be competent and committed to stabilization. Moreover, price expectations depend on how people think others will react to the government's policies. How these 'second order' expectations (Phelps 1983; Di Tata 1983) are evolving cannot be confidently assessed before actual market reactions are observed.

Thus, any incipient stabilization has to pass through a period in which agents still refuse to make long-run commitments of the sort that require expectations to be held with confidence. One important consequence of this lagged response is that the demand for public debt is unlikely to recover immediately. Therefore, the government will remain cash constrained during the transition. The promise of future surpluses will not make current deficits irrelevant.

The uncertainties of the transition also limit the government's ability to determine all the particulars of its policies in advance. A stabilization attempt certainly has better prospects of success if guided by a well-defined policy strategy right from the start. But no such programme can do without some amount of 'learning along the way'. Consequently, the government faces a tough choice between making strong commitments and maintaining the flexibility to respond to new information. Strong commitments will prove costly if they cannot be honoured. The lack of them runs the risk that the programme may appear too open-ended to be credible. In actuality, policy-makers are apt to mix concrete measures with more or less vague pronouncements, and to combine changes in policy intended to be permanent with a variety of transitory moves.

The 'stabilization game' has to be played out over time. The initial policy package does not decide the eventual outcome. Still, the early stages of a programme are crucial since they will determine whether the effort can be continued or must be abandoned. History shows us several types of programmes. The pattern of policies used against the hyperinflations of the 1920s differs from the 'heterodox shocks' against high inflations in the mid-1980s, and these again differ from still more recent programmes in several Latin American countries.[1] This history of stabilization efforts confirms that achieving and maintaining fiscal control is a necessary condition for success. But it does not suggest that a particular 'class' of plans provides us with the sufficient conditions. The authorities need not only move toward fiscal balance, they must also find ways to accomplish the transition at reasonable social cost. To that end, the private sector must be induced to adapt its behaviour to the new policy course. This, in turn, requires that the stabilization plan be adapted to its time and place so as to be credible to the public. While each historical situation is unique, policy-makers have to pick a combination and a sequence of actions from a more or

---

[1] There is a considerable literature that describes and analyses these experiments. The episodes of the 1920s are treated, for example, in Keynes (1923), Graham (1930), Bresciani-Turroni (1937), Robinson (1938), League of Nations (1946), Yeager (1981), Sargent (1982), Dornbusch (1985), Heymann (1986), Llach (1987), Bernholz (1988*a*, 1988*b*, 1989), Végh (1992). An overview of the mid-1980s programmes of Argentina, Bolivia, Brazil, Israel, Mexico, and Peru can be found in Bruno *et al.* (1987, 1991), Dornbusch and Edwards (1991).

less standard menu. The items on that menu and some of the trade-offs between them are discussed below.

FISCAL POLICIES

Cash management and fiscal reform

It is rare that a disinflation strategy can be plotted against the backdrop of a fiscal consolidation that is well under way. It does happen. Mexico in 1987 is an example. But it is an exception. To the extent that progress on the fiscal front has already been made, the authorities will gain some freedom of manœuvre in how they manage the disinflation. In the milder forms of high inflation, governments may perhaps be sufficiently in control of the situation that significant fiscal moves can be made without waiting for inflation first to abate. But, in the more common case, the escape route from high inflation is along a tightrope of strict day-to-day management of state finances.

A reasonably well-designed and well-supported programme will halt the flight from money. But it cannot count on financing sizeable deficits in the market, except through the very risky expedient of offering bonds with high real yields and short maturities. Although the increase in the demand for money that follows immediately upon disinflation will temporarily offset part of the loss from the inflation tax, any temptation to delay fiscal adjustment on this account had better be resisted. The magnitude of the increase in real money holdings cannot be predicted with any precision and it can be reversed very quickly if the public sees no tangible evidence that the government will in fact be able to do without central bank financing. So, prudence dictates low deficits in the early stages.

To satisfy this condition is likely to be painful even if employment were to keep up in the process. The increase in real tax revenues when the fiscal-lag effect goes into reverse will help, but it will not suffice. The instruments at the government's immediate disposal will be few and of a kind that had better not be relied upon for more than a short period. These short-run fiscal expedients typically include (i) deep cuts in real government salaries, (ii) reduced maintenance of infrastructure and delays in those ongoing investment projects that are not abandoned, (iii) steeply increased tax rates wherever collection is the easiest, and (iv) dramatic increases in the prices charged by public enterprises. While such tactics are expedient in the emergency, they move both revenues and expenditures away from the configuration desired over the longer run. Moreover, some of these measures have the immediate consequence of raising prices. Thus, many programmes start with a sudden fit of what is euphemistically called 'corrective inflation'.

These transitory elements of the initial policy package will not be effective for long. Emergency taxes added to a badly administered, ramshackle tax structure do not put the government on a sustainable fiscal basis. Spending cuts decided as a matter of short-run expediency soon meet political resistance. When they also result in a noticeable worsening in the quality of services, tax increases become even less acceptable to the public. If extraordinary expenditures loom large in the deficit, a renegotiation of reparations or debt service may go a long way towards establishing fiscal balance. But in most cases, a high inflation is rooted in a more deep-seated crisis of the fiscal system. Although a first round of disinflation can be achieved without it, thorough-going fiscal reform is necessary if a recurrent cycle of short-term belt-tightening and belt-loosening episodes is to be avoided. A government that has managed to disinflate cannot delay for long those more permanent measures that will allow it to stabilize, or the opportunity to do so will slip away. Lack of timely action sealed the fate of the Argentine 'Austral' plan of 1985, for instance. In that episode, the fiscal deficit was brought down quite sharply at first, but shot up again later when the effects of various temporary measures petered out and more permanent ones were not forthcoming.

Beyond the initial disinflation phase, the task of replacing the original patchwork of fiscal measures with a more permanent fiscal structure becomes the big hurdle (cf. Sanguinetti 1992). Until this is done, the possibility of a relapse into high inflation will be ever present. But even if people can be persuaded that the government will somehow avoid monetary financing so that such a relapse is not an immediate threat, the hurdle must be tackled without delay, for the public's uncertainty over how the coming fiscal measures are going to affect the profitability of various activities impedes the return to business as normal.

The consistency condition that the stream of revenues should finance the normal stream of spending does not dictate a particular composition of those flows. In general, fiscal stability is compatible with a variety of choices with regard to the size of the public sector and the allocative and distributional patterns of its activities. Price stabilization need not follow a particular recipe in these matters. However, in the particular case, the available options are likely to be limited and more or less confined to those revenue and spending categories where past performance has been the weakest. A country with a very ineffective tax system, for example, will do best by concentrating on measures to increase revenues, while another will gain more by pruning 'inflated' expenditures.

To consolidate the stabilization requires both a return to meaningful budgeting and a broadly based political agreement on the main features of the tax system. Disinflation will by itself reduce the short-run volatility of real revenues and make it easier to forecast expenditures. It thus allows better programming of the public finances. Making the most of this opportunity requires a well-functioning administration, however, and this is apt to be lacking. To rebuild the administrative apparatus of government will take time, and to rebuild the public's confidence in it even more so. Yet it is a straightforward matter when compared to the task of finding a lasting political compromise. To restore the government's solvency on a firm basis may require a 'new politics' that redefines the claims that different groups can legitimately present to the State. This is far more demanding than reaching an interim truce in the distributive game so that a disinflation can be attempted. The transition towards fiscal stability will sorely test the cohesiveness of the coalition which backs the programme and the effectiveness of the social institutions which arbitrate distributive claims.

Privatizations

In times past, it was not uncommon for financially hard-pressed governments to sell state property or to concede exclusive rights to perform certain activities to private parties (cf. Hicks 1969, ch. 6). Privatizations are back in vogue and have become a standard feature of recent stabilization programmes.[2]

Privatization of large public firms can accomplish a number of things:

(i)   It can change the system of incentives within the firms that are privatized and, depending on the regulatory framework of the industry, it may also modify the rules governing competition in important markets.

(ii) It can be used to signal the government's intention to direct its policies according to 'market principles', quite apart from the privatization projects themselves.

(iii) It can be used to build support for the government among groups interested in controlling the activities which the State now leaves to the private sector.

(iv) When the new operators are better able than the State to provide resources for investment, it can be a means of bypassing financial constraints which prevent the expansion of the activities in question.

(v)   It can serve to improve the balance sheet of the State, by swapping assets for old debts.

(vi) It can increase the government's 'net worth', if it is possible to capture in the selling price either the expected efficiency gains from the transfer or the price increases that were not politically feasible for a state enterprise to make.

(vii) In the absence of a well-developed market for public debt it can serve as a financing expedient that will relax the government's short-run cash constraint.

Actual privatizations will combine these elements in various ways. In the first phases of a disinflation programme, it is to be expected that the government stresses short-run objectives. A rapid pace of privatization sends strong signals of reassurance

---

[2] We are referring here to privatization in the Western sense only, i.e., to the sale of large state-owned enterprises, usually public utilities, in economies where most activities are already carried out by the private sector.

to wealth holders and may make them moderate their resistance to new tax measures or spending cuts. More directly, the sale of real assets will provide much-desired resources to a government which lacks credit and may already be heavily indebted. Besides relieving immediate financial pressures, the transfer of state enterprises also allows the public sector to retrench so that available funds and scarce administrative resources can be focused on its basic functions.

But there are also costs to acting in haste. The performance of the firms to be privatized is likely to have deteriorated in the inflation. Selling them before stabilization has run its course will reduce the price that the government can obtain. The authorities may then be tempted to attract bids by offering to protect the prospective new owners from competition. At worst privatization can end up replacing badly-working state enterprises by a new breed of powerful monopolies.

Privatization ventures differ with respect to the market structure that results from the sale, the type of regulatory power that the government retains over the activity in question, and the price it receives. From a narrow financial perspective, they are a means to soften the credit constraint that the authorities face. As long as they do not take the form of 'distress sales' to fund current expenditures, they can provide some measure of more durable relief by helping to reduce the public debt. But fiscal consolidation will not come from the one-time sale of property. Only decisive action to bring the permanent flows of taxes and expenditures into line will do.

Foreign debts, reparations

In high inflation, the government cannot make ends meet. The charge that governments have in some historical instances consciously promoted inflation in order to prove their inability to pay is of doubtful validity. What is not in doubt is the virtual impossibility of servicing debts in a normal manner under conditions of extreme economic instability. This becomes especially apparent in those cases where the real exchange rate depreciates dramatically (as was the case with Russia in 1992–3, for example). Moreover, it is unlikely that a heavily indebted high inflation economy could stabilize while repaying its debts as originally contracted. During the first stages of disinflation, therefore, it is common to find governments in some type of *de facto* moratorium, where they reduce actual payments to a minimum. This, of course, cannot be sustained for very long. Stabilization requires a more permanent arrangement, which makes clear what commitments the government will honour and what relief it is able to obtain. Creditors are not likely to enter into renegotiation of debts or reparations until they see a serious disinflation programme being implemented. A successful renegotiation, however, can give a significant boost to a stabilization process already under way by bolstering expectations and reducing the uncertainty that limits the demand for government debt. There are several historical instances of this. For example, the 1924 renegotiation of German reparations under the Dawes plan helped to consolidate the stabilization programme then in progress (cf. Dornbusch and Fischer 1986; Llach 1987; Maier 1975). The reschedulings of Latin American debts under the Brady plan brought lower interest rates in the countries concerned and seem to have improved the terms on which their governments can borrow.

MONETARY REFORM AND MONETARY POLICIES

Changing the rules

To disinflate, monetary policy has to change. To stabilize, the monetary regime must be changed. It is plain enough that government has to reform its ways. What is more difficult to decide are the rules of behaviour that such monetary reform should comprise and the extent to which these rules ought to be formalized, i.e., be put into law as binding constraints on the central bank and on the executive branch. Assurance of monetary stability can be sought by moving either towards control of the domestic money supply or towards external fixed-rate convertibility. Either strategy will raise a number of questions concerning how rules and discretion are best to be balanced.

The programmes that put an end to the various post-war hyperinflations combined deficit reduction with strict limitations on the monetary financing of governments. The constraints imposed included mandatory limits on the nominal value of bonds held by the central bank and commitment to a fixed exchange rate. In several cases, adherence to the new monetary and fiscal rules was to be monitored by external supervisors (Santaella 1992). More recently, the 1991 programme in Argentina put into law a strict form of convertibility to be enforced by the central bank (cf. Canavese 1992).

Yet, explicit monetary reform is neither a necessary condition for disinflation, nor a sufficient condition for lasting stabilization. In some of the above mentioned episodes, the new monetary regime was put in place *after* prices had stopped rising, not before. In most of them, moreover, it was not altogether clear initially whether the government would be able to manage the public finances within the limits implied by the monetary rules. But the announcement of such reforms generally had a strong effect on expectations none the less.

Ultimately, stabilization cannot be achieved without a definite change in the monetary regime. An explicit monetary rule puts into law the limits to what the central bank can and cannot do. It constrains the monetary managers who can no longer oblige the demands of the Treasury. The fiscal authorities must therefore operate under a hard budget constraint. To the extent that private sector agents find the monetary rule credible, they will adapt their price expectations and their demand for assets.

Although closing the central bank door to the government is the first requirement for stabilization, monetary reform cannot stop there. It must, for instance, close the back door too. Whether or not it is done through explicit legislation, the central bank's 'quasi-fiscal' operations must be brought under control. When the central bank pays interest on bank reserves, for example, or when rediscounts are extended on worthless paper to favoured sectors, the line between monetary and fiscal policies blurs. The lack of a strict demarcation line invites trouble.[3]

---

[3] The Argentine 'Austral' plan of 1985 failed in part because it did not get

If the hardening of budget constraints does not apply also to the central bank itself, some of the pressures for subsidies will be transmitted to it and, when accommodated, undermine the fiscal adjustment. The role played by the Central Bank of Russia in 1992–3 may serve for all time as the paramount example of how quasi-fiscal operations by a central bank can make stabilization impossible.

Beyond merely ensuring against the subservience of monetary policy to fiscal exigencies, a monetary regime should specify the kinds of transactions the central bank has the right or the duty to execute, and the bounds within which it can exercise discretion. Here, the first question to be answered is whether assurance of nominal stability is to be sought through control of the quantity of money or through maintenance of external convertibility. In the wake of true hyperinflation, it is understandable that the designers of monetary reforms choose convertibility. By fixing the exchange rate, the authorities avoid the problems of defining a particular monetary aggregate on which to exercise quantity control, and they allow the money supply to vary more or less with the 'needs of trade'. This is particularly convenient at a moment when the demand for real balances is likely to be extremely variable and correspondingly hard to predict. In addition, exchange rate 'anchoring' influences prices more directly than does a fixed money-growth rate rule or similar scheme (see below).

A lengthy period of high inflation will leave the reputation of the monetary authorities badly damaged. For convertibility at a fixed exchange rate to be credible, therefore, the discretion of the central bank has to be constrained fairly severely. The straightforward way to do this is to require the bank to maintain a high ratio of foreign exchange reserves to liabilities but this, of course, means that such reserves must be on hand in sufficient volume in order to get the system started. At a somewhat deeper level, the credibility of the convertibility regime hinges on whether the independence of the central bank from the treasury can be made credible to the public at large. If it is going

the central bank's quasi-fiscal operations under control in a timely manner, for example.

to maintain tight convertibility the central bank cannot monetize a substantial government deficit. In the event that fiscal and monetary policies were the clash in the future, which side would come to dominate? Stability cannot be guaranteed by the central bank alone. It requires the active co-operation of the fiscal authorities.

The government will have its own credibility problem. Its creditworthiness will not be restored overnight. Until the market for public debt can be restored, deficit spending cannot be used to stimulate real activity. Strict convertibility similarly limits what the central bank can do to offset disturbances. Major changes in the stock of base money must necessarily have their counterpart in foreign exchange operations, and for monetary authorities to move the real exchange rate they must engineer a change in the domestic price level. In particular, a sizeable real depreciation can only be brought about through internal deflation and this, of course, may come at the cost of serious recession.

A tight monetary rule does not allow the central bank to adapt its policies to contingencies. Under a simple non-contingent rule, it either ignores large shocks or is forced to break it. This is not without risks (cf. Flood and Isard 1989; Lohmann 1992). Traditionally stable economies accord their monetary authorities flexibility, because they are trusted to exercise restraint in normal times. But when this confidence is not present, only strict (and credible) legal constraints will support expectations of low and stable inflation rates. The lack of reputation has to be paid for by renouncing flexibility. Governments which find other ways to prove their commitment to long-run stability need not 'tie the hands' of their central banks too tightly; those who cannot, and opt for very rigid monetary systems, have to give up the discretionary use of monetary policy for counter-cyclical purposes. The loss of these policy instruments is one of the lasting costs of high inflation.

Dealing with a domestic debt overhang

Nominal instability will teach lenders to demand high nominal rates and short maturities as a hedge against sudden price level movements. The government's short-term nominal debt will then not be wiped out by high inflation. It may even survive hyperinflation. Although a coherent disinflation programme can be counted on to reduce nominal interest rates sharply, the government cannot realistically expect to market long-term debt very soon, and it has to consider the possibility that *ex post* real interest rates will remain high for some time.[4] Even if the nominal debt is not large, the accumulation of interest from rolling it over can add up to a significant fiscal burden. Moreover, the cost of contractionary monetary policies during the initial transition is considerably increased by their effect on the government's interest expenditures. If the demand for government bonds does not recover quickly—and even well-designed and strongly-supported programmes cannot take this for granted—a growing domestic debt can put the disinflation in danger.

One way to deal with this danger is to programme a sufficient primary surplus in the fiscal accounts. More easily said than done! Privatizations may also be a way to reduce the debt burden as long as they are not used as a short-run expedient to finance current deficits. The more drastic way out of the predicament is simply to repudiate the domestic debt, wholly or in part, or to force the refinancing of it. Although the recent experience of Argentina[5] suggests that such action need not cause permanent damage to the government's reputation, it is hard to predict in the abstract how it will affect perceptions of the risks involved in holding assets within the country. The public can take the intervention as a one-shot declaration of bankruptcy to be followed by prudent management, or it can see it as the first in a series of desperate measures likely to follow further down the road. The general attitude of the government towards asset holders will have some influence on what the reac-

---

[4] Cf., e.g., Bernholz (1988*b*) concerning the behaviour of real interest rates following the post-World War I stabilizations in Germany, Hungary, and Poland, and his (1988*a*) on the 1985 Bolivian stabilization.

[5] The Argentine government undertook an operation of this type in late 1989 when, following a short-lived attempt to disinflate, it found itself faced with a run from domestic to foreign assets and decided to force a swap of short-term bank deposits for dollar bonds of long maturity.

tion will be. But forced refinancing can do no more than 'clean the slate' in any case. Unless the chances of achieving a sustainable budget are very good it is an extremely hazardous gamble.

Bluebacking in practice

If prices suddenly stop rising in an inflationary economy, previously held expectations are falsified. As a consequence, the real values of payments due on contracts concluded in nominal terms (or with lagged index clauses) will come to differ from what the parties had originally anticipated. When the volume of such contracts is large, the revaluation of real debts that an abrupt disinflation can produce not only redistributes wealth in an arbitrary manner, but may also threaten a wave of defaults in an economy which is already financially fragile.

If the initial situation is one of an inflation running at a constant, predictable rate, the effects of an unanticipated disinflation on the real outcome of financial contracts can be exactly neutralized by establishing a legally enforced schedule that converts pre-contracted payments so as to make them depreciate in nominal terms from the date of stabilization onward at a rate equal to the growth rate of prices in the inflationary period. This 'blueback scheme' (see Chapter 3) ensures that, in these hypothetical conditions, the real value of payments is equal to what it would have been had the inflation continued and also to what the parties expected when entering into the contract.

Of course, the actual conditions under which disinflations have to be attempted never conform exactly—and seldom conform closely—to the assumptions of that exercise. The blueback scheme presupposes that the authorities drawing up the conversion schedule can reliably infer what expectations were entertained when the payments due at some particular date were originally agreed upon. But under most conditions this is simply not possible. Expectations of future prices are apt to vary not only over time but also across individuals at any time. Consequently, a measure which only considers the date at which payment is due will not validate expectations. In those cases where the parties originally acted on inconsistent fore-casts, moreover, it is obviously impossible to validate the expectations of both.

Nevertheless, this kind of 'neutralizing' intervention can be a useful device under certain conditions. First, the size of the potential redistribution should be large, given the average length of the contracts outstanding and the drop in the inflation rate that is being planned. This condition is likely to be satisfied only in some high inflations but neither in moderate nor in hyperinflations. Second, inflation must have been more or less steady for a period comparable to the longest term to maturity for which there is a substantial volume of contracts outstanding. Lastly, the government must be confident that it can produce a low inflation rate for a similar time interval into the future. If these requirements are met, the policy-maker can avoid bitter controversies over the fairness of the policy by setting a rate of nominal depreciation for pre-contracted payments that agents can recognize as producing real outcomes reasonably close to those originally expected.

This conversion scheme was used in the 1985 'Austral' programme in Argentina and variants of it were used in other programmes around that time. Under the right conditions the scheme eliminates the wealth effects of a sudden, unanticipated disinflation. It ceases to have practical effects when old contracts mature; so long as pre-existing contracts are overwhelmingly of short maturity, therefore, it need not extend beyond the first stages of a stabilization programme. But the blueback scheme can do no more than smooth the initial transition. Use of it has no bearing on whether, later on, the disinflation is successfully maintained or eventually gets reversed.

PRICE ANCHORING AND SHORT-RUN MONETARY POLICIES

To float or to anchor: the exchange rate and monetary management

Forming reasonable expectations in the wake of a large shock is not an easy matter. Prudent people are not likely to let their price forecasts be guided altogether by government announcements but will wait to revise their plans until they see pricing behaviour actually changing in the markets. Even when government fiscal and monetary announcements are accorded a great deal of credibility, therefore, it is not plausible that the expectations of all agents will suddenly stabilize in unison, unless the evidence is utterly convincing that price increases will indeed stop, or until the evidence is in that they have already stopped (cf. Dornbusch and Simonsen 1987; Simonsen 1988). Moreover, the feedback from price expectations to the credibility of policies should not be disregarded. Anticipated real tax revenues, for example, vary inversely with the estimate of future inflation.

Managing a disinflation by regulating the money supply while the exchange rate is left to float becomes a complicated business. Agents may react to the government's fiscal and monetary measures by increasing their demand for real balances and by slowing down the increase of the prices that they set. But if, for lack of a convincing signal, the adjustment is only partial, the inflation rate may hover in an intermediate range, while firms search in vain for some simple and reliable criteria by which to set prices. If the economy is initially in hyperinflation, firms may not abandon 'dollarization' altogether but neither will they find it a good idea to keep prices fixed in foreign exchange. This can produce the curious phenomenon of a sizeable local 'dollar inflation'. Argentina went through one such episode in 1990 when the prices of goods quoted in dollars rose quite rapidly.

A 'dirty float' combined with tight money is not likely to do much better than free floating in putting an immediate brake on price increases. Continued price drift will create an excess demand for money and cause an incipient nominal appreciation of the currency (cf. Dornbusch 1976). But this strengthening of the domestic currency could easily be reversed and will not be perceived as permanent. Local prices will not respond immediately to it, therefore. The monetary authorities then face a dilemma. Either they buy foreign currencies (and accommodate the ongoing inflation) or else they stand by and allow a sizeable real appreciation. Meanwhile, in an atmosphere of great uncertainty over the future behaviour of prices and the exchange rate, the monetary crunch will delay the recovery of output and keep real interest rates at high levels. Both effects have unfavourable consequences for the government's finances.

Fixing the exchange rate, on the other hand, predetermines one of the main variables directly influencing pricing decisions. This sends a strong message to price setters. It may be especially effective in the wake of a hyperinflation, allowing agents quickly to co-ordinate their short-run forecasts on a low inflation path. A programme which combines fiscal retrenchment with exchange rate anchoring is likely to produce more rapid initial convergence of inflation and interest rates than if this second element were missing.

But fixing the exchange rate brings its own dilemmas (cf. especially Calvo and Végh 1993, 1992; Guidotti and Végh 1992). First, the choice of the initial exchange rate is not an easy matter in practice. If it is set too low, the programme risks a quick erosion of confidence and may face a costly realignment further ahead; if too high, the risk is a sizeable 'residual inflation'. The inflationary pressure of too high a rate can be contained if the government generates a high enough primary surplus that it can buy foreign exchange in the market without increasing the money supply. But sterilization of a balance of payment surplus will be but one of many worthy causes competing for the use of scarce fiscal resources.

Second, as inflationary expectations abate an excess demand for money will emerge. Since the central bank will be trying to decelerate the growth of its domestic assets, the result will be a balance of payments surplus. Although the central bank has relinquished ultimate control over the money supply by pegging the exchange rate, it will still have some capacity to sterilize foreign reserve flows. The choice has to balance the dangers of allowing the money supply to increase too fast, accommodating residual inflation and causing it to persist, against those of increasing the public debt and keeping interest rates at high levels. The bank cannot take for granted that the private sector will automatically generate just the 'right' money supply growth to keep creeping inflation in check. On the other hand, high interest rates will not only weigh heavily on the budget but may also endanger the solvency of indebted firms. Overall, monetary sterilization seems a risky and expensive way to regulate aggregate demand in the initial stages of a disinflation.

Third, the commitment undertaken when the fixed exchange rate is introduced may vary by degree. It can range from a *de facto* peg hardly distinguishable from a very dirty float to a law completely depriving policy managers of discretion. The authorities have to decide whether to fix the exchange rate 'for the time being' or to commit themselves to enforce a pre-set parity indefinitely.[6] Pegging as a transitory measure leaves open the question of what may happen when the anchor is lifted. This will cause 'peso-problems'—interest rates and prices will incorporate premiums against the possibility of a discrete devaluation.[7] To commit to a fixed rate indefinitely, on the other hand, is to gamble that the inflation will soon enough come down to international levels and that the real exchange rate will remain at a value that proves sustainable.

What usually happens at first is that an excess supply of foreign exchange develops even as the currency appreciates in real terms. In part, the appreciation may be due to a capital reflux which could reflect a permanent shift in the public's willingness to invest within the country's borders. But it may also derive simply from an overshooting of prices in response to growing

---

[6] Recent programmes show both types of choices. Israel and Mexico, for example, initially fixed the exchange rate, but later devalued their currency at moderate speeds; the Argentine convertibility plan of 1991 obliged the central bank to sell dollars at a fixed price for an indefinite period.

[7] Cf. Krasker (1980).

domestic demand. The real exchange rate then becomes too low, in which case the reserve flows will sooner or later reverse, forcing what could be a wrenching adjustment of the trade balance (cf. Dornbusch 1980; Rodriguez 1979). Once again, the immediate results of the programme in the first disinflation phase—results that obviously are crucial to the chances of the plan ultimately succeeding—have to be balanced against the problems that it bequeaths to the future.

Incomes policies

Economists in general disapprove of incomes policies and price controls. But a good case can be made for their use in the transition out of a high inflation. How to use them and when to abandon them (before they interfere seriously with the allocation of resources) become delicate questions of judgement, however.

In high inflations there is, typically, no single variable which serves as a standard for revising nominal prices. Moreover, explicit or implicit contracts, that exist in large number, may cause wages and prices to continue rising even when nominal demand and the exchange rate have stabilized. Such 'inertial' price increases will, in turn, feed back on expectations. It is more difficult, therefore, to co-ordinate a disinflation out of a high inflation than out of a hyperinflation. To disregard inflationary inertia and its expectational repercussions is to gamble. Even if the fiscal fundamentals of the programme are sound, it remains a gamble (cf. Kiguel and Liviatan 1988; also Heymann 1990, 1992).

Some resort to incomes policies is in fact unavoidable. The government cannot escape the responsibility for managing public sector prices and government wages in any event. A programme that failed to dictate a sharp deceleration of these variables is hard to imagine; indeed, a pre-announcement about their course for some time to come may be required. Moreover, the authorities have ways to influence private prices and wages short of legal coercion. The alternatives range from gentle persuasion to public denunciations to negotiated agreements.

Governments attempting a decisive disinflation can—and do—exercise this influence even if they consciously avoid imposing officially enforced price controls.

Can brute price fixing be useful in breaking inflationary inertia? The use of such measures is of course exceedingly controversial. The reasons are familiar. Controls set prices at arbitrary values. If strictly enforced, they cause 'repressed inflation' and result in shortages or black markets. In addition, they open up a new arena for high-stakes lobbying games between private interests and the government (cf. Jonung 1990).

These objections acquire particular force when no obvious benchmark can be found by which to gauge how prices should be set so as to ensure that they will be sustainable at least over the short run. Such benchmarks will be particularly hard to find, when many prices have already been subject to controls for some time. In hyperinflation, they are altogether missing. Furthermore, incomes policies can easily have unfavourable, rather than favourable, expectational effects if people associate their use with a history of futile attempts to combat inflation without dealing with the fiscal deficit and its monetization.

It is foolish to forget or discount the seriousness of these traditional objections to the use of price controls. But, that said, transitory incomes policies can serve a purpose within programmes that do address the fiscal problem. A temporary freeze, for instance, can reinforce public confidence in the near-term fiscal outlook since it increases the probability of a positive Olivera–Tanzi effect. It may also dilute fears that an early contraction in activity will tempt the central bank into excessive reflation (cf. Cukierman 1988). A credible freeze puts a halt to the rise of the general price level and can, if circumstances are right, break the momentum of prices. If fiscal and monetary policies restrain the growth in aggregate demand, many of the government-imposed price ceilings will not be binding.[8] The

---

[8] The factual evidence from recent stabilization efforts is mixed but it underscores the connection between demand management and the results of incomes policies. For example, the price freeze imposed in Brazil during the 1986 Cruzado plan quickly gave rise to shortages. But the 1987 Mexican programme (which administered prices more flexibly than a simple freeze) did not create generalized shortages and neither did 1985 freezes in Argentina and Israel.

imposition of controls obviously overdetermines prices but this does not necessarily cause more confusion than leaving price-setters with inconsistent expectations to grope their own ways through the transition.

The costs of this overdetermination of prices are bound to increase with time, however. Incomes policies, which may have served a purpose in the initial phase, must therefore be abandoned or redefined quite soon or their microeconomic costs will soon swamp the transitory macroeconomic benefit. Once the problem of co-ordinating the disinflation has been overcome, it should be left to market participants to revise their prices in response to market feedback. At this stage 'microeconomic' measures to promote competition or stimulate supply in markets that were previously subject to inappropriate regulation may help to put the recovery on the right course.

Trade liberalization

The removal of barriers to international trade, like the dismantling of regulations, modifies the allocation of resources over the long run. On the whole, these policies should be evaluated in that context. But trade policy has price effects too, and needs to be considered also as one possible component of disinflation strategies.

Trade liberalization can alter the way in which prices are determined in major markets. It is at its most effective when quantitative restrictions are eliminated, since this exposes formerly non-traded goods to international competition. Trade reform may also modify the incentives of the parties in wage negotiations by strengthening the employment effects of wage increases that are not matched by movements in the exchange rate. The likely end result of liberalization is that movements in the price level become more closely linked to those of the exchange rate. In this respect, it reinforces the effect of an exchange rate anchor.

As the economy moves toward stability, a number of factors tend to produce a real appreciation of the currency. The removal of import restrictions will help to offset this tendency to some extent. It is likely to reduce the rate of inflation relative to the rate of nominal exchange depreciation in the short run and also to raise the real exchange rate that is sustainable over the longer run (cf. Edwards 1989). The authorities then have two options in order to maintain external balance. Either they set the initial exchange parity so as to make foreign currencies more expensive initially than would have been required if trade liberalization were not part of the programme, or else they must restrain the growth of nominal domestic demand, non-traded goods prices and wages. It is worth noting that, in the latter case, macroeconomic policies have to be managed with more restraint, not less, when the economy is opened up to foreign competition.

If aggregate demand is allowed to expand too rapidly, the symptoms will show up less in prices and more in quantities once trade has been liberalized. Gradually, current account deficits will grow excessive while domestic output and employment become biased towards non-tradable commodities. At an early stage, these developments are not easy for policy-makers to detect or to interpret accurately and they need not set equilibrating market forces in motion as long as residents can borrow abroad or repatriate funds. By the time the need to adjust becomes obvious, the authorities may find it hard to resist protectionist pressures.

Maintaining a restraining influence on aggregate demand becomes even more important—but no less difficult—if the country is also opened to the international movement of capital. The ill-fated programmes of pre-announced exchange rates used in Argentina, Chile, and Uruguay in the late 1970s gave rise to a lively debate about the interaction between exchange rate, trade, and financial policies. In these episodes, financial deregulation at first stimulated capital inflows which helped to induce booms in domestic spending and mounting overvaluation of the currencies. When eventually the capital flows reversed, the economies were abruptly forced to undergo major structural and macroeconomic adjustments. The lesson widely drawn from this experience is that unfettered capital mobility may generate wide swings in both aggregate demand and relative prices, and that these swings confound output and investment decisions; consequently, it is advisable to carry through the liberalization of output markets before moving on to the liberalization of capital markets (cf. for example Bruno 1988). In some cases, however, the 'dollarization' of portfolios is already such that the authorities can exercise little influence on the degree of capital mobility.

The upshot of all this, we believe, is that the success of macroeconomic policies is far more important to the success of trade liberalization than vice versa.

BEYOND DISINFLATION—OR BACK TO HIGH
INFLATION

Stabilization programmes differ in both strategic design and tactical detail. The soundest strategy, in our judgement, combines fiscal retrenchment with some form of nominal anchoring.[9] Whatever their tactics—and whether in the end they succeed or fail—these programmes meet roughly the same market reactions at the start and also encounter a series of characteristic difficulties which have to be overcome to keep the stabilization on track. This sequence of problems deserves some commentary.

The announcement of the programme typically prompts a sharp about-turn in short-term expectations. People increase their demand for cash balances and dis-hoard foreign currencies. Nominal interest rates drop abruptly. The magnitude of the decline varies from case to case but interest rates generally remain high relative to the low rates of inflation and external depreciation that the programme promises. Prices may keep on rising for a while, especially if the plan starts with a devaluation

[9] In what follows we omit discussion of plans following the Chilean strategy of the mid-1970s. This Chilean programme produced a drastic decline in the fiscal deficit, but did not attempt to anchor either the exchange rate or prices. It succeeded in bringing down the inflation rate, albeit after a sharp recession, but it took several years before inflation fell below the 100% annual mark. Cf. Corbo and Solimano (1991), Edwards and Edwards (1987), Kiguel and Liviatan (1988), Ramos (1986).

and increases in public sector prices, but they decelerate sharply in a short time. Consumers no longer rush purchases and they engage more actively in comparison shopping. At this stage, although firms are still reluctant to cut their unit margins, some may offer rebates on products that are found significantly over-priced.

Output rates may fall at first. However, if the economy was initially in hyperinflation or near it, its cessation is more apt to normalize the supply of goods. Moreover, the lowering of the inflation tax increases disposable incomes, particularly those of low income groups whose spending depends strongly on current receipts. Thus, a tight fiscal policy need not be contractionary but can have the opposite effect—*if* it succeeds in bringing infla-tion down at the same time. Real aggregate demand will also be helped by a widespread revival of credit as suppliers come to expect prices to behave more predictably. Initially, credit is offered only at high interest rates. But agents who were previ-ously cash-constrained will none the less increase their spend-ing. Furthermore, if interest rates are governed primarily by the rate of devaluation expected in the near future, and if this is lower than expected inflation, the *ex ante* cost of credit will appear low to some agents.

The combination of these influences soon brings an upturn in production. Within relatively stable monetary regimes, a drop in output and employment may be the normal result of reduc-ing the rate of inflation. The move away from an unstable high inflation regime towards a more stable low inflation regime faces no such unavoidable dilemma. Instead, 'expansionary dis-inflations' have become the common experience.

Argentina, Bolivia, Brazil, Israel, Mexico, and Peru all initi-ated major disinflation programmes in the 1980s. With only one exception, the average rate of growth of GDP was *higher* in the two years following that in which the plans started than in the two preceding years. On this method of calculation the short-lived Brazilian Cruzado plan becomes an exception, but Brazil was actually in a feverish demand boom during the entire period the disinflation lasted. Moreover, those countries that succeeded in sustaining the disinflation show better output performance in the subsequent years than those which relapsed into high inflation.[10]

Although, at the very start, the government may have to meet urgent payments by borrowing at the central bank, a well-conceived programme will soon put a stop to this. But a favourable balance of payments will make the money stock grow rapidly none the less. The rate of inflation typically does not come down to zero even if the budget is balanced and key prices are 'anchored'. Industrial prices may remain more or less constant at first, but those of services and primary goods usually drift upwards. Some price movements are of course to be expected since disinflation will change relative prices. The danger is that residual inflation of this sort will set a floor under price expectations and be propagated forwards. The programme is not necessarily bound to fail if the economy fails to converge rapidly to a very low inflation rate, but it is a clear warning that success in the initial transition will not guarantee maintained stability.

Some months after its start, a programme may enjoy a period of comparative tranquility, with inflation much lower than in the past, a balance of payments surplus, production on the rise and, possibly, a recovery in real wages. But these favourable indicators may well mask growing pressures that will soon have to be confronted.

Beyond this first disinflation stage, two major tasks remain to be accomplished. First, the nominal anchors have to be managed and those which may have been 'overdetermined' at the start of the programme dismantled at some point. Second, the fiscal position has to be consolidated. If the government fails to move quickly, especially on the fiscal front, it gets trapped in the day-to-day management of a still very unstable system. When there is no immediate prospect of fiscal reform and fiscal institutions do not work well, the game of coping with sectoral

---

[10] The evidence on the behaviour of real activity from the hyperinflation stabilizations of the 1920s is less clear-cut. In Germany, aggregate output recovered but a number of business sectors went through 'stabilization crises'. In other Central European countries unemployment increased, although the cost of disinflation in terms of lost output does not seem to have been large.

demands one by one is soon renewed. As the goal of stability fades into 'avoiding the worst', the familiar combination of inadequate taxing capacity and multiplying claims on the public purse produces an erratic deficit which again tends inexorably to grow to high inflation levels. The government's intermittent efforts to resist demands for spending or to raise taxes come more and more to be seen by the public as short-lived fits of fiscal rectitude without a comprehensive strategy or clear purpose. Thus, they fail to budge expectations.

The central bank must then choose between simply accommodating deficits or risking an explosive increase in the public debt. As the economy relapses into the high inflation syndrome, the authorities find themselves in the constant quandary of either letting the exchange rate and public sector prices increase, so as to maintain realistic real values, or delaying these nominal adjustments in the hope that inflation will decelerate for a while.

It does not take long before policy-makers have to face dilemmas that are at least as serious as those encountered in the preceding high inflation period. In some recent episodes, such as those of Argentina and Brazil in the late 1980s, governments failed to find a steady course and frequent policy swings produced large fluctuations in the inflation rate and in relative prices. At this stage, the authorities may try to clamp down on money supply growth at intervals, but market operators are quick to learn that decompression will soon follow that will allow the exchange rate and prices to shoot up. Cycles in incomes policies become anticipated as well. In periods of accelerating prices, firms, which come to expect that controls will soon be tightened, increase their mark-ups. The entire syndrome is amplified as a result (Kiguel and Liviatan 1991). Once the programme falters, it becomes increasingly difficult to avoid a return to extreme instability. The public quickly loses confidence in economic policies, and successive 'policy packages' produce weaker and weaker results until they are abandoned.

Stabilization programmes have to make progress against ingrained patterns of behaviour. But the record shows a number of cases where governments gathered sufficient strength from the initial results of the programme to overcome the successive hurdles encountered later. For this to be possible, it is crucial that they gain control of nominal demand. The fiscal deficit has to be kept within narrow bounds as the transitory elements of the initial package are dismantled. Once the manifest 'state of emergency' has passed, interest groups will step up their claims and must be kept at bay. If these conditions can be met, redundant price anchors can be removed with little risk that the inflation will erupt again.

Some private sector responses will make things easier. As sellers gradually 'unlearn' their inflationary habits, their planning horizons lengthen and their pricing practices begin to change. The risk lessens that occasional movements in a few prices will propagate through the system and create an inflationary trend. Finding themselves in a less erratic and more competitive environment, firms will trim precautionary mark-ups and begin to return to more cost-conscious management.

None the less, this second phase of disinflation becomes problematic even for the best of programmes. The spectacular successes of the first phase cannot be repeated. The abrupt plunge of the inflation rate coupled with a strong recovery in output can happen only once. Beyond this stage, the government is out of moves that 'make almost everybody better off and nobody worse off'. Now, the real value of the prices which have been used as anchors must not be allowed continually to deteriorate or the deleterious consequences will start to build up. As the anchors are let loose and begin to rise, it becomes necessary to clamp down even harder on aggregate demand to keep the residual inflation within safe limits. Unless efficiency gains mature quickly into lower costs on a wide front and inflationary expectations fall nicely into line, the authorities may have to be prepared to face a slowdown in real activity.

At some point, the policy-makers have to decide what range of inflation rates they will eventually settle for. The hyperinflations of the 1920s were brought back down to near zero inflation. In societies with long experience under the gold standard, this was a natural ambition for policy-makers to pursue,[11] particularly since expectations of an eventual return to this 'normal' state of affairs were widespread. By contrast, the programmes that succeeded best against high inflation in the 1980s—i.e. those of Israel, Mexico, and Bolivia—managed to sustain relatively moderate, but not near-zero, inflations.[12] A society's 'inflationary memory' fades away but slowly. The persistence of inflation above international standards poses issues that are not easily resolved, particularly with regard to exchange rate policy (cf. Bruno and Meridor 1991; Ortiz 1991; Dornbusch and Fischer 1991). No professional consensus has yet been reached on whether it is wise for a country, that has recently escaped from a long history of high inflation, to make the further effort to vanquish moderate inflation.

A successful disinflation does not automatically bring rapid growth or an end to distributive conflict. But stabilization will improve the economy's performance, which does benefit people with low incomes, and it removes important obstacles to growth. Investors' 'animal spirits', dulled by instability, do recover. Although it takes considerable time for long-term financial markets to get re-established, credit also expands. Some financial developments may actually occur too rapidly and create new uncertainties. In particular, capital reflux can suddenly swing relative prices against internationally traded goods in an economy where not long ago foreign currencies were everyone's favoured store of value.

Stability, after a very high inflation, changes practically all aspects of economic life. Resources must be reallocated in a myriad ways. Sustainable relative prices are altered. New taxes are imposed and old subsidies removed. Activities which were

[11] Note, however, that while the hyperinflations of the time were brought under control, the concerted attempt by the major trading nations to stabilize the international economic order on a gold exchange standard failed with the outbreak of the Great Depression.

[12] In this respect, the Argentine convertibility plan of 1991 set for itself an objective more resembling that of the earlier programmes in that it established strict convertibility of the peso into dollars at a fixed parity. The programme followed two dramatic bursts of hyperinflation and a difficult and partial disinflation from the last one in early 1990. Inflation was quickly brought down to a very moderate level but it took about 2 years to reduce the rate of CPI inflation to less than 10% per annum.

profitable in an inflationary environment become unattractive. Opportunities appear where they previously went unperceived.

In this new environment, people will revise their subjective wealth estimates—in most instances upward. But expectations have to be formed in a situation where past experience provides little guidance. Individual wealth perceptions need not be based on consistent beliefs but may well overshoot. The recently stabilized economies seem prone to fluctuations arising from intertemporal co-ordination failures. The shift in the inflationary regime even changes the macroeconomic analysis most applicable to the economy. Traditional business cycle theory regains its relevance as the focus of immediate concern moves away from the short-run behaviour of government, the volatility of expectations, and the high-frequency pricing decisions of firms.

INFLATION AND STABILIZATION IN THE FORMER SOVIET UNION

To put the historic cataclysm that the former communist countries are undergoing in the same context as the high inflations of Israel or Argentina is to trivialize it. Yet, the 'orthodox shock' therapies that the West is urging these countries to adopt draw much of their inspiration from Latin American stabilization experience. High inflations do exhibit systematic features. It seems useful, however, to take note of some of the differences between the Latin American high inflations and the present situation in the former Soviet Union (FSU).

For present purposes, we may characterize that situation— very schematically, to be sure—by the following five observations.

(i)   The former unitary state has disintegrated. The hegemony over the former 'satellite' states has been lost. It is uncertain, moreover, whether the ethnic tensions that threaten further political splintering within several of the fifteen republics will be contained.

(ii)   The institutions of the command economy have been fatally damaged and 'can't be put together again'.

(iii) Little progress has been made towards creating the public finance systems adequate to modern mixed economies.

(iv)   Progress towards fulfilling the minimal institutional requirements for a private sector market economy to function has been spotty at best. In some areas (routine law enforcement) matters are getting worse, rather than better.

(v)   Financial institutions are as yet rudimentary and quite inadequate to handle the control functions and credit needs of an economy of the former USSR's size.

These factors have no counterpart in Latin American experience.[13] A clear perception of the role of the first two in particular is crucial to an understanding of how the inflationary depression in these countries differs from experiences with extreme instability in various Western market economies. It is appropriate to begin with 'initial conditions'—in this instance, the economy that Gosplan built (Leijonhufvud 1993a, 1993b).

The manufacturing sector built up under central planning is characterized by a high degree of vertical industry integration and reliance on very large plants. Individually, these plants tend to be technologically inflexible, and so is the entire system consisting of such plants. The planners had exaggerated notions of the economies of plant scale and little understanding of the systemic economies of scale external to the plant. Their 'gigantomania' left a very vulnerable legacy: many large plants depend on a single or at least dominant supplier for some of their raw materials or intermediate inputs and, similarly, have one dominant customer. If one such gigantic plant ceases to operate, others are left without supplies or without customers. Even when other suppliers or customers exist elsewhere, the inadequacies of the transportation and distribution system are such that switching to an alternative pattern of deliveries can be all but impossible in the short run. Failure in one part of the system,

---

[13] The generalization cannot quite be broadened to take in the European hyperinflation cases of the 1920s since the disintegration of the USSR has its counterpart in the dismemberment of Austro-Hungary after World War I. Still, the former citizens of that empire did not experience a total change in the economic system.

therefore, can cascade through a large part of it. Such failures have been occurring on a large scale and constitute the most intractable part of the recent crisis in the FSU economy and the aspect of it, moreover, that is not at all amenable to traditional macroeconomic prescriptions.

The Gosplan system was not only larger than Russia, it lapped over the borders of the Soviet Union into the 'satellite' Eastern European nations. The plan prices underlying the terms of trade between political units bore little relation to potential market prices. Trade was based not on mutually recognized gain but on Moscow's political hegemony. The loss of it, therefore, has a lot to do with the breakdown of the system. The collapse of Comecon trade already demonstrated its vulnerability. From early 1991 onwards, new tensions among the republics of the Soviet Union began to disrupt trade between them also. The threat to withhold deliveries became part of the political game between republics even before the breakup of the USSR and the creation of the CIS. The Gosplan legacy of vertically integrated industries of gigantic plants made such threats highly effective: cessation of deliveries from one republic could seriously disrupt production in others. Following the breakup of the Soviet Union, the relationship between the CIS republics came to be negotiated very largely through threat games of this sort.

The Gosplan legacy would have made rapid progress on market reform exceedingly difficult in any case. The basic problem is not political, although it is greatly exacerbated by political disintegration. The vertical integration theory of the firm helps make the problem clear. The standard metaphor in discussing it is the assembly line. The different workstations on such a line cannot be made into separate firms, buying their respective intermediate good input from the preceding station and selling to the succeeding one, because these 'firms' would be without alternative suppliers for their inputs and without alternative customers for their outputs. The assembly line would turn into a chain of bilateral monopoly relations for which no stable equilibrium could be found. The analogy likening the Gosplan system to a set of such assembly lines is easily overdrawn, of course. But the parallels are instructive:

(i) If one workstation on an assembly line breaks down or fails to receive required intermediate inputs, the whole line comes to a halt.

(ii) The workstations on an assembly line cannot be made into individual firms, each one selling its output to the next, because of the near-impossibility of finding terms of trade that will prove stable for such a chain of bilateral monopolies.

(iii) The physical assets that together make up the assembly line have little market value separately. The whole is worth more than the sum of the parts.

Privatization is no panacea when dealing with a productive structure of this kind, and liberalizing prices will not automatically replace the arbitrary plan prices with market prices truly reflecting relative resource scarcities. It is obviously true that the inherited, utterly arbitrary system of prices offers hardly a clue to what enterprises are socially efficient or inefficient. It is a widespread opinion that rationalization of the FSU economies can only be achieved by privatizing all enterprises and letting the market weed out the inefficient ones—and the faster the better. But the 'sink-or-swim' test of what enterprises deserve to survive can very easily go horribly wrong. It will go wrong not only because some plants will fail that would survive if prices were competitive, but because forcing individual loss-makers into bankruptcy may force a cascade of failures up and down the vertical chain of plants. The gain from eliminating the losses recorded at one plant can easily be completely swamped by the social loss resulting from a vertical cascade of failures. The unemployment and capital destruction that might result in such cases will be of a kind, moreover, that is not to be remedied through traditional macroeconomic stimulus.

The vulnerabilities of the vertically integrated structures that are the Gosplan inheritance also help explain why enterprise subsidies have become the crux of the ruble zone inflation problem. The state enterprises, which never operated under hard budget constraints in the communist past, have proved quite effectively resistant to such constraints in the non-communist present. With the help of the ministries that once controlled them, many of the vertically integrated industries try to keep going with much the same plant-to-plant delivery patterns as before—transacting at arbitrary prices, but without settling accounts out of their own revenues. Instead, they turn to the government for subsidies to keep production going and unemployment from skyrocketing. If subsidies are denied, 'enterprise arrears' are allowed to pile up so that some money creation is postponed. If they are granted, the money presses roll at once.

Why does not the government impose hard budget constraints on these enterprises? Three observations will make at least a partial answer. First, Soviet enterprises never had to maintain a sound financial working capital position to operate. The present FSU enterprises are largely without financial working capital. Were the stream of subsidies (and/or permitted arrears) to suddenly dry up, many of them would simply lack the wherewithal to continue production. Second, the financial institutions or securities markets that might be able to provide the required working capital on business-like terms do not exist. Third, the government cannot credibly threaten large enterprises with bankruptcy, particularly not if it concerns the dominant enterprise in a particular location or if the failure would 'cascade'. There is still much ambivalence and controversy over the extent to which activity levels in the economy and the fate of firms should be regulated by the monetary-financial control system.[14]

High inflations, as we know, have destroyed the financial systems of countries with long and unbroken experience with the market system. Russia and the other former Soviet republics cannot hope to create functioning intermediaries and securities markets under conditions of high inflation. So far Estonia is the only republic to have stabilized its own currency by relying on a (somewhat modified) currency board arrangement. For the others, the conditions are far off under which capital formation in significant volume can resume.[15]

---

[14] Cf. Chapter 4 above.

[15] The efficiency with which existing resources are utilized (never very high) is almost surely more seriously impaired in the FSU than in countries with more experience both with free markets and with high inflation. Standard accounting practices are little known in these countries, for example, and inflation accounting is totally unknown. Under high inflation conditions, most former Soviet enterprises will have little or no idea of whether they are running at a profit or a loss.

7

High Inflations and Contemporary Monetary Theory

There cannot, in short, be intrinsically a more insignificant thing, in the economy of society, than money; except in the character of a contrivance for doing quickly and commodiously, what would be done, though less quickly and commodiously, without it; and like many other kinds of machinery, it only exerts a distinct and independent influence of its own when it gets out of order.

John Stuart Mill

People who pierce the veil of money rarely return with their faculties altogether intact.

Daniel Patrick Moynihan

THE AMBIVALENCE OF MONETARY THEORY

Mill's famous dictum gives concise expression to a view of the foundations of monetary theory that still governs virtually all work in the subject. It has been quoted innumerable times as a well-formulated piece of time-honoured wisdom suitable for trotting out on ceremonial occasions. But there is something puzzling about its popularity. For, surely, there is a tension between the two parts of Mill's statement that at least borders on outright contradiction: Why should it matter when an 'intrinsically insignificant thing' gets 'out of order'?

The tension can, of course, be resolved in one of two ways. On the one hand, one might suppose that when the contrivance gets out of order, the rise in transactions costs will cause people to conduct their regular business somewhat 'less quickly and commodiously' without money. If their real transactions were largely unaffected, that would prove money to be 'intrinsically insignificant' all right. On the other hand, one might suppose

that severe monetary disturbances have the 'distinct and independent influence' of seriously disrupting real activities for prolonged periods of time—in which case there is nothing
'insignificant' about the contrivance of money.

The tension is not resolved, one way or another, in the modern literature, although the more purely theoretical literature
leans one way and the applied literature the other. On the
applied side, monetarist writers, for instance, warn that monetary mismanagement is capable of bringing on great depressions. At the same time, on the theoretical side, the search for
an intellectually satisfying way to introduce money into general
equilibrium models is still on and with no end in sight. The
problem is to demonstrate that a general equilibrium system
can*not* operate *equally* 'quickly and commodiously' without
money. By various contrivances, money can be grafted on to
the theoretical trunk but what sprouts is usually only one of
money's functions not all the traditional four. In overlapping
generations models, money finds a place as a store of value (at
least in hypothetical worlds where there are no other such
stores), but there is no reason for it to serve the function of a
medium of exchange. Cash-in-advance models force money's
use in exchange, but do not explain the prevalence of nominal
contracting.

Which way should one lean? In the previous chapters, we
have presented, first, a summary of standard inflation theory
(somewhat 'annotated') and, then, a fairly detailed description
of what high inflations are like and what problems stand in the
way of their stabilization. Between these two parts, the same
conceptual tension creeps up again.

A note of caution is perhaps required. We cannot claim that
our description of high inflations is entirely atheoretical or
'purely' empirical; on the contrary, it is obviously already struc-
tured by our theoretical beliefs. But *any* account is bound to
produce this dissonance between the 'out of order' reality of
high inflations and the 'intrinsic insignificance' of money in the
core of standard inflation theory.

NEOCLASSICAL MONETARY THEORY: TRADITIONAL AND MODERN

Contemporary monetary theory sharpens the contrast. In Mill's time, monetary theory dealt with an economy that was basically a system of spot markets. Intertemporal markets were not totally excluded, of course. The creation of bank money against 90-day real bills was a central topic in nineteenth-century monetary debates, for instance. But intertemporal contracts and, in particular, organized markets for such contracts were on the whole treated as exceptional. In reading the British monetary economists of that time, one gains the impression that they regarded the London gilt-edged market (and particularly, the consols) as one of the peak achievements of Victorian civilization. Markets for long-term contracts were not to be taken for granted—after all, the natives of less fortunate countries had to manage without them for the most part.

Modern monetary theory, in contrast, takes as its starting point an Arrow–Debreu complete markets system. Directly or indirectly, agents are able to make exchanges between any two dimensions of the contingent/dated commodity space. In the modern view, it is departures from this complete markets scenario, not the assumption of it in the first place, that require analytical justification. 'Missing markets' become exceptions to be explained by technical obstacles.

The modern theory is forced into this position by its prior methodological commitment to the description of individual rational behaviour in terms of constrained optimization as the only firm foundation for economics. Optimization requires that the opportunity sets and preferences of agents be specified over all dimensions of the relevant commodity space; *a priori* restrictions on the dimensionality of this space are in general not to be had. When, then, a competitive equilibrium is assumed to co-ordinate the plans of all agents, the result is a description of the economy's motion corresponding to the solution of an all-knowing Pareto-motivated social planner's decision problem. Departures from social optimality can be obtained in a variety of ways: incomplete market participation (as in OLG models), asymmetric information, and the like. But the basic framework commits agents to a once-in-a-lifetime contingent programme, and it forces the reconciliation of all such plans without clarifying the role of markets and the relevance of the transactions structure in co-ordinating individual activities.

Money itself has no secure place in this complete markets general equilibrium framework. When all future contingencies can be handled in the present, there is no reason to postpone commitments[1] or delay transactions. With everything settled from the start, money will not be demanded either as a liquid ('flexible') store of value or as a means of exchange.

This brand of monetary theory is merging with finance theory. Just as the somewhat older tradition modelled the 'real' economy first, as if it functioned perfectly well without money, only to turn next to the problem of finding a significant role for money, modern finance theory is formally carried out entirely in 'real' terms with the subsequent conversion to money asset prices done in entirely *ad hoc* fashion. The merger brings into monetary theory the Modigliani–Miller theorem in generalized form:[2] consistent pricing in intertemporal general equilibrium means that financial structure cannot matter.

THREE PROBLEMS

The economic performance of high inflation economies is far worse than that of economies enjoying monetary stability. At this point, we take this as established. It is the phenomenon we must try to understand. The line between order and disorder in the system is shifting as an economy moves into high inflation.

---

[1] Certain physically irreversible investments may be postponed when the various uncertainties concerning their profitability will be resolved with the passage of time. In that case society may hold physical resources in a 'flexible' form until the investment date. But the commitment to undertake these investments *contingent* on how the uncertainty is resolved will be made in the present.

[2] As well as associated lemmas, in particular, Ricardian equivalence and the irrelevance of open market operations.

Economies in the grip of serious monetary instability do not converge—behind a fluttering 'Veil of Money'—to some 'real' equilibrium that differs from what it would be under assured monetary stability only by the inflation tax distortion. Instead, it settles into far less well co-ordinated and less productive states. The non-neutrality of a money 'out of order' goes deeper than the inflation tax.

We cannot deal with the whole welter of theoretically 'dissonant' observations. In attempting to draw some lessons for monetary theory from our material, we will focus on three broad areas:

(i)   The staying power of domestic money. It continues in general use even at extremely high rates of 'taxation'.

(ii) The disappearance of markets. High inflation countries end up with an extremely impoverished structure of intertemporal markets.

(iii) The excess variability of relative prices.

THE MEDIUM OF EXCHANGE FUNCTION

A line of theoretical inquiry begun by Ostroy 20 years ago (Ostroy 1973) and recently surveyed by Ostroy and Starr (1990) provides insight into our first problem, the 'staying power' of money in ordinary day-to-day transactions. Work along this line has also helped to clarify how general equilibrium theory has to be modified in order to accommodate a significant transactions role for money.

Ostroy and Starr ask what is required for it to be possible actually to carry out the individual trades needed to reach a general equilibrium. To limit the inquiry to that question, they assume that the equilibrium price vector has been arrived at (by some procedure independent of trading activity[3]). The problem is to make it feasible for each transactor to move, by some sequence of trades, from his endowment to his optimal consumption vector, while at the same time enforcing budget

---

[3] Kiyotaki and Wright (1989) make progress on this front.

constraints so as to prevent people from getting away with more than they are entitled to. If the economy is restricted to 'barter', the necessity of policing budget constraints will immensely complicate the logistical problem of finding a pattern of trades that will realize the general equilibrium. The equilibrium will in general *not* be realizable, for instance, if agents are restricted to sequential pairwise barter trades each of which has to obey a strict *quid pro quo condition*. A medium of exchange will solve the problem. In a decentralized economy where agents trade sequentially, people use money as evidence of having made a measured contribution to the welfare of some members of society that, in turn, will legitimize their appropriation of goods and services from other members. Money in effect does the record-keeping required to enforce budget constraints over time in multilateral exchange.[4]

Earlier monetary equilibrium models were 'dichotomous' in the sense that, although money was hitched on as a store of value, the 'real' equilibrium would be achieved whether or not money was present (cf. Hahn 1965; Clower 1967). Models of the Ostroy–Starr type introduce a 'real' role for money as a transactions medium. If real balances were not present in sufficient volume in the system, it will not be capable of reaching its first-best equilibrium. Here, finally, theory is edging away from portraying money as 'intrinsically insignificant' and begins to inform our understanding of what money 'out of order' might entail.

However, knowing that an economy will not do well without a medium of exchange does not tell us what instrument will fulfil that role. Although high inflations show signs of widespread currency substitution, a tax of one per cent per day on cash

---

[4] Readers who find the budget enforcement argument too abstract to be convincing may want to consider the collapse of the manufacturing sector in the former Soviet republics. Once co-ordinated (after a fashion) by Gosplan, the enterprises have been unable to find their way to a decentralized equilibrium. For a period, most of the system kept on running with totally 'soft budgets', building up enormous payments arrears. As the issue of enforcing budget constraints eventually had to be faced, the system contracted rapidly. Short of real money balances, enterprises tried all kinds of barter but were not able in such manner to piece together a functioning system.

holdings—or even several months of inflation running much above that level—will not drive domestic money totally out of existence. This is not because alternatives are unavailable: the hoards of US dollar bills held by Argentine residents in the late 1980s, for example, may well have been larger than the stock of domestic money. But these dollars did not come into circulation so as to eliminate the use of the local currency.

The staying-power of domestic means of payment that this demonstrates indicates the strength of the social convention[5] supporting the use of the national money. To establish a new convention around a different means of payment will require people to make the transition in co-ordinated fashion. Such a transition is not easy to organize. The fact that the government persists in conducting its business in its own currency may also be significant. People have to hold government issued paper money at least for the purpose of settling accounts with the public sector. It may be that this introduces just enough 'friction' into individual currency substitution decisions to generate a demand for that money also for the purpose of small-scale transactions between private agents. But this is speculation.[6] The point remains that we do not have a clear picture of what ultimately supports the demand for domestic money—and of what might make this ultimate support vanish.

[5] Kiyotaki and Wright (1989) model the general acceptability of a means of exchange as a Nash equilibrium. But the staying power of money in high inflation remains a riddle also in their framework: 'If [the per-period storage cost of holding money] gets sufficiently large, however, then there cannot exist any equilibrium where money is acceptable . . . *A sufficiently bad money has no hope of serving as a medium of exchange.*' (Kiyotaki and Wright 1992, p. 20, italics added).

[6] Note, however, that when in the final stages of the post-World War II Hungarian hyperinflation, the government introduced the 'tax-pengö' (a currency that was indexed daily and accepted in payment of taxes), the inflation rate measured in regular pengö become truly astronomical (6×10^7 *per month!*) and the real stock of standard money shrank to virtually nothing. Since at this point nothing was being done about the fiscal problem, the inflation rate in tax pengös rose quite high as well. See Bomberger and Makinen (1980, 1983).

THE ADDING-UP PROBLEM

The Ostroy–Starr analysis concentrates on the institutional arrangements needed to prevent people from violating their budget constraints. It presupposes that they know what those budget constraints are. We can press the analysis a bit farther by asking what institutional arrangements may be necessary to make this possible.

Again, it is helpful to start with a centralized economy as a bench-mark. In modern representative agent models (or social planner models), it is assumed as a matter of course that the representative agent knows his lifetime budget constraint. For simplicity, let us focus on the measurement of wealth. The representative agent must have this number right or he cannot possibly arrive at the correct solution to his overall allocation problem.

For the economy as a whole, the aggregate of individual wealth perceptions will determine the rates of saving and capital accumulation. But each agent measures his own wealth by guessing the market conditions that he will face in the future. With incomplete markets, people have no way of determining either the physical volume of their future sales or the relative prices that will prevail. What, then, assures that individual wealth perceptions will *add up* consistently in an actual economy composed of millions of transactors? Better put, what error correction mechanisms does the economy possess that will bring the aggregate wealth estimate back into the near neighbourhood of its 'true value' whenever it wanders off?

Wealth perceptions may be inaccurate for various reasons. Here we are interested in errors that do not sum to zero across the population.[7] The simplest such cases have to do with falsifications of the Ostroy–Starr cumulative record of past net sales

---

[7] Cf. Yeager (1960): 'Precisely one of the characteristics of a disequilibrium situation, and one of the reasons it cannot endure, is that real incomes appear different to people from what they can actually be.' For general discussions of disequilibrium wealth perceptions and macroeconomic outcomes, cf. Leijonhufvud (1968) and Heymann (1983).

that money is supposed to provide. Private counterfeiting can do this but the more important case is, of course, that where a government acquires resources by simply printing money. Either case is likely to produce transitory aggregate overestimates of wealth. The rules for correcting the errors differ, however. When counterfeiting is discovered, those who had accepted counterfeit notes will be forced to take a corresponding capital loss. Government issued money, on the other hand, will stay in circulation and the price level must rise so as to distribute the capital loss as an inflation tax on everybody's cash balances.

Government issued fiduciary money may also be thought of as a 'debt' of sorts. What matters is whether the government is spending more money than it takes in either in present *or* in future taxes.[8] Whenever it does, the inflation tax will sooner or later come into effect to bring perceived private sector wealth back to what it can be. When it becomes apparent that a private promise to pay will not be honoured, the adjustment is made by making the holder of the IOU bear the loss.

Imagine, for a moment, an economy where the monetary record-keeping function is handled by a centralized bookkeeping agency (CBA). All credits and debits created in the course of sales and purchases of goods and services are registered with the agency as they occur. Suppose also that the agency prevents the accumulation of debits in excess of credits on individual accounts and that borrowing and lending are not allowed. (We may have to start the system off with everyone endowed either with a limited overdraft right or with a positive balance of 'outside' credits.) In a system of this sort, would it matter whether debit balances were ever extinguished by *payment*? As long as the CBA sees to it that no one gets away with appropriating goods and services from the economy without having contributed equal value, it would seem that insisting on payments would be to little purpose. Balance sheets could be left to grow

---

[8] Cf. Sargent (1987*a*), where the definition of money appropriate to the determination of the price level in intertemporal equilibrium models is 'outside money *net of future government surpluses*'. It is not obvious how that definition is going to be made operational.

to indefinite length as long as credits and debits indeed did balance. In a Modigliani–Miller spirit, the total volume of credit outstanding would not matter.

Next, let borrowing and lending be allowed. Entrepreneurs sell their IOUs, for instance, in order to gather up enough of other people's accumulated credit balances to finance sizeable investments. Imagine, as before, that the system keeps going by keeping debits and credits to individual accounts in balance and without an operating payments mechanism. Now, however, suppose that it is discovered that, because of fraud or miscalculation of returns to investment, many of the outstanding IOUs will not be honoured. Just before this discovery, people believed themselves wealthier in the aggregate than is consistent with the system's production possibilities. To bring individual estimates of wealth into line with what is feasible, the current holders of the defaulted IOUs should be made to bear the loss. But they may have borrowed or bought on credit on the presumed strength of the IOUs they held—and be unable to assume the entire loss as a consequence. The CBA would then have to track down the agents who had sold to them on credit in order to make these people take the loss, and so on. In a system where (by assumption) debits are never extinguished by final payment, all transactions in effect involve the extension and the acceptance of credit. A's ability to honour his commitments is conditional on B's, whose ability to pay is similarly conditional on C's, and so on. Thus there is no telling where the process of locating the ultimate losers will end up. The financial structure that we are imagining is a dense web of such endless chains of conditional promises. Hence everyone would be at risk. It is an endogenous risk, not the exogenous risk of Arrow–Debreu constructions. Such a system is *financially fragile.*[9]

For the basic *adding up problem* to be solved correctly, agents must first find out who is and who is not solvent and what commitments, therefore, are or are not good. When widespread fraud is discovered or miscalculation revealed in a financially

---

[9] The theme of many writings by Hyman Minsky (e.g. 1977).

fragile economy, sorting the good credit risks from the bad ones can, in the absence of a CBA, only be accomplished by shortening the chains of promises-conditional-on-promises until an overview of the situation is achieved. This is done, of course, by demanding *payment* from debtors and prospective customers. Under conditions of financial fragility, however, the switch from credit expansion to credit contraction will not just sort out the negative net worth balance sheets from the positive ones. It is likely to lump the merely illiquid with the bankrupt. The demands for payment *now* rather than later will bring down also many of those who have borrowed short to lend long or to invest in capital with long payback periods. There are bound to be many such agents because any well-developed financial system has as one of its most important functions the piecing together of large, durable investments from many small and short-lived acts of saving.

In such a credit crash, therefore, the system goes from one wrong answer to the adding-up problem to the opposite one. In our example, aggregate wealth was overestimated initially. The miscalculation is discovered but, in the decentralized economy, the *monetary* process of ascertaining its magnitude and determining the incidence can easily fail to screen the sound but illiquid debtors from those who have been over-optimistic or fraudulent. Aggregate wealth is then underestimated. This error can be both large and persistent if debt deflation sets in. The way to insulate oneself from the contagion of a credit collapse is to demand payment on one's claims and to pay off one's debts, so as to cut oneself out of the collapsing web of conditional promises.[10] When the representative agent[11] decides to

[10] If contracts were in kind, the usual barter difficulties would of course arise in this context as well, i.e., what your 'debtors' owe you would not be acceptable to your 'creditors'. It is by settling with a *means of payment* that transactors save themselves in this situation. For much the same reason, the adding up has to be done in a monetary unit of account and not, say, in apples. Being long in apples will not save you from bankruptcy.

[11] In the present context, of course, the representative agent is *not* to be construed as having a per capita share in the *consolidated* balance sheet of the closed economy, but rather as having accounts receivable and payable of average size—and commensurably 'average' worries about the creditworthiness of others.

take this course, he will increase the excess supply of goods and services and the excess demand for final means of payment in the economy. By increasing the real value of outstanding debts and claims, the ensuing deflation reinforces the prevailing uncertainty about who will and who will not be able to pay in full. This deviation-amplifying process can keep the system away from its equilibrium price level and equilibrium aggregate wealth estimate for a considerable time.[12]

Great depressions are caused and amplified by widespread insolvencies within the private sector. High inflations are caused by the insolvency of governments covering their deficits with 'bad debt' money. Each can be alleviated by the sector (if any) whose credit is healthy. Depressions can be cured by a credit-worthy government's expenditures and transfer payments financed by borrowing.[13] High inflations can be cured by the private sector allowing itself to be taxed.

BOTTOMS UP

In each of two preceding sections we have dealt with the problem of *finding a feasible procedure* such that a decentralized economy could reach an efficiently co-ordinated state. The economic system has, in effect, to *calculate* solutions to these problems. One concerns the medium of exchange function of money, the other the unit of account and standard of deferred pay-

---

[12] It is well known, of course, that the Modigliani–Miller theorem in its original application to corporate finance does not hold when bankruptcy risks are significant (cf. Stiglitz 1969). It is not surprising, therefore, that we find ourselves escaping the macroeconomic tyranny of generalized Modigliani–Miller theorems once we introduce default risk.

[13] Cf. Leijonhufvud (1973). To associate, as is so frequently done, the efficacy of Keynesian remedies with the stickiness of wages and fix-prices is both superficial and dangerously misleading. For deficit spending (and particularly bond-financed spending) to be effective in raising real incomes and employment, the State should be operating well within its capacity to tax, and its spending or transfers should alleviate binding liquidity constraints in the private sector. Keynesian counter-cyclical policies require a solvent government. The general inability of high inflation governments to alleviate recessions is at bottom due to their lack of credit, not to any inability on their part to inflate surprisingly fast.

ments, but aspects of the two problems are similar. In considering the logistics of executing multilateral exchange, Ostroy and Starr contemplate the complications of long (and perhaps endless) chains of 'indirect barter' transactions. The 'adding-up' problem of the previous section is seen to involve long (and perhaps endless) chains of promises-conditional-on-promises.

Throughout the discussion of these two problems, we continued to use the standard general equilibrium model as the benchmark reference. That construction presupposes that agents know all there is to know about their environment, that they calculate optimal plans accordingly, and that the corresponding individual activities are, somehow, perfectly co-ordinated. We have argued, first, that for the system to come anywhere close to this equilibrium, individual budget constraints have to be monitored and individuals must be able to know what their budget constraints are and, second, that money, in its various functions, is required for both the determination and the enforcement of budgets. So, money is not a veil. Disturb its functioning sufficiently and the system will not achieve as 'rational' an equilibrium as it otherwise would.

In all of this, we have not modified the standard picture of what individual agents are like. The individuals of which the system is composed remain Arrow–Debreu planners, perfectly capable of optimizing over infinite dimensional spaces, and all the rest. The problems of record-keeping and of financial fragility are systemic imperfections. Although most people like to think that they are smarter than the organizations for which they work, it may be that we should pay attention also to the limits to the ability of agents to process information, to manage complexity, and to co-ordinate their activities in an unstable environment. The trouble of course is that, from the standpoint of economic analysis, this means venturing into rough country where the economist will have to do without many of the accustomed comforts of home.

A sideways glance at what is going on in other fields can sometimes help one's perspective. The field of 'artificial intelligence' is in the grips of a controversy between those who advocate a 'top down' and those who favour a 'bottom up' approach. The 'top down' approach relies on the sheer crunching power of a centralized processor eventually to replicate whatever human intelligence can do. The 'bottom up' approach, or 'distributed AI', relies on interacting networks of relatively simple processors and attempts to make neural nets evolve that, by parallel processing, will handle tasks far beyond the capacities of the components.

Neoclassical monetary theory is, in these terms, quintessentially 'top down'. There is little purpose to economists choosing sides and doing battle as if these two approaches were mutually exclusive across the entire discipline. But to get a handle on such ill-co-ordinated processes as high inflations (or, for that matter, Keynesian depressions), we may do better to view the system from the 'bottom up'. For the present, this means simply two conjectures, stated in very general terms:

(i)   That the economy is best conceived of as a network of interacting processors, each one with *less capability* to process information than would be required of a central processor set to solve the overall allocation problem for the entire system.

(ii) That money is used in the economy *because* people lack the kind of rationality presupposed in complete markets models. That monetary calculation, nominal contracting, and monetary payments practices are essential to the integration of the computations of the 'boundedly rational' processors of local information.

MARSHALL'S CONSUMER

It is conceivable (isn't it?) that people may not be terribly good at the rational calculation of complicated optima. Taking this possibility seriously goes against fashion but we think it is worth exploring. We choose to do so by considering a simple example, namely, the Marshallian consumer.

The economic system as a whole, we have argued, requires a computational procedure, an *algorithm* in effect, to find a solution to the overall allocation problem. The network of linked market mechanisms and the underlying rules that govern interactions in markets are the means for implementing this algorithm. Algorithms are *sequential*, step-by-step procedures for reaching an answer.[14]

In standard theory, an agent's activity vector is the result of just one single choice. Consider the complexity of the problem. The Slutsky consumer chooses a basket of n consumer goods; if the economist puts him in a temporal context, he will obediently choose an nT-dimensional timepath; if faced with the uncertainty of c possible states of nature per time-period, he will unerringly precalculate his contingent paths through this nTc-dimensional jungle, unfazed by the multiplication of margins at which optimality conditions have to be checked. In each instance, there is just a single decision.

This modern conception of rational choice may be contrasted, for instance, to that of Pareto, who was willing to postulate a rationality in the economic realm that he did not expect elsewhere in the social sphere because he conceived of economic behaviour as consisting largely of *frequently repeated actions* the outcomes of which could be checked against intentions in a direct and reliable manner. Pareto's agents *learn to be rational* through trial-and-error. The modern Slutskyite's lifetime consumption choice is not such a repeated action.

If Slutsky demand theory were more concerned with actual consumer behaviour, it might be considered a weakness that it has trouble explaining 'shopping'. Alfred Marshall's demand theory may have other weaknesses, but his consumer can go shopping—making up her mind on what to buy as she goes along. Marshall's consumer is able to break down her Slutsky cousin's horrendous decision problem into a *sequence* of manageable pieces. Her main trick is knowing the marginal utility of money, but it helps a lot that she has a cardinal, additive utility function.[15]

---

[14] In a market system, obviously, numerous such sub-routines would be running in parallel at any one time. Cf. Waldspurger *et al.* (1990); Huberman (1990). Huberman's decentralized programme for parallel computation organizes itself on basically market-system principles.

[15] Although, for our illustrative purpose, we stick with it in the text, Marshall's generalized additivity is hardly to be taken seriously. The hierarchical additivity of Strotz's 'utility-tree' should. See Strotz (1957) and also

The conceptual experiment goes as follows. The consumer receives her income as periodic money payments. Into the present period she carries with her the memory of the 'final' utility of the last shilling spent in the latest pay-period. This historical magnitude she treats as a constant. She has a marginal utility function for each separate consumer good. This marginal utility, however, is a subjective magnitude that cannot be meaningfully communicated to others. To express demand for the good it has to be made subject to the 'measuring rod of money'. The number of utils anticipated from consuming the third package of tea divided by the constant number of utils attached to a shilling equals the number of shillings she is willing to pay for a third package of tea. The consumer's decision-rule is: If the demand-price for a good, calculated thusly, exceeds the market price—Buy! Knowing 'the value of money' (to herself, in utils), she will thus be able to weigh it against market prices of goods in simple pairwise comparisons, make *sequential* 'shopping' decisions, and still end up at the optimal point on her *n*-dimensional budget-constraint. The procedure is a low-cost algorithm for finding this solution—or, rather, for approximating it (cf. Leijonhufvud 1974).

A rule-of-thumb decision strategy of this sort spares one's mental health from contemplating all marginal rates of substitution in n-space before buying a cup of coffee. It is in the nature of rules-of-thumb, however, that they may introduce error. Using the rule, Marshall's pragmatic British consumer can *act* when her Russian or French cousins would be paralysed by the existential indeterminacy of it all. She can set out to spend her money without knowing beforehand all the goods that may be offered for sale, or all the prices, or even her own tastes in all dimensions of the commodity space. Each area of ignorance, naturally, becomes a potential source of allocational error.[16]

Gorman (1959). Note that Strotz motivated his additivity assumption, not as a primitive property of the sensations induced by consumption, but as a decision strategy evolved to simplify calculations.

[16] To the Slutskyite or Walrasian consumer, in contrast, any such area of ignorance makes the consumption allocation problem ill-defined and therefore insoluble from the very start.

Suppose, in particular, that the consumer spends a major portion of her income on commodities whose prices have not changed before discovering—too late—that other goods, which she had been used to consuming, have become significantly more expensive. This will mean that, when the budget is exhausted, various marginal rates of substitution are out of line with relative prices. Such a discovery teaches her in effect that she has been calculating her demand-prices with the help of a measuring rod that has 'stretched'—i.e., on the basis of a subjective evaluation of what money is worth that, though learned in the past, no longer applies. She must then 'recalibrate' the marginal utility of money, as best she can, before setting out to spend next month's wages, and so on. In times of rapid inflation, therefore, this behaviour pattern relies on learning of a type subject to a rapid depreciation—and this depreciation is one of the social costs of inflation.

The irregular leads and lags in price-rises on the different goods in her regular basket, will make it difficult for this Marshallian consumer to put together a reasonable approximation of the optimal basket. Inflation compels the household constantly to recalibrate the marginal utility of money, as best it can, before setting out to spend each successive paycheck. The recalibrating is a *guess* at the utility of the 'final shilling' of that paycheck. Shopping on the basis of this guess becomes in effect a speculative activity.

The informational and computational simplifications of this Marshallian decision procedure depend in *essential* ways on the use of money. The consumer is using it as a personal 'standard of value' in decision-making. But sequential shopping, as opposed to simultaneous commitment to a complete allocation, also requires the household to retain a measure of *flexibility* (cf. Lippman and McCall 1986). It does so by carrying the socially accepted means of exchange (albeit for short periods only).

It may well be that the informational and computational economies of such a decision procedure (or something pretty much like it) are so important to people that they are unwilling or unable to give up these cognitive shortcuts even in times of rapid and ragged inflation. As we have seen, in high inflations,

certain large transactions, such as in real estate, are often con-
ducted in foreign currency, just as certain large contracts, such
as union contracts, are indexed. Obviously, it is worth incurring
considerable decision and transactions costs for these large and
infrequent transactions. But nominal pricing and payment in
domestic currency persist precisely in the realm of Pareto's
'repeated actions'.

THE DISAPPEARANCE OF MARKETS

The problems that high inflation monetary regimes would add
to monetary general equilibrium theory stem from the uncertainty about the government's fiscal and monetary policies now
and in the future. The Arrow–Debreu complete markets theory
can, it would seem, be generalized in a natural (and by now
almost instinctive) way to encompass the complications that
uncertain policy adds. To that end, one would simply expand
the shared decision-space of agents by multiplying the
Arrow–Debreu dated goods/natural contingencies by the various 'states of the State' that may with some probability be associated with each date/state of nature.[17] At a formal level, all
theoretical problems would now appear solved: as long as he
can keep track of the added notation, the student of general
equilibrium finds 'nothing new'. But he should discern trouble.
The theory predicts that random walk inflation would *multiply
markets*. There is some of that: new types of indexed contracts
do emerge that are not seen in countries enjoying monetary stability. But the dominant phenomenon is the opposite one: the
disappearance of markets.[18]

At a less rarefied level of theory, we still have a puzzle. High
risk will not by itself eliminate an asset from the efficient port-

[17] Sargent (1987b) contains a number of exercises of this variety.
[18] In fact, there is trouble not only on the empirical but also on the purely
theoretical front. In trying to calculate his optimal allocation in Arrow–Debreu
space, the representative agent has posed for himself a problem that is already
not computable (cf. Lewis 1985; Rustem and Velupillai 1990). The trick of
expanding this infinite-dimensional space further to take in the conditional fiscal strategies of the government does not add plausibility to this line of attack.

folio. Risk and aversion to risk will not make markets disappear. Moreover, differences in opinions about future prospects provide a motive for trading. Why then do not heterogenous expectations about inflation prospects produce thicker rather than thinner intertemporal markets?

Two different departures from standard decision theory promise help with these puzzles. One is Bewley's recent work on Knightian uncertainty,[19] the other Heiner's earlier theory of reliable interactions.

Bewley's Knightian agent is uncertain in the sense that he does not know which of a number of alternative probability distributions over outcomes will apply. His inability to evaluate risks over this range of uncertainty means that his preference ordering over risky prospects will be incomplete. Bewley postulates that agents will prefer one prospect to another if and only if it has higher expected value for each and every probability distribution deemed relevant. An additional 'inertia' postulate ensures that agents will choose to stay put as long as the *status quo* is preferred, at going prices, for at least one of the relevant probability distributions.

Consider then the conditions under which such an agent would be willing to sell (or buy) a particular asset. For each of the probability distributions among which he is uncertain, he can compute the supply price (demand price) at which he would be willing to sell (buy) *if* he were confident that this was the true distribution. The price that he actually sets has to dominate the *status quo* for each and every distribution, i.e., it will be the highest of the supply prices (or the lowest of the demand prices). Increasing uncertainty—adding probability distributions that have to be judged possible—will raise his supply prices and/or lower his demand prices. This obviously reduces the chances that he will find willing trading partners.

For our purposes, the main point of Bewley's formulation is

---

[19] Cf. Bewley (1989) and for a related line of inquiry, Dow and Ribeiro da Costa Werlang (1988). Dow and Werlang, drawing on earlier work on non-additive subjective probability by Schmeidler and Gilboa, show that 'uncertainty aversion' will produce a range of prices over which agents will choose not to take a position, one way or another, in an uncertain asset.

his extension of the old proposition that people with the same opinion about prospects will find no mutual gains from trade. The most straightforward illustration concerns simple bets. Consider whether a bet on the occurrence of a particular event would be made between two individuals both of whom are uncertain about the likelihood of the event. Uncertainty, here, means that they do not know which probability among a set of possible alternatives applies to the occurrence of the event. A 'Knightian' individual, considering a bet based on the occurrence of the event in question, will agree to make it (move from his *status quo*) if and only if, at given odds, the bet has a positive expected value to him for *each* of the probabilities in the interval that he deems potentially relevant—and so, of course, will the individual betting against the occurrence. Now, suppose that there is at least one probability that both feel they had better take into account. For that probability, the bet has a positive value to one and a negative value to the other (unless, by chance, zero to both). Hence, when the two subjective probability intervals intersect at all, the two parties will not be able to agree on a bet.

The generalization of this proposition to financial transactions and intertemporal contracts in general would require that one take into account how preferences and endowments, and not only expectations, affect the willingness to trade. But the qualitative features of the simple betting illustration are preserved. In particular, increasing uncertainty shared by the community of potential traders will make agents take into account a wider range of possible distributions, for all of which the *status quo* has to be inferior in order for exchange to take place. Consequently, the volume of trade will decline.

If an economy of Bewley's Knightian agents were to be exposed to steadily increasing uncertainty, we should expect its intertemporal markets to thin out and eventually to disappear when the loss of volume makes it uneconomical to operate them. As a market gets thinner, its 'representative traders' are the first to leave and agents with extreme expectations (or very atypical endowments) come to dominate. In a thin enough market, this might easily lead to abnormal price volatility.[20] But even in markets where volume remains very substantial, such as the foreign exchange market, uncertainty aversion on the part of the majority of traders will change the way the market functions. When no one, or almost no one, is willing to take a position on 'average market opinion', the market price can move far away from it without inducing stabilizing speculation.

The point of departure for Heiner's theory[21] is his observation that as we ascend the hierarchy of the more or less standard decision problems in economics, from the two-dimensional blackboard illustrations to the infinite dimensions of Arrow–Debreu, the competence of the imagined decision-maker is always stepped up so as to be fully adequate at each stage to the added complexity. This leaves out of economic theory any and all questions of what behaviour to expect when the complexity of the environment increases relative to what the agent can routinely handle. Thus standard theory implies, in effect, that added complexity always results in commensurably more sophisticated decision strategies on the part of the typical agent. This implication, Heiner maintains, is false. In his own theory, increasing complexity will beyond some point cause agents to simplify their strategies instead.

A Heiner agent has to decide whether or not to include certain actions in his entire repertoire of actions. For concreteness, we may think of him as regularly engaged in certain current transactions and, for instance, in investing money and perhaps extending credit to certain customers for periods up to t weeks. His problem may be whether to transact also in money of $t + 1$ maturity or else whether to extend credit to some customers that are new arrivals. He is an *imperfect decision-maker* so that the uncertainty he faces is determined not only by the complexity of the environment in which he considers to act but also by the limits to his cognitive abilities.

[20] Possibly, it may also produce 'winner's curse' phenomena in markets where you would not normally expect to find them. To substantiate the incidence of the 'curse' would, however, require an extensive study of high inflation business failures.

[21] Heiner's research programme is mapped out in his (1983) whereas Heiner (1986) is probably the most pedagogical exposition of his model.

Suppose now that the Heiner agent has to make a sequence of decisions over time on whether to transact in $t + 1$ money. In each instance, he must try to judge whether, given the nominal market rate of interest, the inflation over the next $t + 1$ weeks will make him lose or gain in real terms on the transaction. To form that judgement he must try to make the best inferences of which he is capable about government actions and about market reactions to those actions over the period in question. The further into the future is $t + 1$ the longer the string of hypothetical actions and reactions that the agent must calculate with. Some people are pretty good at that sort of thing, others less so. It is a matter of being *reliable* in discriminating between situations that are favourable or not favourable to undertaking the transaction in question.

The central feature of Heiner's model is the *reliability condition* which must be satisfied for the particular action or type of activity to be a viable part of the agent's behavioural repertoire. The condition states that a measure of the agent's reliability in discriminating between favourable and unfavourable conditions must equal or exceed a 'tolerance level' determined by objective factors. What is considered tolerable in a given environment will depend on the relative frequency of favourable and unfavourable conditions—if favourable conditions are extremely rare, for example, the decision-maker must be exceedingly reliable in recognizing them—and also, obviously enough, on the rewards for being right and the penalties for being wrong that the environment imposes. In the case we are considering, violation of the reliability condition would entail cumulative losses over a succession of transactions.

Consequently, the agent must regulate his behaviour in such a way that the reliability condition is fulfilled. He raises his reliability by being more conservative and by imposing rules of thumb on himself. 'I must remember never to break the speed limit on this stretch of the highway—here *you never know when the highway patrol is around*.' These rules may involve ignoring potentially useful information that a more reliable agent would cue on. The general proposition, of course, is that reliability is achieved by 'taking fewer chances', which in this instance means transacting only when very confident, and therefore less frequently, in the market for $t + 1$ money. For certain categories of actions, a particular agent may well be unable to meet the reliability condition no matter how far he lowers the frequency of such moves. He will then exclude these actions altogether from his repertoire.

Under a Random Walk Monetary Standard, the longer is the sequence of government actions and market reactions that must be forecast, the more difficult will it be to make reliable decisions. The likelihood that a particular agent will choose not to engage in intertemporal transactions involving money will increase, therefore, with term to maturity and, for given maturities, with the variance (step-size) of the monetary authorities' Random Walk.

For our purposes here, the implications of Bewley's and of Heiner's theories are quite similar. Both have an inertia property—when the respective agents cannot reliably judge exchange opportunities, they stick close to their endowments. In Heiner's theory, as in Bewley's, it should be the case that a very atypical endowment could cause an agent to trade in a market that is so uncertain that most transactors have withdrawn.

INTERTEMPORAL CO-ORDINATION

What are the consequences of the disappearance of markets? Our usual benchmark, the competitive general equilibrium model, is of limited use in this instance. It sets a standard of perfect but impossible pre-co-ordination. Individual plans spanning a shared high- or (usually) infinite-dimensional goods/dates/contingencies space are co-ordinated by competitive equilibrium prices. Pick any two goods in this space and any two transactors. Their marginal rates of substitution between the two goods will be the same[22] (and, where applicable, equal to the marginal rate of productive transformation) at the respective activity rates chosen. This, of course, will be as

[22] We need not look into every Kuhn–Tucker corner in the present context.

true for goods dated far apart in time and contingent on low probability events as it is for the bread and butter of today. It is as if everyone has communicated with everybody else about everything. No arbitrage possibilities are left unexploited. Gains from trade as well as gains from productive transformation are exhausted in the system.

Actual economies, obviously, are not like that. Even under ideal conditions of monetary stability, they do not pre-reconcile the plans of all agents in all dimensions of Arrow–Debreu space in some once-and-for-all *tâtonnement*. Instead, trade takes place sequentially, with only a subset of future trades precommitted. Some economic systems—the highly developed ones—co-ordinate the activities of a greater proportion of their decision-makers over larger regions of commodity space than do others. Clearly, high inflation economies do particularly badly in co-ordinating plans over time. As we have seen, they end up poorly equipped with intertemporal markets and such time-spanning markets as survive are thin. The temporal depth over which individual intertemporal substitution and transformation opportunities are effectively communicated is shallow and the subsets of agents brought into line are small. The question is: what does it matter that markets are missing?

The most trivial of the reasons why trade is sequential is that it simply is not worth the average consumer's while to precontract for the delivery of all those consumer goods that she knows will be in competitive supply. Instead, she will concentrate on deciding how much generalized purchasing power to carry over into future periods and how best to balance risk and return in so doing. For many goods, over the near future, under conditions of monetary stability, producers and consumers alike may be able to form more or less accurate expectations of what the future price will be. Under certain circumstances, then, rationally expected prices will substitute perfectly well in the intertemporal planning of agents for the market-clearing prices that might have been determined in the 'missing markets'.[23] To

---

[23] Lucas (1981a) suggests along these lines that rational expectations may 'sometimes (though certainly not always)' render missing markets innocuous in equilibrium models. The absence of intertemporal markets will not be

argue along this line that actual economies behave 'as if' they had complete markets would go too far, however. It would end us up with a theory in which it does not matter how large the set of actually operating markets is.[24]

The disappearance of markets raises three alliterative concerns: calculation, co-ordination, and commitment.

Consumers require accurate estimates of future prices in order to evaluate their wealth correctly just as firms do to *calculate* the value of investment opportunities. Consider how the errors and inconsistencies that they are likely to commit increase as we deprive agents of information in stages: (i) Take away the Arrow–Debreu future markets prices. This we are used to in all 'realistic' macro. (ii) But we usually assume that people are guided by a market-determined real interest rate. That requires knowing the nominal interest rate and having identical inflation expectations. Inflation expectations become incoherent even in moderate inflations, so that the relevant 'Law of One Price' ceases to hold in the main intertemporal markets. (iii) In the high inflation economies, nominal market-determined interest rates beyond the next month or two also disappear. (iv) Indexation improves the picture somewhat. It may sustain some longer-run financial contracts. But agents still have the problem of estimating the real rate of interest in terms

---

innocuous if we deal with a system where conditions may sometimes change in an unprecedented manner. When a change occurs such that the economy has to find a new equilibrium growth-path, genuine communication about intertemporal plans between consumers and producers might well be required, calling up the echo of that long-ago observation: 'An act of individual saving . . . depresses the business of preparing today's dinner without stimulating the business of making ready for some future act of consumption' (Keynes 1936).

[24] The rather extensive literature on 'missing' or 'incomplete markets' seems of limited relevance to our present concerns. It investigates whether Arrow–Debreu planners, when deprived of various subsets of markets, will or will not be able to do as well as they do with complete markets. The image is one of perfect decision-makers trying to get around the constraints of the imperfect system in which they happen to find themselves. We meet a perspective closer to our own in Oliver Hart's introduction to the 'incomplete contracts' literature: 'many aspects of incompleteness are intimately connected to the notion of bounded rationality, a satisfactory formalization of which does not exist' (Hart 1987).

of the goods they trade under conditions where relative prices are extremely volatile.

Thus, not much is left of a rational basis for decentralized intertemporal economic calculation.

Co-ordination fails on two grounds. Intertemporal supplies and demands are not reconciled and intertemporal valuations are not made consistent. Individual marginal rates of substitution will not converge either to each other or to the socially attainable marginal rates of productive transformation. In short, resources fail to move into their most valuable uses.

To understand the implications of the disappearance of contractual *commitments*, we need to take a fresh look at the production side of the economy. Standard production theory still has the Ricardian farm as the representative production unit: constant returns when both land and labour can be varied, smoothly diminishing returns when labour is varied with land constant.

Suppose, instead, an economy made up of Smithian factories (cf. Leijonhufvud 1986b). Here, 'the division of labour depends upon the extent of the market'. Increased division of labour is productive so that the average product of inputs increases with the rate of output.[25] A highly articulated division of labour, moreover, tends to be associated with a high degree of complementarity between specialized inputs. The extreme case is that of an assembly line which will come to a halt if one machine breaks down, if one worker leaves his workstation, or if one intermediate goods supplier fails to deliver. Such a structure is vulnerable to a breakdown in co-operation also because the markets for some of these specialized inputs will be thin so that alternative suppliers are not quickly and easily to be found.

The manufacturing sector of a modern economy is not much like a giant Ricardian farm. It is better thought of as a nonlinear input–output system composed of Smithian factories in

---

[25] As a simple concrete illustration, consider a firm consisting of a single assembly line. If 'the extent of its market' were to double, it could build a second parallel line. But some machines (and their operatives) on the first line are not operating continuously. If we suppose that one of them is operated only half of the time, this workstation could serve both lines. The firm is then able to double output with less than double the initial inputs.

which each firm produces under increasing returns to scale and also uses one or more intermediate inputs produced by other increasing returns firms. A structure of this kind requires the support of innumerable *credible precommitments* to reduce the risks faced by individual producers to manageable proportions. When producers decide that high inflation makes intertemporal *contracts* into independent sources of risk so dangerous as to outweigh their prospective benefits, they will also retreat into a less specialized, more nearly linear, less productive structure—and everyone will be poorer as a consequence. The high inflation economy cannot sustain as complex a division of labour as a stable one.

EXCESS RELATIVE PRICE VARIABILITY

There is by now quite a large literature on the inflation-induced variability of relative prices. Most of the papers on the subject presume that this increased variability must be due to the stickiness of some subset of money prices and that the object of the game, therefore, is to explain why they stick.

The presumption here is that, in the natural course of events, all prices would rise at 'the' inflation rate, were it not for 'frictions' of one sort or another that cause some of them to adjust only spasmodically. The underlying notion is that relative prices are determined by 'real factors' and that money plays no role in determining the equilibrium of the 'real sector' except for the inflation tax which is in itself a 'real factor'. The interpretation which attributes excess relative price variability to frictions fits comfortably into the intertemporal general equilibrium models favoured in contemporary monetary and finance theory (and, of course, into a dominant tradition going back at least as far as David Hume). On this interpretation, all that is required is an explanation of why some price-setters will find it optimal to let their prices 'stick', and the phenomenon of excess relative price variability is safely put in its proper place as a footnote to familiar theory.

'Menu costs' has become the accepted term for costs that

must be incurred to change prices. Originally, these costs were conceived of as those necessary to communicate new prices to consumers. The term referred to restaurants which, because of the cost of reprinting menus, would change their prices only at discrete intervals.[26] It is now sometimes used to refer to costs that include the time and trouble required to make the pricing decisions. This broader concept has more substance than the 'technological' interpretation of menu costs—but will not fit easily within standard theory. Taking it seriously forces the modeller to recognize bounded rationality.

The positive statistical relationship between the inflation rate and relative price variability gets weaker at very high rates of inflation. This nonlinearity has been interpreted as confirmation of the hypothesis that the phenomenon is due to 'stickiness'. Since the cost to a seller of letting his or her price stick obviously increases with the inflation rate, high inflation would tend to overcome the postulated 'frictions' in the price system, whatever their nature. As the inflation rate increases from moderate to high levels, the rising frequency of fix-price revisions will add to the recorded relative price variability. Beyond some point, however, the overcoming of frictions should allow more and more prices to conform closely to 'the' rate of inflation until, presumably, relative price variability should actually decrease.

We know of no clear evidence, however, of actually *decreasing* relative price variability at very high rates of inflation. One may surmise that this is likely to happen in the terminal stages of a hyperinflation if, at that point, virtually *all* prices become dollarized. The collapse of demand for the domestic currency would then be associated with a collapse of the cross-sectional dispersion of price changes.[27] This may have happened in the

---

[26] The term was probably invented in the US. In high inflation economies, of course, the standard menu is printed without prices which are, instead, filled in by hand whenever changes are called for. As Tommasi (1992, p. 501) notes: 'In inflationary environments, technologies that minimize such costs are adopted.'

[27] Note, however, that this would be associated also with a collapse of the intertemporal correlation of prices measured in domestic money, since the variability of the exchange rate becomes extreme as the demand for real domestic money balances approaches a minimum.

Bolivian hyperinflation, for example. It is extremely unlikely however, that such a decrease of relative price variability would occur short of the total abandonment of the domestic unit of account.

The assertion that the relationship between price variability and inflation disappears at high inflation rates has been made with particular reference to Argentinian data. However, Carlos Dabús (1993) finds that relative price variability is significantly higher in Argentine hyperinflation episodes than in 'ordinary' high inflation periods. Relative price variability keeps on rising even as the frequency of price adjustment increases. There is clear evidence here that higher inflation overcomes frictions, but no evidence at all that, in so doing, it dampens the noise in relative prices.

The impression that beyond some point additional inflation will not add to relative price variability is almost certainly false. In his comprehensive study of the Mexican inflation experience, Palerm (1990) found that the variance of the price change distribution decreases dramatically as the frequency of observation is reduced.[28] Furthermore, the ratio of the variance based on monthly observations to that based on longer intervals increases with the inflation rate. Thus we may infer that the 'flat portion' of the relationship hides a substantial rise in intra-month price variability. We do not have the broad-based, highly disaggregated, high-frequency data to *prove* it, but the inference is certainly in accord with abundant anecdotal as well as statistical evidence.

Consider, then, the contrast between two possible pictures of what may lie behind the behaviour of the various measures of relative price variability. At one extreme, all the flex-prices closely track 'the' inflation rate while the fix-prices ratchet upwards, zigzagging around the trend determined by flex-prices. In this picture, excess relative price variability is due to the low-frequency adjustment of fix-prices. At the other extreme, 'the' inflation rate is basically set by the non-synchronous but more

---

[28] Tommasi (1994), working with weekly data on a sample of food products in a number of stores, finds the same decrease in variability for longer intervals of observation.

or less concerted revisions of fix-prices while the individual flex-prices wander around this trend. This conception pictures relative price variability as due to the excessive volatility of flex-prices.

Neither extreme will do. The record will not yield up a 'pure' case. If we think of 'stickiness' in general terms as dependence on the past (and not only on the expected future), then there is some of that, as we have seen, due to the use of indexation. Somewhat paradoxically, indexation introduces a mechanical reliance on memory into agreements that have to cover a future time span beyond what can be reliably forecast. While it imparts inertia to the inflation rate rather than to the price level, it does so by ratcheting up the indexed prices at discrete intervals.

But Palerm's findings, based on monthly data for the least aggregative subcomponents available of the Mexican WPI (1940–84) and CPI (1969–84), tend to undermine the price stickiness interpretation.[29] Distinguishing between fix- and flex-prices on the basis of the frequency of price revisions found in the data, he finds that:

(i)   fix-prices 'conform' better to the time paths of the aggregate indices than do flex-prices;

(ii)   in devaluation episodes, fix-prices react more promptly and strongly than flex-prices do;

(iii)   accelerations of inflation are associated with a larger-than-average number of fix-prices being adjusted and with increases in the positive skewness of the distribution of price increases;

(iv)   deviations of current inflation from trend do not generally stem from movements in flex-prices, but from synchronized revisions of fix-prices;

(v)   a high proportion of relative price variability is explained by changes in flex-prices.

Palerm's research demonstrates that the first conception is untenable in anything close to its pure form. The balance of his findings suggest, in fact, that the volatility of flex-prices is *more*

[29] Cf. also Palerm (1991): 'Fresh examination of the data, freed from this preoccupation with producing "Keynesian" results, reveals a far richer variety of price setting procedures.'

important in generating the phenomenon than is the stickiness of fix-prices. The evidence may not be conclusive in this respect, but it does establish the important role played by the movements of flex-prices in generating the observed variability of relative prices.

How can that be? The usual presumption is that maladjustments of prices arise when 'the law of supply and demand' is not allowed to determine price. We need to take a broader view of the problem in order to understand what excess relative price variability reveals about how inflation affects the economy's functioning.

The equilibrium of a market can be characterized either in terms of quantities demanded and supplied being equal at the going price or in terms of demand-price and supply-price being equal at the going transactions volume. Correspondingly, we have two directions of departure that may be taken in considering less well co-ordinated states of that market. The first is the 'Keynesian' one which focuses on the failure of desired demands and supplies to mesh at 'the' given market price. The alternative stresses the multiplicity of individual demand- and supply-prices at which the actual volume is transacted.

The *failure of market clearing* approach has recommended itself to generations of economists as a natural way to describe situations of high and persistent unemployment. For a preliminary characterization of what goes wrong with the co-ordination of activities in high inflations it is more helpful to focus on *violations of the law of one price.*[30] More generally, in the multi-market setting, we are looking for violations of the *no arbitrage* condition. The inefficiencies that arise in this way are less obvious than the large-scale unemployment in a depression. Since by hypothesis prices are inconsistent, moreover, it is not clear how one would attach an aggregative value to the social loss that they entail. What is clear, however, is that this loss may be large although aggregate employment remains high.

---

[30] Beyond a preliminary stage of analysis, obviously, there will be no such clear-cut distinction between types of market disco-ordination. A market that does not clear, for instance, is bound soon to show price dispersion (cf. Arrow 1959).

Non-market-clearing macro-models have, of course, been the targets of sharp attacks in recent years: rigid prices (or rigidities in other terms of contracts) mean that gains from trade are not exhausted; rational agents should be able to do better, and so forth. Much the same strictures will apply to a theory in which price differentials are not perfectly arbitraged. The states described are not rational from a social point of view and it is unclear how they emerge and how they can persist in a system of rational agents.

Note one aspect of the problem: highly inflationary economies seem less well co-ordinated than they would be if they enjoyed monetary stability. That an economy may vary over time in the degree to which activities within it are well co-ordinated is a notion that fits at best uneasily in the corpus of economic theory (Leijonhufvud 1981b). We have had models of economies in which nothing ever goes right and of economies in which nothing ever goes wrong—and great factional struggles where believers in the one faith try to evict those of the other from Parnassus—but as yet not much in the way of modelled examples of systems that work well under some conditions and not under others. Possibly, it might be useful to develop a class of models with ill-co-ordinated inflationary equilibria to go along with the standard models of perfectly co-ordinated equilibria. But the uneasy coexistence of 'Keynesian' theory (with its 'unemployment equilibria') and general equilibrium theory of years past is not the sort of situation one would wish to recreate. Instead, we should try to understand the nature of the *phase-transition* that an economy undergoes as it passes from relatively well-co-ordinated interaction under monetary stability into the ill-co-ordinated processes of high inflation.

One dimension of this phase-transition is familiar to us already: As inflation rises, the structure of intertemporal markets shrinks, starting in the long end. In moderate inflations, it is only the markets for very long bonds and fixed-rate mortgages that disappears. In high inflations, the longest-term surviving instruments may be index contracts with a term of a few months and money loans of a few weeks. The paralyzing limit of this process is reached when sellers put up the sign 'Closed for the Lack of Prices'. The excess variability of relative prices should be put in the same context as the disappearance of markets. Both result from the cognitive difficulties that agents confront in an unstable monetary environment.

As inflation rises, precedents become as useless as forecasts become unreliable. The usable memory in the system shortens as does the useful foresight. Economists are too fond of purely teleological models where expectations determine prices and the role of memory in forming expectations is suppressed. Actual economies rely heavily on memory to co-ordinate activities. The knowledge needed to find equilibrium prices is not created *de novo* each trading day. The trouble with hyperinflations is that forecasting has become terribly difficult; that is so because memory is no guide. This must be our starting point.

Excess relative price variability results from increased variability in the rate at which individual prices rise, and from lack of synchronization between those prices. Three aspects of the phenomenon need to be discussed. First, the weakening of the 'market forces' normally at work to keep relative prices in line; second, the impulses perturbing the system of relative prices; and, third, the mechanisms propagating the process.

'Market forces', of course, is just a somewhat obscurantist term for the readiness of traders 'to buy low and sell high'. Many transactions that in more normal circumstances are regarded as routine arbitrage operations become risky speculations in high inflations. The supply of arbitrage services shrinks, therefore, and it requires higher than normal expected price differentials to induce traders to take a position, however temporary. We have encountered this already: it is the unwillingness of traders to enter intertemporal markets that causes these markets to thin out and disappear. The disappearance of such markets is in itself the extreme case of violation of the law of one price, since the very mechanism for accomplishing the equalization of individual marginal rates of substitution disappears from the system.

The weakening of intertemporal substitution, of which the disappearance of the corresponding markets is the extreme symptom, means that intertemporal 'smoothing' of activity rates and of prices will not be undertaken to the extent normal under monetary stability. The markets for individual goods become increasingly 'segmented' in time: discrepancies between output and consumption rates are not averaged across time in a normal manner through inventory management. Consequently, the prices for these goods show increased volatility around their respective average rates of inflation.

In the markets for ordinary consumer goods, the law of one price is normally policed by comparison shoppers. But at high rates of inflation, the price information gained through search depreciates very rapidly. At the margin of search activity, this decrease in the average duration of the benefit stream gained from search has to be balanced by an increase in the expected value of the immediate gain. Whether people will spend more or less time and effort in search is indeterminate. But the time and effort that they do spend will do less to compress price dispersion in the market (cf. especially Tommasi 1992*a*, 1994). The elasticities of substitution that are effective in the market place decrease and sellers come to face more inelastic short-run demand schedules. At very high rates of inflation, it is not just the relative prices of different goods that vary with increased frequency, but the law of one price will be found violated for the same good, at almost the same time, in very nearly the same location.[31]

Thus high inflations erode market mechanisms, causing what should be thick markets to thin out and to fragment. They weaken the substitution relationships over time, across space, and between agents that normally will tightly constrain the amplitude of price variations. They do so by depriving people of a reliable basis for comparisons and calculations.[32]

Monetary and fiscal impulses emanating from government

[31] Decompositions of the total variance of relative prices into variance across goods and variance across sellers of the same good show the latter component to account for 80–90% of the variability both in the Tommasi and the Lach and Tsiddon (1992) samples.

[32] The signal-extraction problem central to the Phelps–Lucas 'islands' model seems a far more promising starting point in familiar theory than do the various menu cost models for coming to an understanding of high inflation pricing practices, therefore.

and the public sector will feed into the excess price variability process. When the demand for public debt more or less disappears in high inflation, the government becomes unable to smooth its cash-flow deficit. The result is a variable, high-frequency nominal impulse. In addition, when the government is responding in emergency fashion to different pressure groups in succession, the brunt of this nominal impulse shifts from sector to sector. The injections of new money, therefore, are not neutral but tend to set up movements in relative prices.

Two hypotheses to account for excess relative price variability (without resort to 'frictions') suggest themselves. The first is basically stochastic. In the absence of stabilizing speculation, markets reveal not only permanent but also transitory changes in relative scarcities. Relative price movements, that would normally have been smoothed out, come to reflect not only the random disturbances that an economy is always exposed to but also the microlevel randomness in the timing of many routine activities. The second hypothesis is chaotic: that what we are observing is, in effect, 'turbulence' in the markets.

Chaos has become such a fad in recent years that one hesitates to advance the notion. In economics, the literature on the subject consists mostly of demonstrations that the logical possibility of chaos inheres in dynamic versions of many familiar models. The excess variability of relative prices, in contrast, may be a genuine empirical phenomenon exhibiting complex dynamics. The extreme shortening of time horizons induced by high inflation might well bring about chaotic behaviour.[33]

In any case, price setting will be based on some mix of (selective) memory and (imperfect) foresight. The cost component of price is backward-looking, the mark-up forward-looking. The mark-up will of course be anything but constant under high

---

[33] Simple adaptive market models in which both price and output are feedback-governed easily go chaotic, for instance. Overlapping generations models generate chaotic motions where otherwise similar models of infinitely lived consumers show perfectly 'smooth' behaviour. Cf., e.g., Benhabib and Day (1982). If the infinitely lived consumers have very high subjective rates of time discount (or some other form of imprudent myopia), they too can go chaotic, of course. Liquidity constraints preventing the consumer from smoothing his consumption over time might induce chaos as well. Cf. Bewley (1986).

inflation conditions. Sellers will routinely seek to compensate themselves for cost increases but they are also forced to speculate on what their costs of restocking inventory or repurchase inputs will turn out to be. In more tranquil conditions, retailers' prices may be co-ordinated on their respective wholesalers', who in turn co-ordinate on the manufacturers' price, with everyone in the chain using conventional mark-ups. The higher the inflation, the less guidance price-setters find in historical costs. In choosing a mark-up, it is everyone for himself. High dispersion of prices is to be expected. Relative price variations are bounded, however. The bounds are presumably wider, the higher the inflation rate, but they are still present.[34] The underlying fundamentals of production possibilities and consumer tastes have some effect even when people are unwilling to take positions on the basis of them. Price-setters who have ended up close to the bounds, by choosing extreme mark-ups at a particular time, will not stay there.[35] In markets fragmented by low cross-elasticities of demand, individual sellers may come to hogcycle on their own even as output aggregates show little variation.

TURBULENCE ON THE EXCHANGES

In the absence of high-frequency data on the prices of individual goods at individual points of sale, an irreducible element of speculation will remain in the theoretical discussion of relative price variability. The foreign exchange market does provide high frequency data, however, and we may buttress the inferences made previously by drawing on what we know about the relationship between the exchange rate and prices in a 'triple

---

[34] When the market for one of two goods being compared disappears, this should of course not be interpreted as the relative price going to infinity (or zero). It is a matter of the range of prices for which there would be a demand for the good not overlapping with the range for which a supply would be forthcoming, so no price is being quoted.

[35] Tommasi (1992*b*) again provides interesting evidence: close to 20% of the price changes in one of his samples were *decreases*. This in a period when the inflation rate averaged 4% per week.

standard' economy. At the same time, it affords us a closer view of what a dynamic phase-transition into a higher inflation regime looks like.

Figure 7.2 shows the seismographic record of two hyperinflation 'quakes' in the Argentine exchange market in 1989 and 1990. The hyperinflation episodes are sharply demarcated in the day-to-day changes in the domestic currency price of the dollar. What strikes the eye is more the extreme volatility than the average rate of appreciation of the dollar. In the April to July 1989 episode, the average rate of increase of the rate was 4.8 per cent per day, but with a standard deviation of 9 percentage points. Between December 1989 and March 1990 the exchange rate increased on average 3 per cent per day with a standard deviation of 10 points![36]

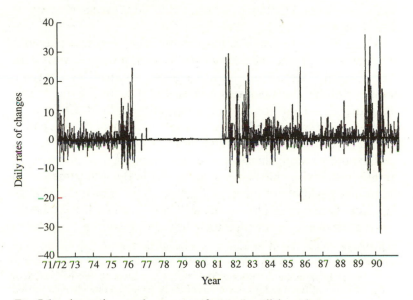

Fig. 7.1. Argentina: exchange rate, free or parallel market

[36] As seen most clearly in fig. 7.1, the volatility of the exchange rate under 'more ordinary' high inflation conditions was considerably lower. Over the 18-month period from January 1987 to July 1988, for example, (fig. 7.2) the standard deviation for daily changes in the exchange rate was 1.67 and in the 4 months plus between the two hyperinflation episodes in Figure 7.2 it was 3.05.

A second contrast between high and hyperinflation is also striking. In the Argentinian data, the standard deviation of the daily rate of growth of base money is somewhat higher than that of the daily rate of appreciation of the dollar under most high inflation conditions. In the hyperinflation episodes, however, not only is the relationship reversed, but the standard deviation for daily increases in the exchange rate is 1.5 to 2.5 times that of base money growth.[37]

How do we understand this behaviour and what consequences does it have? Taking the central government's deficit as our point of departure, it is clear that neither the central bank nor the banking system can or will do much to smooth the nominal impulse of the daily cash-flow deficit. The central bank does not have a government bond market that functions well enough for it to smooth the rate of monetary injections by open market operations. The banks will not hold any excess reverses at all, if they can help it.

The banking system's behaviour in these respects may not change much in the transition into hyperinflation, however. In the non-bank sector, on the other hand, balances of domestic money will be managed as buffer stocks only to the most minimal degree feasible, once hyperinflation takes hold. Changes in money holdings, therefore, will spill over into the exchange market more quickly and fully. Next to no trade credit will be outstanding among firms, moreover. Monetary impulses that might otherwise have been cushioned by adjustments in accounts payable are more likely now to go into the exchange market. Quite generally, firms will go through the exchange market in trying to manage their liquidity positions.

All the above-mentioned measures correspond to 'market determined' (not officially pegged) exchange rates.

[37] In the hyperinflation episode from mid-April through the first week of July, the ratio of the standard deviation of daily exchange rate changes to that of base money changes was 9.39/6.10; in the second episode from mid December to mid March 1990, it was 9.70/4.12. Excluding two weeks of transition in mid July, the period between the two episodes shows the more 'normal' relationship of 3.05/4.45. In the 6 months following the second hyperinflation episode, however, the variability of the exchange rate remained a bit higher than that of base money growth—by our measure 1.93/1.76. None the less, the 'stylized fact' remains clear.

In the exchange market itself, stabilizing speculation has all but evaporated. Although broad classes of agents hold considerable balances abroad, and larger real balances in dollars than in domestic currency at home, minor impulses will move the rate on any given day. Few are willing to take a position on average market opinion. The market sometimes becomes so 'thin'[38] that it may be possible to trace certain price movements to the decisions of particular firms moving funds into domestic currency, for instance, to pay wages.

The volatility shown in Figure 7.2 translates directly into relative price volatility. As the economy goes across the brink into hyperinflation, more prices are quoted in dollars although, as we have seen, dollarization of prices remains incomplete. In most markets payment is still taken in the national money. Conversion of dollarized prices into domestic money is made at the exchange rate as of the moment of purchase. The result is that these dollarized prices, measured in domestic money, respond not only to the excess market demand for the respective products, and to changes in inflation expectations, but also to the excess demand in this very volatile exchange market. On a day-to-day basis, in fact, the state of the exchanges becomes more important than the state of the market for the good itself in determining its price. The dollarized prices will share the high-frequency movements of the exchange market which, as the data show, are of very large amplitude. These exchange rate movements are not reflected directly in non-dollarized prices. The end result is a corresponding short-run volatility of the relative prices between the two sets of goods.

It is an extreme, but not for that reason less instructive, illustration of the disorganizing force of 'money out of order'. Economists are inculcated with a great faith in the power of simple, self-interested individual reactions at a million margins to bring order and coherence to all the complexities of social interactions. The efficacy of the Invisible Hand is often wondrous to behold. But it too has its limits.

---

[38] We are using 'thin' here, not in the sense of few market participants or low volume, but in the sense of price sensitivity to temporary 'blips' in excess demand.

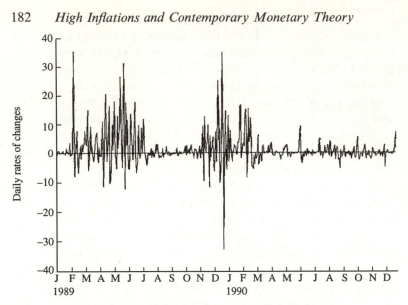

Fig. 7.2.   Argentina: exchange rate, free or parallel market

MONEY AND THE SOCIAL CONSTRUCTION OF REALITY

This chapter has offered not a theory or a model but a theoretical collage, composed of attempts to push our understanding of high inflation phenomena a bit beyond the analytical description of these phenomena in the earlier chapters. A coherent, encompassing, formal synthesis of these pieces of theorizing is beyond what we can do, certainly at this stage.

A moment's reflection should convince the reader, however, that standard theory is a collage as well. The elements are more familiar, some of them comfortingly formalized, but an integrated whole they do not make. No single formal model in the literature will give us all the traditional four functions of money, for example. But the two collages are plainly different, even though we have made much use of standard theory throughout. It remains to try to characterize and to motivate this difference.

Consider the elements of standard theory that we have drawn

upon. Retracing the 'chain of causation' for the last time, we encounter in succession:

Political economy models. These game theoretic models[39] of how deficits and their monetization are determined implicitly recognize that the economic costs and socio-political consequences of inflation are substantial.

Dynamic inflation-tax models. Within these structures the costs of inflation are more or less trivial. Focusing on price level dynamics, the models attempt no explanation either of the deficits or the pricing practices that they assume, leaving one set of questions to political economy and the other 'up for grabs'.

Price setting models. Here the literature presents us with a proliferation of models, each one with its own special assumptions, each one focusing on its own more or less narrow problem, be it (i) inflation inertia, (ii) search behaviour, (iii) market segmentation, (iv) expectations formation, or (v) relative price variability.

Undergirding the models in the chain, we have the *models of money*. These obviously have to be key to our understanding of inflation but at the present stage they leave crucial questions unanswered: Why is money used? Why are the four functions combined? What would cause the use of money to be abandoned? What is the true functional form for money demand?

Economists have not fitted and cannot fit all of this together. It is not clear that they should even try. At this point, collage is the appropriate *genre*. The best that can be done is to draw insight from the various classes of models for different aspects of the overall problem. That overall problem is one of extreme and awesome complexity.

The argument is certainly not that economists ought to be able to model the system's behaviour in all its complexity. It is, rather, that they ought not to assume that agents typically are and do. Are agents forming rational expectations of this collage? The pieces do not all fit together. Yet, each of the models is derived 'as if' we could be sure of the appropriateness of its axioms and assumptions. The totality of this collage, it seems to us, virtually implies that the typical economic agent can*not*

---

[39] Cf. especially Persson and Tabellini (1990).

be like the agent assumed in each of its elements. She has to be more like the agent in *our* collage.

Standard theory suffers from a distorted perspective on the relationship between the economic system and the agents that are its constituent parts. It portrays a system that is simple in structure (and in its dynamics) relative to the cognitive capabilities of the agents. In this kind of theory, there are no problems too complex or difficult for the 'rational' decision-maker to handle. These perfect decision-makers have to cope with the imperfections of the system. It is as if 'design flaws' in the system prevent the full exploitation of the representative agent's capabilities. Some 'friction' has to be found in the system to explain why people use money. Some externality has to be responsible if co-ordination failures occur.

This is all backwards. Complex systems are built from simple parts. The obstinate refusal to look at the economy in that way is productive of nothing but riddles of the type: How do you get money into a general equilibrium model? The modern economy is complicated, as Hayek would put it, 'beyond human comprehension', too complicated by far for individual decision-makers to confront directly in their planning. The typical agent could not begin to cope with all the opportunities and options that the economy offers, let alone with the infinite-dimensional goods-dates-contingency space of modern general equilibrium theory.

It is odd that economists routinely make obeisance to the point when discussing the division of labour, that is, specialization in production. In that context, the representative agent is not supposed to know and master everything.[40] In the theory of exchange, in contrast, cognitive limitations have traditionally been more or less ignored. And monetary (and finance) theory from Patinkin onwards has been pursued altogether within the framework of exchange theory, with production and (therefore) specialization of knowledge eliminated as inessential complications.

Innumerable people all over the world contribute value added

---

[40] One must note, though, that the Ricardian farm has more or less driven the Smithian factory out of production theory. And the Ricardian farmer is competent at all his chores.

to the consumption basket of the average citizen of one of today's industrialized countries. These globe-spanning structures of co-operation have developed to this degree of complexity not because the world economy is populated by agents typically endowed with commensurate cognitive skills but, on the contrary, because ways to *simplify* individual decisions and tasks and to *simplify* the co-ordination of individual activities have gradually emerged. The complex dynamic structures of a modern economy are not some sort of belated system response bringing the economy closer to the full exploitation of the cleverness that its inhabitants have possessed all along. Rather, the economy has evolved to a complexity beyond human understanding because, gradually and fitfully, people with limited cognitive capabilities have devised ways of getting along that do not require them to confront the full complexity of the system of which they are part.

These simplifying strategies are a combination of collective institutional arrangements and individual cognitive short-cuts adapted to one another. Both money and organized markets belong in this category of institutional arrangements. Perhaps the technicalities of economic theory tend sometimes to obscure the point. It may be helpful to step back a bit and take a broader view for a moment.

Stable patterns of social interaction presuppose the ability of individuals to predict other people's reaction to their own actions—and, therefore, the outcome of action conditional on the behaviour of others. This requires a shared perception of reality and this shared perception has to be constructed as bridges between the subjective selves of the individuals composing the social group. This interpersonal reality is a social construction.[41]

---

[41] Our title for this section is taken from Berger and Luckmann, *The Social Construction of Reality*, a well-known work in phenomenological sociology. This branch of sociology may not be much known among economists today but it has some economic ancestry. Berger and Luckmann build on the work of Alfred Schütz, a member of the Vienna *Geistkreis* in the 1920s of which Hayek, Haberler, Morgenstern, and Machlup were prominent members (cf. Craver 1986). Schütz had been trained in the subjectivist tradition of the Menger school.

The most intuitive illustration of the social construction of reality is language. One does not have to go whole hog deconstructionist to recognize that words do not have the *same meaning* to two different individuals, if by that we mean that they call forth *exactly* the same set of associations for both of them. Reliable communication requires a sufficient intersection between the two subjective sets, plus some knowledge of what is likely to be idiosyncratic and what interpersonally shared. There may be realms of experience about which reliable communication is not possible and others where it is possible only between people of very similar backgrounds.

Other simple examples have to do with the interpretation of gestures, postures, actions. For reliable interaction in society it is obviously vital that friendly intentions not be mistaken for hostile ones (and vice versa).

Now, a language is a set of social restrictions on the meanings that audible noises may have. These restrictions are immensely helpful in making predictable interaction possible. Language is, in this sense, a social institution. Arthur Okun (1981, p. 287) saw *money* in the same light: 'The nation's investment in the dollar as a meaningful yardstick is a "reality" not a "money illusion". It is analogous to our investment in the English language.' In high inflation economies, the analogy suggests itself not only as a useful metaphor, but as a distillation of vivid experience: 'the first thing you have to rebuild is the currency. It is to the economy what language is to society: A country without a currency is a tower of Babel in which you can't communicate.'[42]

It is an old insight. In British Classical economics 'computational costs arising from the absence of a common unit of account, not to mention the inconveniences of barter, were regarded as an essentially impossible barrier to trade'.[43] People do not grope towards the equalization of marginal rates of substitution and of transformation in very large commodity spaces

---

[42] Domingo Cavallo, the Economics Minister responsible for the 1991 stabilization programme in Argentina, in interview with T. Kamm, *Wall Street Journal*, September 11, 1992.

[43] Laidler (1991), p. 9.

by transmitting $n(n-1)/2$ 'barter price' signals to each other. Marshall's 'common measuring rod of money' does not only help individual consumers to fashion a rational shopping strategy and entrepreneurs to calculate profit, it also provides the essential code by which they communicate.

By taking non-monetary general equilibrium as the starting point for monetary economics, modern theory makes regaining that old common-sense insight a task of forbidding technical difficulty. But the starting point is ill-chosen and much of the ingenuity expended on the question, 'Why money in general equilibrium?', is ill-spent. Historically, monetary exchange systems did not develop out of non-monetary exchange systems. Money has not emerged as a belated innovation in systems that already possessed the property rights and commercial law of full-blown exchange systems. Non-monetary systems rely on reciprocity and redistribution, not exchange, to co-ordinate the division of labour. Barter is always a marginal phenomenon, hardly more important in non-monetary economies than it is in systems relying primarily on monetary exchange.

We should not allow ourselves to be misled by the central role given to non-monetary general equilibrium constructions in modern theory. It is money that makes possible exchange systems that co-ordinate activities over large subsets of the commodity space among large subsets of agents. Obviously, no actual economy comes at all close to co-ordinating the plans of all the people over all goods and contingencies for all time. But if we suppose a system with n tradables, it is easy to imagine that, in the absence of money, the types of exchanges of good-for-good that might be observed would exceed $n-1$ and perhaps come to approach $n(n-1)/2$. But the number of 'markets' in which competition would enforce the Law of One Price would surely be far smaller. Without money, the patterns of co-operation that people would be able to achieve would be far more primitive, far less complex and articulated than what we in fact observe.

High inflations destroy social institutions and arrangements that would not have existed in the first place if the rationality of economic agents were unbounded. By insisting on the assumption that individual decision-makers are not subject to any relevant cognitive limitations, we fail to find a solid foundation for monetary theory and fail to understand the social and economic consequences of inflation and, therefore, the benefits of monetary stability.

Appendix

This appendix develops some of the arguments of Chapters 2 and 4 more formally. Its main purpose is to illustrate those discussions with several 'prototype' models embodying different assumptions about the determination of the price level. Section A1 analyses the government's budget constraint, emphasizing the relationship between fiscal and monetary policies. Sections A2 through A5 deal with models of price level dynamics for given fiscal policies. A 'political economy' model of the fiscal deficit and the steady-state inflation rate is outlined in section A6.

A1   THE FISCAL DEFICIT AND THE MONEY SUPPLY: A STYLIZED DESCRIPTION

As long as there is some room for bond-financing, the government's budget constraint can be expressed in discrete time as:

$$(A1) \quad D_t + R_{t-1}B_{t-1} + R_{t-1}B^c_{t-1} = B_t - B_{t-1} + B^c_t - B^c_{t-1}$$

where D_t is the 'primary' deficit (i.e., net of interest payments) in nominal terms in period t, R_{t-1} is the nominal interest rate on loans made at $t-1$ and due at t, B_t the nominal value of government bonds held by the public at the end of period t and B^c_t the stock of bonds in the central bank. Expression (1) assumes that the central bank charges market interest on its loans to the government. The assumption is not crucial in what follows. If the assets of the central bank consist only of government bonds and its liabilities only of non-interest-bearing base money, its balance sheet simplifies to:

$$(A2) \quad B^c_t = M_t + NW_t$$

where M_t is the stock of base money at the end of period t and NW_t the central bank's net worth. The profits of the central bank can be approximated by:

(A3) $$NW_t - NW_{t-1} = R_{t-1}B_{t-1}^c$$

Expressions (1) through (3) can be used to determine the budget constraint of the 'consolidated' public sector, including the government itself and the central bank:

(A4) $$D_t + R_{t-1}B_{t-1} = B_t - B_{t-1} + M_t - M_{t-1}$$

The LHS of the equation shows the nominal financing requirements of the public sector as the sum of the primary deficit and the nominal interest accrued on the debt outstanding. This has to be matched (RHS) by an increase in public sector liabilities, i.e., bonds held by the private sector and base money.

Equation (4) is equivalent to:

(A5) $$d_t + r_{t-1}b_{t-1} = m_t - m_{t-1} + m_{t-1}\frac{\pi_t}{1 + \pi_t} + b_t - b_{t-1}$$

Lower-case letters denote variables measured in real terms: d_t is the real primary deficit, b_t is the real stock of public sector bonds held by private agents, and m_t is the real value of the stock of base money; r_{t-1} denotes the *ex post* real interest rate on one-period loans due at t. The variable π_t indicates the inflation rate in period t.

The LHS of expression (5) is often referred to as the 'operational' deficit. It is financed in three ways, namely: (i) 'pure seigniorage' (i.e., the increase in real base money balances), (ii) the 'inflation tax', which is equal to the real depreciation of the public's cash holdings at the beginning of the period, and (iii) the increase in the real value of interest-bearing public debt.

The analogue of expression (5) in continuous time has the form:

(A5') $$d_t + r_t b_t = \dot{m}_t + m_t \pi_t + \dot{b}_t,$$

where r_t indicates the instantaneous real interest rate and $\dot{m}_t$, $\dot{b}_t$ are the time derivatives of real money balances and the public sector debt in real terms, respectively.

Another useful way of writing the budget constraint (5') is:

(A5'') $$d_t + r_t b_t = \mu_t m_t + \dot{b}_t$$

where μ_t denotes the rate of growth of nominal base money at time t.

A2 SIMPLE MODELS OF THE INFLATION TAX

When there is no market for public debt and the central bank follows a policy of passive accommodation of the government's borrowing requirements, $b_t = 0$ for all t and the rate of money growth depends directly on the real primary deficit. In continuous time, (A5') and (A5'') then become:

(A6) $$d_t = \dot{m}_t + m_t \pi_t = \mu_t m_t$$

where d_t is considered an exogenous variable with respect to μ_t.

If the demand for base money is treated as a standard money demand function in continuous time:

(A7) $$m_t^d = y_t f(\bar{r}_t + \pi_t^e)$$

where y_t denotes real income, $\bar{r}_t$ the *ex ante* real interest rate at time t and π_t^e the anticipated rate of inflation. Under the assumption that real income and the *ex ante* real interest rate are given and constant,[1]

(A7') $$m_t^d = m(\pi_t^e)$$

Equation (A7') does not dictate any definite restrictions on the form of the money demand function beyond the requirement that $m'(\pi_t^e) < 0$. Consequently, we cannot specify a shape that the 'inflation-tax curve', $m(x)x$, necessarily must have. We will assume in what follows that the curve is single-peaked and that it tends to zero as the argument x grows very large. An example of a money demand function which implies such as inflation tax curve is Cagan's function: $m(\pi^e) = A \exp(-\epsilon \pi^e)$.

---

[1] In discrete time, equation (A7') would become $m_t^d = m(\pi_{t+1}^e)$ where π_{t+1}^e is the expectation formed in period t of the inflation rate in period $t + 1$.

The portfolio balance condition implies:

(A8) $m_t = m_t^d$

Equations (A6), (A7′), and (A8) determine a system of differential equations in the supply and demand of real balances and actual and expected inflation, under the assumption of a fixed *ex ante* real interest rate and market-clearing prices. The system is closed by specifying how price expectations behave. We deal in turn with the cases of perfect foresight and of adaptive forecasts.

A2.1   Perfect foresight

In this case, $\pi_t^e = \pi_t$, and the system reduces to:

(A9) $d_t = \dot{m}(\pi_t) + m(\pi_t)\pi_t = m'(\pi_t)\dot{\pi}_t + m(\pi_t)\pi_t$

For a constant real deficit, given that $m'(\pi) < 0$, the dynamics of the inflation rate are governed by the sign of $d - m(\pi)\pi$.

(A9′) $d - m(\pi_t)\pi_t = m'(\pi_t)\dot{\pi}_t$

Figure A1 shows that as long as $d < \tilde{d}$—the deficit is lower than the maximum attainable inflation tax revenue—the system has two steady states.[2] Moreover, the low inflation steady state is 'dynamically unstable', while the high inflation rest point is stable, since there are many possible paths, consistent with the differential equation, which converge to that point. The model is an example of multiple equilibria in that it specifies a family of solutions, not just a single one.

A2.2   Adaptive expectations

Here, expectations vary according to:

(A10) $\dot{\pi}_t^e = \theta(\pi_t - \pi_t^e)$.

where $\theta > 0$ is the coefficient of adaptation.

---

[2] If $d > \tilde{d}$ the model leads to the conclusion that inflation is ever decreasing: if $d > m(\pi)\pi$, it must be that $\dot{m} > 0$. This paradoxical result can be eliminated, for example, by assuming that real balances adjust gradually and sufficiently slowly to their 'long-run' value given by equation (A7). The stability properties of the two steady states are then also reversed (cf. Kiguel 1989).

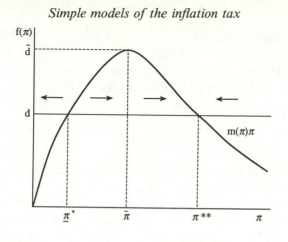

The system is now formed by equation (A10) together with:

(A11) $$d = m'(\pi_t^e)\dot{\pi}_t^e + m(\pi_t^e)\pi_t$$

It is straightforward to reduce the system to a differential equation in π^e:

(A12) $$d - m(\pi_t^e)\pi_t^e = \left(\frac{m'(\pi_t^e)}{m(\pi_t^e)} + \frac{1}{\theta}\right)m(\pi_t^e)\dot{\pi}_t^e$$

It is clear that $\dot{\pi}^e = 0$ iff $d = m(\pi^e)\pi^e$, and then, by (A10), $\pi = \pi^e$. Therefore the steady states of the system coincide with those obtained under perfect foresight. From expression (A12), it can be seen that, as long as the semi-elasticity of money demand ($|m'(\pi^e) / m(\pi^e)| \equiv \epsilon$) is larger than the inverse of the coefficient of adjustment in expectations (or, equivalently, $\epsilon > 1$) the high inflation steady state is again dynamically stable, while the low inflation steady state is unstable. These results are reversed when $\epsilon < 1$, that is, the inflation will converge on the 'good' steady state if the system adjusts 'slowly' either because the elasticity of expectations with regard to the discrepancy between anticipated and actual inflation is small or because the interest-elasticity of money demand is small. Given that θ and ϵ may vary with π, or π^e, it is possible to have models where both steady states are locally stable: $\theta\epsilon < 1$ for $\pi^e \approx \pi^*$, and $\theta\epsilon > 1$ for $\pi^e \approx \pi^{**}$. There would then exist a critical point $\tilde{\pi}^e$ located between the steady states which separates the regions of attraction of the stationary points (cf. Bruno 1985).

A3   MONETARY POLICIES

As long as monetary policy has some independence from government financing requirements, the rate of money growth, μ_t, can be a policy instrument. If the stock of public debt may vary, the system can be described by the public sector budget constraint (A5″)—or in discrete time by (A5)—together with an equation expressing the identity between the rate of growth of real balances and the difference between the rate of increase in the stock of money and the inflation rate (cf. Drazen 1985, on which the following exposition is based; also Blanchard and Fisher 1989, chapter 10).

$$(A13) \qquad d + r_t b_t = \mu_t m_t + \dot{b}_t$$

$$(A14) \qquad \dot{m}_t = (\mu_t - \pi_t)m_t$$

Under perfect foresight, $m_t = m(\pi_t)$, so that there is a one-to-one correspondence between the time path of the real money stock and that of inflation. If expected and actual inflation coincide and the *ex ante* interest rate is constant (or, equivalently, if the public debt is perfectly indexed and bears a fixed real rate), $\bar{r}_t = r$. Then equations (A13) and (A14) result in a system of differential equations in m and b.

In order for the system to be in a steady state, the rate of money growth must be equal to the inflation rate, and such that the inflation tax matches the operational deficit. The steady-state locus in the m–b space is described by the equation:

$$(A15) \qquad d + rb = \pi(m)m$$

Figure A2 shows this locus, *SS*, when the inflation tax curve is single-peaked. The figure indicates that, for a given primary deficit there is no steady state if the public debt exceeds $\bar{b}$. When

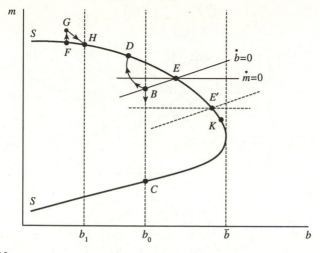

Fig. A2

$b = \bar{b}$, the operational deficit is equal to the maximum revenue obtainable from the inflation tax. Consequently, a higher level of debt implies a deficit which cannot be financed on a steady-state basis. Clearly, the value of $\bar{b}$ falls with increases in the primary deficit. If $b < \bar{b}$, the system has two steady states: one with high real balances (low inflation) and another with low real balances (high inflation).

Each point on *SS* corresponds to a different value of the rate of money growth: μ increases as one moves 'down' along the curve. For a given value of μ, the dynamics of m and b are governed by equations (A13) and (A14), and are described qualitatively in Figure A3 (cf. again Drazen 1985), where μ is supposed to be consistent with the existence of a steady state A, on *SS*.

If monetary policies are constrained to finance the operational deficit—and thus keep constant the real value of the debt—the inflation rate evolves as described in section A2.1: the 'bad' steady state is stable. A path which starts at a point like B in Figure A2, and must follow the constant-debt curve b_0, converges to the low-real-balance, high inflation steady state c. Consider, however, the case where monetary policy makes μ

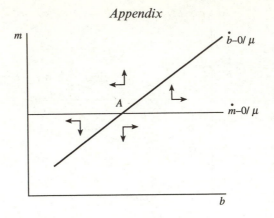

Fig. A3

higher than the value which would make $b = b_0$. The central
bank not only finances the fiscal deficit but engages in expansionary open-market operations. Then, the movement from B
follows the dynamics originating at a point like E', and the
point (m, b) moves to the north-west: the rate of inflation and
the real stock of debt both fall. Thus expansionary monetary
policies can make the system follow a path from B that converges to a point like D, which is located on the 'good' branch
of the inflation tax curve and implies an inflation rate lower
than that of the steady state with $b = b_0$. The argument can be
extended to the case where the expectations that enter as an
argument of money demand are adaptive with coefficient θ
such that $\theta\epsilon > 1$. These not-too-intuitive results were described
qualitatively in footnote 13 of Chapter 2.

   The analytical framework can also be used to derive conclusions of the 'unpleasant monetarist arithmetic' (cf. Sargent and
Wallace 1981). Suppose that the system is located initially at a
steady state such as F (see Figure A2). The central bank now
unexpectedly[3] reduces the rate of growth of the money supply,
and keeps μ constant at the new level until b reaches a certain
value b_1; afterwards, it finances the operational deficit, so that
b remains fixed at b_1. Then, under perfect foresight, the (m, b)

---

[3] As usual, the exercise disregards the contradiction implicit in disturbing a
perfect foresight path.

pair follows the path *FGH*. On impact, the monetary deceleration causes a fall in the price level, since individuals raise their
demand for real balances. The inflation rate is initially lower
than at the initial steady state but increases over time, and eventually settles at a higher level due to the accumulation of public debt, the interest returns on which must be monetized. The
perfect foresight assumption guarantees that there is no discrete
jump in the price level when the policy of tight money is abandoned. If, when the contractionary monetary policy is started,
the economy is at a point like *K*, where the *SS* curve is steep, it
is possible to obtain the 'spectacular result' that the reduction
in μ increases the price level and immediately raises the inflation rate above its level at *K*.

A4 INERTIA, RELATIVE PRICES, AND WAGE–PRICE SPIRALS

In order to discuss 'non-monetary' models, it is convenient to
start from a decomposition of the growth rate of the price
index:

$$(A16) \qquad \pi_t = \alpha\mu_t^F + (1 - \alpha)\pi_t^A$$

The inflation rate in period *t* is written as a weighted sum of the
rate of increase of flexprices (π_t^F) and fix (or 'administered')
prices (π_t^A), with the weights being those of the aggregate price
index, here assumed for simplicity to be calculated as a geo-
metric rather than an arithmetic mean:

$$(A17) \qquad \pi_t^A = \lambda_1 W_t + \lambda_2 S_t + K_t^*$$

The rate of increase in fix-prices is assumed to depend linearly
on the rate of growth of the components of unit costs: wages
(W_t) and public sector prices[4] (S_t), with coefficients adding up

[4] In the analysis of an open economy, the rate of change of the nominal
exchange rate is added to these variables. The particular formulation in the text
assumes that public sector prices and the exchange rate enter the inflation
equation only through their effects on manufacturing costs. To incorporate
direct effects of these variables on the price level requires only minor changes
in the model.

to one; the term K_t^* allows for the possibility of changes in the mark-up ($K_t^* > 0$ if mark-ups increase in period t) and may incorporate productivity effects.

(A18) $W_t = \pi_{t-1} + W_t^*$

Price inertia can be generated by staggered forward-looking wage contracts (cf. Blanchard 1983) or by backward-looking indexation. We concentrate here on the second case; for simplicity, we assume nominal wage adjustments to be synchronous. Equation (A18) assumes that the rate of growth of nominal wages is set before the start of period t; the two components are the indexation term and a term for the 'target' increase in real wages, W_t^*, resulting from prior agreements that come into effect in period t. The unit time period in expression (A18) corresponds to that of the indexation scheme in force; this period is typically shorter the higher the 'normal' inflation rate.

Equations (A16) to (A18) can be combined to give:

$$(A19) \quad \pi_t = \pi_{t-1} + \frac{\alpha}{(1-\alpha)\lambda_1}(\pi_t^F - \pi_t) + \frac{\lambda_2}{\lambda_1}(S_t - \pi_t) + \left(W_t^* + \frac{K_t^*}{\lambda_1}\right)$$

This expression includes an 'inflationary persistence' term whose relative importance in determining the inflation rate depends on the share of fix-price goods in the consumption basket and the share of labour in the cost of producing those goods. The two following terms represent relative price changes: the inflation rate increases, *ceteris paribus*, when flex-prices or public sector prices rise relative to the aggregate price level. The less than   self-explanatory term $W_t^* + (K_t^*/\lambda_1)$ in equation (A19), finally, can be given either a 'cost-push' or a 'demand-pull' interpretation. If labour's reservation real wages are set under the presumption that real earnings will rise (so $W_t^* > 0$) but at the same time there is no matching decrease in mark-ups, inflation will accelerate. This term can be interpreted in several ways: as a 'distributive conflict' effect that would find expression in wage demands and mark-ups or as an occasional result of pricing inconsistencies stemming from incoherent expectations. The term, however, can also be viewed as the channel through which aggregate demand affects wages and prices.

A5 MIXED MODELS: SOME EXAMPLES

The class of models in which the inflation rate is influenced both by inertial or relative price effects and by aggregate demand is large. The dynamics of prices and output that result from these models are generally sensitive to the details of the specification. However, many of these models share the properties that, in the steady state, the inflation rate is governed by the rate of money growth while output is at its 'normal' value. This section presents two exercises using models of this type: one in discrete time and another in continuous time. Both are expositional devices, relying on drastic simplifying assumptions.

A5.1 *Inflation and public sector prices with inertia and constant money velocity*

This exercise is based on Heymann and Canavese (1989). The model is summarized in three equations:

(A20) $\pi_t = \pi_{t-1} + \beta_1 (\bar{S}_t - \bar{S}_{t-1}) + \beta_2(y_t - 1),$ $\beta_1, \ \beta_2 > 0$

(A21) $$d(\bar{S}_t, y_t) = m_t - m_{t-1} + m_{t-1} \frac{\pi_t}{1 + \pi_t}$$

(A22) $$m_t = y_t$$

The first equation is a variant of (A19), which incorporates an aggregate demand term: the inflation rate is expressed as the sum of an inertial term, the change in the real price of public sector goods ($\bar{S}_t$ denotes that relative price in period t) and the deviation of real output, y_t, from a normal value, set to one by choice of units. Equation (A21) indicates the government's budget constraint in the absence of bond-financing; the real value of the deficit is written as a (decreasing) function of real public sector prices and real income. The final equation simply states

the quantity-theory proposition that real balances are proportional to output.[5]

For a given real price of public sector goods, the inflation rate
is constant whenever output (or the real value of money bal-
ances) is at its normal level, $y = 1$ and, as long as $0 \leq d(\bar{S}, 1) < 1$
that is, as long as the deficit at normal output is lower than the
maximum which can be financed through the inflation tax, there
is a (unique) steady state. Figure A4 indicates the position of
the steady state and the qualitative behaviour of the (m, π) pair
when the system starts away from the stationary point.

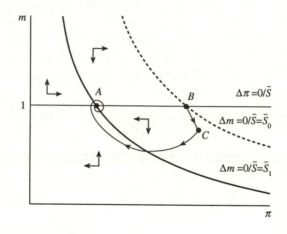

Fig. A4

It can be checked that a steady state like point A is locally
stable. The convergence may be oscillatory if the parameter of
aggregate demand in the price equation (β_2) is sufficiently large.
Consider now the following experiment. The system was located
at a stationary point B. The government now adjusts public sector prices more rapidly than the inflation rate prevailing until

---

[5] The hypothesis is obviously unrealistic. If real money demand was treated
in the usual way, as a function of output and anticipated inflation, the system
of difference equations (A20)–(A22) would be of higher order, except in the
case where expectations are assumed to extrapolate current inflation, i.e.:
$\pi^e_{t+1} = \pi_t$.

then, and makes the real value of those prices increase from $\bar{S}_0$ to $\bar{S}_1$. From then on, real public sector prices are adjusted so that $\bar{S}_t = \bar{S}_1$ for every period. Since the normal output real deficit is now lower, the new steady state will be at a point (A, say) with a lower inflation rate. However, on impact when public sector prices are over-indexed, the inflation rate will accelerate. It can be verified that the increase in $\bar{S}$ implies an initial fall in real money balances and, if the coefficient β_2 is not too large,[6] also a higher initial inflation rate. Therefore, the system will move to a point like c—that is, there will be a period of 'stagflation'—and then converge to the steady state through a path such as BCA in Figure A4.

A5.2 Money demand dynamics with price inertia and perfect foresight

This exercise postulates an 'accelerationist' aggregate supply curve, the continuous time counterpart of an inertial model with a 'Phillips curve' effect. Accelerations in the inflation rate, therefore, are supposed to be proportional to deviations of output from a normal value. The money supply process is given by the condition that seigniorage equals a fixed deficit—for simplicity, the government's real financing requirements are taken to be independent of output. Real money demand depends on output and anticipated inflation. The expectations that enter into this function are assumed to be of the perfect foresight variety.[7] Then, the system is described by:

(A23) $$\dot{\pi}_t = \beta(y_t - 1), \quad \beta > 0$$

(A24) $$d = \dot{m}_t + m_t \pi_t$$

(A25) $$m_t = y_t \, k(\pi_t)$$

---

[6] The condition is $_1(1 + a_2) > {}_2 a_1$, where a_1, a_2 measure (in absolute value) the sensibility of the real deficit with respect to public sector prices and output, respectively.

[7] Under adaptive expectations, the following system of differential equations is of third order, instead of second order.

The qualitative evolution of the (m, π) variables is shown in Figure A5, under the assumption that money demand is such that the normal-output inflation tax curve $(\pi k(\pi))$ is single-peaked and there are two steady states. In each steady state, output is at its normal level, $y = 1$.

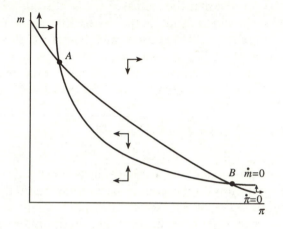

Fig. A5

Near the steady states, the dynamics of (m, π) are governed by:

(A26) $$\dot{m}_t = -\pi^* m_t - m^* \pi_t$$

(A27) $$\dot{\pi}_t = \beta \frac{m_t}{m^*} + \beta \epsilon \pi_t$$

Where (m^*, π^*) represent steady state values, ϵ is the semi-elasticity of money demand at the steady state and the variables (m, π) are now expressed as deviations from their steady-state values. The sign of $1 - \epsilon\pi^*$ is that of the derivative of the normal-output inflation tax with respect to the inflation rate. Consequently, $1 - \epsilon\pi^* > 0$ at the low inflation steady state, and $1 - \epsilon\pi^* < 0$ at the high inflation one. This means that point B is saddlepath stable, while point A is stable if and only if $\pi^* - \epsilon\beta > 0$. Therefore, if 'frictions' in price adjustment are sufficiently strong (β small) the low inflation equilibrium will be a stable point.

A6   FISCAL INCONSISTENCIES AND HIGH INFLATION

The models of 'high inflations traps' summarized in the previous sections are based on the dynamics of inflationary expectations conditional on a constant fiscal deficit. States of high inflation can also be rationalized as the outcome of 'policy games' where the fiscal deficit is determined endogenously. The argument sketched here (based on Heymann and Sanguinetti 1994) is a variant of existing game-theoretic models of inflationary taxation (cf. Calvo 1978; Barro 1983; Grossman and van Huyck 1986). The model has clear limitations: it does not consider price-setting behaviour and ignores the difficulties agents may face in forming expectations. In exchange, these simplifications allow one to draw straightforward conclusions.

Assume government decisions derive from a loss function which depends on the rate of inflation and the discrepancy between a 'target' level of spending—taken as an exogenous parameter for the sake of the exercise—and actual expenditures. The argument is carried out in discrete time. Period t losses are represented by:

$$(A28) \qquad L_t(g_t, g^*, \pi_t) = \tfrac{1}{2}(g_t - g^*)^2 + \tfrac{1}{2}\alpha\pi_t^2, \quad \alpha > 0$$

where g_t is realized spending and π_t the inflation rate in period t. Note that the government is not modelled as an expenditure-maximizer, since it would not choose to use resources beyond the level g^*.[8]

The authorities can draw revenues from regular taxes and from inflation. Regular tax receipts are subject to the fiscal-lag effect. The model postulates that the 'capacity' to collect taxes in real terms is fixed. Standard tax receipts are given by:

---

[8] This is the main difference between this formulation and the one in Bruno (1990), where the government's loss function is assumed to be linear in the revenue from the inflation tax.

(A29) $$h(\pi_t) = h_0 + \frac{h_1}{1 + \pi_t},$$

where h_0, h_2 are the parameters describing the tax system: $h_0 +$ h_1 indicates the maximum (zero-inflation) attainable tax revenues, and h_1 measures the exposure of the system to the inflationary erosion of real revenues.

Revenues from seigniorage in period t are:

(A30) $$S(\pi_t, \pi_{t+1}^e, \pi_t^e) = m(\pi_{t+1}^e) - m(\pi_t^e) + m(\pi_t^e)\frac{\pi_t}{1 + \pi_t}$$

It is assumed that $m(\pi_t^e)$ is a well-behaved money demand function which depends on expected inflation, such that $m'(\pi^e)$ < 0, $m(\pi^e) \to 0$ when $\pi^e \to \infty$, and $\pi^e\, m(\pi^e)$ is single-peaked. Combining (A29) and (A30), the government's budget constraint is:

(A31) $$g_t = h(\pi_t) + S(\pi_t, \pi_{t+1}^e, \pi_t^e)$$

As is common in the literature, the model postulates that the inflation rate is a choice variable of the government. In addition, the public is assumed to form (correct) forward-looking expectations, and the analysis concentrates on non-reputational equilibria of the game,[9] with a constant $g*$. In a discretionary policy regime, therefore, the government's reaction function in period t results from the minimization of that period's loss.

Thus, the inflation rate in period t solves the problem:

(A32) $$\min \tfrac{1}{2}(g_t - g*)* + \tfrac{1}{2}\alpha\pi_t^2$$
$$ST\ \ g_t = h(\pi_t) + S(\pi_t, \pi_{t+1}^e, \pi_t^e),$$

taking as given the inflationary expectations π_{t+1}^e, π_t^e.

---

[9] Trigger strategies in infinite-horizon games of this sort are known to generate multiple equilibria, and require that atomistic agents somehow co-ordinate their expectations so as to 'agree' on a strategy to discipline the government's choice (cf. Rogoff 1989). Also, the single-period Nash equilibrium, if unique, is the single solution of finite-horizon game. It can be noted that backward-looking expectations would make the decision problem explicitly intertemporal: future levels of money demand would depend directly on the government's current actions.

The corresponding FOC defines implicitly the government's reaction function $\pi_t(\pi_t^e)$:

(A33) $$(g_t - g^*)\frac{(m(\pi_t^e) - h_1)}{(1 + \pi_t)^2} + \alpha\pi_t = 0$$

Imposing the perfect foresight condition, $\pi_t^e = \pi_t$, (A33) implies the Nash equilibrium which describes the path of the inflation rate:

(A34)
$$\left((m(\pi_{t+1}) - m(\pi_t)) + m(\pi_t)\frac{\pi_t}{1 + \pi_t} + h_0 + \frac{h_1}{1 + \pi_t} - g^*\right)\frac{(m(\pi_t) - h_1)}{(1 + \pi_t)^2} + \alpha\pi_t = 0$$

For a fixed g^*, the problem admits a steady state solution[10] in which $\pi_{t+1} = \pi_t = \pi$ and:

(A35) $$\left(m(\pi)\frac{\pi}{1 + \pi} + h_0 + \frac{h_1}{1 + \pi} - g^*\right)\frac{(m(\pi) - h_1)}{(1 + \pi)^2} + \alpha\pi = 0$$

It can be seen that interior solutions $0 < \pi < \infty$ are such that $g < g^*$ and $m(\pi) > h_1$. Since inflation is costly, loss minimization implies that spending will fall short of the target g^*. The second inequality means that the equilibrium inflation rate will always be smaller than $\bar{\pi}$, the value at which $m(\bar{\pi}) = h_1$ and where the revenues from the inflation tax are exactly compensated by the income loss from the fiscal-lag effect.

Expression (A35) can be rewritten as:

(A36)

$$g^* - h_0 - h_1 = d^* = \frac{\pi}{1 + \pi}(m(\pi) - h_1) + \frac{\alpha\pi(1 + \pi)^2}{m(\pi) - h_1} \equiv R(\pi) + H(\pi)$$

---

[10] It can be shown that equation (A34) implies that when the steady state is unique, it is dynamically unstable. The system either settles down at the steady state or it moves along a divergent bubble. We disregard the possibility of such bubble paths in what follows.

This equation implicitly relates the inflation rate to the 'desired' zero-inflation deficit d^*. The expression

$$R(\pi) = (m(\pi) - h_1)\, \pi/(1 + \pi)$$

measures inflation tax revenues net of the inflationary losses on regular taxes: it is a single-peaked function which reaches a maximum at $\pi = \tilde{\pi}$ and equals zero at $\pi = 0$ and $\pi = \bar{\pi}$. The second term on the RHS of (A36), $H(\pi)$, is an increasing, convex function which tends to infinity as $\pi \to \bar{\pi}$. The shape of $R(\pi) + H(\pi)$ depends on the value of α. For large enough values of α, $R(\pi) + H(\pi)$ is an increasing function of π; for small α, it has a local maximum and a local minimum (see Figures A6a and A6b).

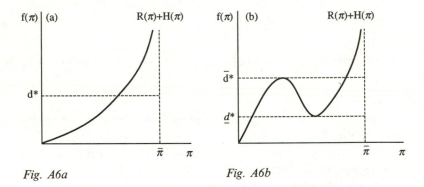

Fig. A6a   Fig. A6b

Therefore, if α is large enough, the inflation rate increases monotonically with d^*. For low values of α, there is an 'intermediate' range of target deficits for which there are multiple equilibrium inflation rates compatible with d^*; however, the

[11] For small α, the $\pi - d^*$ correspondence is S-shaped. Other models find similar relationships between inflation and indicators of fiscal policies (cf. Calvo 1988b). Systems for which such correspondences apply may show path-dependent behaviour, and also 'catastrophic' jumps in inflation for small changes in fiscal policies. However, numerical simulations with this model suggest that the case with a large α is more descriptive of actual economies (cf. Heymann and Sanguinetti 1994).

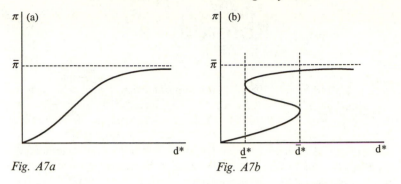

Fig. A7a   Fig. A7b

solutions are unique for both small and very large values of d^* (see Figures A7a and A7b).[11] The region of multiple equilibria is located beyond the maximum of the net inflationary revenue. In any case, at high levels of d^*, stronger pressures on the government's budget result in more inflation, but also in an endogenous fall in public spending, so that the measured deficit eventually declines.

Numerical simulations (cf. Heymann and Sanguinetti 1994) indicate that the model can account for high inflation outcomes for plausible values of the parameters describing government 'preferences', fiscal polices and money demand. However, inflation rates in the hyperinflation range are not obtained as solutions except for very low values of α or extremely high levels of d^*. This suggests that it may be difficult to rationalize true hyperinflations as stationary states of a policy game.

References

Ahumada, Hildegart (1988): 'Saldos monetarios reales e inflación. Pruebas de efectos asimétricos usando técnicas de co-integración (Argentina 1971–1988)', CEMYB-Banco central de la Républica Argentina, working paper.

—— (1991): 'Estimaciones de la demanda de dinero en hiperinflación', CEMYB-Banco Central de la República Argentina, mimeo.

—— Canavese, Alfredo, Sanguinetti, Pablo, and Sosa, Walter-Escudero (1992): 'Efectos distributivos del impuesto inflacionario: algunas estimaciones para la Argentina', *Economía Mexicana*, 2, 329–83.

Aiyagari, Sudhaker and Gertler, Mark (1985): 'The Backing of Government Bonds and Monetarism', *Journal of Monetary Economics*, 16, 19–44.

Alesina, Alberto (1988): 'The End of Large Public Debts', in Giavazzi, F. and Spaventa, L., eds., *High Public Debt: The Italian Experience*, Cambridge: Cambridge University Press.

—— and Drazen, Allan (1991): 'Why are Stabilizations Delayed?', *American Economic Review*, 81, 1170–88.

—— Prati, Alessandro, and Tabellini, Guido (1989): 'Public Confidence and Debt Management: A Model and a Case Study of Italy', in Dornbusch, R. and Draghi, M., eds., *Public Debt Management: Theory and History*, Cambridge: Cambridge University Press.

Arida, Persio and Lara Resende, Andre (1985): 'Inertial Inflation and Monetary Reform: Brazil', in Williamson, John, ed., *Inflation and Indexation*, Washington DC: Institute for International Economics.

Arrow, Kenneth (1959): 'Towards a Theory of Price Adjustment', in Abramovitz, M. *et al.*, eds., *The Allocation of Economic Resources*, Stanford: Stanford University Press.

Auernheimer, Leonardo (1974): 'The Honest Government's Guide to the Revenue from the Creation of Money', *Journal of Political Economy*, 82, 598–606.

Aukrust, Odd (1977): 'Inflation in the Open Economy: A Norwegian Model', in Krause, L. and Salant, W., eds., *Worldwide Inflation*, Washington DC: The Brookings Institution.

Bacha, Edmar (1986): 'A Inércia e o Conflito: O Plano Cruzado e seus Desafios', Discussion Paper 131, Department of Economics, Catholic University, Rio de Janeiro.

Bacha, Edmar (1988): 'Moeda, Inercia e Conflicto: Reflexoes sobre Politicas de Establizacao no Brasil', *Pesquisa e Planejamento Economico*, 18, 1–16.

Baer, Werner and Kerstenetzky, Isaac, eds. (1964): *Inflation and Growth in Latin America*, Homewood, Ill.: Richard Irwin.

Bailey, Martin (1956): 'The Welfare Cost of Inflationary Finance', *Journal of Political Economy*, 64, 93–110.

Ball, Laurence and Romer, David (1989): The Equilibrium and Optimal Timing of Price Changes', *Review of Economic Studies*, 56, 179–98.

—— —— (1991): 'Sticky Prices as Coordination Failure', *American Economic Review*, 81, June, 539–52.

Barro, Robert (1972): 'Inflationary Finance and the Welfare Cost of Inflation', *Journal of Political Economy*, 78, 1228–63.

—— (1983): 'Inflationary Finance Under Discretion and Rules', *Canadian Journal of Economics,* 16, 1–25.

—— and Fischer, Stanley (1976): 'Recent Developments in Monetary Theory', *Journal of Monetary Economics*, 2, 133–67.

—— and Gordon, David (1983*a*): 'Rules , Discretion, and Reputation in a Model of Monetary Policy', *Journal of Monetary Economics*, 12, 101–22.

—— —— (1983*b*): 'A Positive Theory of Monetary Policy in a Natural Rate Model', *Journal of Political Economy*, 91, 589–610.

Bénabou, Roland (1988): 'Search, Price Setting and Inflation', *Review of Economic Studies*, 55, 353–76.

Benhabib, Jess and Day, Richard (1982): 'A Characterization of Erratic Dynamics in the Overlapping Generations Model', *Journal of Economic Dynamics and Control*, 4 February, 37–55.

Bental, Benjamin and Eckstein, Zvi (1988): 'Inflation, Deficits and Seignorage with Expected Stabilization', in Helpman, E., Razin, A., and Sadka, E., eds., *Economic Effects of the Government Budget*, Cambridge, Mass: The MIT Press.

Bernholz, Peer (1988*a*): 'Inflation, Monetary Regime and the Financial Asset Theory of Money', *Kyklos*, 41, 5–34.

—— (1988*b*): 'Hyperinflation and Currency Reform in Bolivia: Studies from a General Perspective', *Journal of Institutional and Theoretical Economics*, 144, 747–71.

Bernholz, Peer (1989): 'Necessary and Sufficient Conditions to End Hyperinflations', Universität Basel, Institut für Volkeswirtschaft, working paper.

Berger, Peter and Luckmann, Thomas (1966): *The Social Construction of Reality: A Treatise in the Sociology of Knowledge*, New York: Doubleday.

Bewley, Truman (1980): 'The Optimum Quantity of Money', in Kareken, J. and Wallace, N., eds., *Models of Monetary Economics*, Minneapolis: Federal Reserve Bank of Minneapolis.

—— (1986): 'Dynamic Implications of the Form of the Budget Constraint', in Sonnenschein, Hugo F., ed., *Models of Economic Dynamics*, New York: Springer Verlag.

—— (1989): 'Market Innovation and Entrepreneurship: A Knightian View', Cowles Foundation Discussion Paper 905, April.

Blanchard, Oliver (1987): 'Individual and Aggregate Price Adjustment', *Brooking Papers on Economic Activity*, 1, 57–122.

—— and Fischer, Stanley (1989): *Lectures on Macroeconomics*, Cambridge, Mass.: The MIT Press.

—— and Kiyotaki, Nobuhiro (1987): 'Monopolistic Competition and the Effect of Aggregate Demand', *American Economic Review*, 77, 647–66.

Blejer, Mario (1983): 'The Anatomy of Inflation: The Variability of Relative Commodity Prices in Argentina', *Journal of Money, Credit and Banking*, 15, 469–82.

—— and Leiderman, Leonardo (1980): 'On the Real Effects of Inflation and Relative-Price Variability: Some Empirical Evidence', *Review of Economics and Statistics*, 62, 539–44.

—— and Cheasty, Adrienne (1991): 'The Measurement of Fiscal Deficits: Analytical and Methodological Issues', *Journal of Economic Literature*, 29, 1644–78.

Bomberger, William and Makinen, Gail (1980): 'Indexation, Inflationary Finance and Hyperinflation: The 1945–46 Hungarian Experience', *Journal of Political Economy*, 88, 550–60.

—— —— (1983): 'The Hungarian Hyperinflation and Stabilization of 1945–46', *Journal of Political Economy*, 91, 801–24.

Bresciani-Turroni, Costantino (1937): *The Economics of Inflation*, London: Barnes and Noble.

Bresser Pereira, Luiz and Nakano, Yoshiaki (1987): *The Theory of Inertial Inflation*, London: Lynne Rienner.

Brock, William (1989): 'Reserve Requirements and the Inflation Tax'; *Journal of Money, Credit and Banking*, 21, 106–21.

Bronfenbrenner, Martin and Holzman, Franklyn (1963): 'A Survey of Inflation Theory', *American Economic Review*, 53, September, 593–661.

Bruno, Michael (1986): 'Sharp Disinflation Strategy: Israel 1985', *Economic Policy*, 2, 379–402.

—— (1988): 'Opening Up: Liberalization with Stabilization', in Dornbusch, R. and Helmers, F. L., eds., *The Open Economy*, New York: The World Bank and Oxford University Press.

—— (1989): 'Econometrics and the Design of Economics Reform', *Econometrica*, 57, 275–6.

—— (1990): 'High Inflations and the Nominal Anchors of an Open Economy', NBER working paper #3518, November.

—— Di Tella, Guido, Dornbusch, Rudiger, and Fischer, Stanley (1987): *Inflation Stabilization: The Experience of Israel, Argentina, Brazil, Bolivia and Mexico*, Cambridge, Mass.: MIT Press.

—— and Fischer, Stanley (1990): 'Seigniorage, Operating Rules and the High Inflation Trap', *Quarterly Journal of Economics*, 105(2), May, 353–74.

—— Fischer, Stanley, Helpman, Elhanan, Liviatan, Nissan, and Meridor, Leora, eds. (1991): *Lessons of Economic Stabilization and its Aftermath*, Cambridge, Mass.: MIT Press.

—— and Meridor, Leora (1991): 'The Costly Transition from Stabilization to Sustainable Growth with Price Stability', in Bruno, M., Fischer, S., Helpman, E., Liviatan, N., and Meridor, L., eds., *Lessons of Economic Stabilization and its Aftermath*, Cambridge, Mass.: MIT Press.

Buiter, Willem (1983): 'Measurement of the Public Sector Deficit and its Implications for Policy Evaluation and Design', *IMF Staff Papers*, 30, 306–49.

—— (1987): 'A Fiscal Theory of Hyperdeflations? Some Surprising Monetarist Arithmetic', *Oxford Economic Papers*, 39, 111–18.

Cagan, Phillip (1956): 'The Monetary Dynamics of Hyperinflation', in M. Friedman, ed., *Studies in the Quantity Theory of Money*, Chicago: Univ. of Chicago Press.

Calvo, Guillermo (1978): On the Time Consistency of Optimal Policy in a Monetary Economy', *Econometrica*, 46, 1411–28.

—— (1988a): 'Servicing the Public Debt: The Role of Expectations', *American Economic Review*, 78, 647–61.

—— (1988b): 'Controlling Inflation: The Problem of Nonindexed Debt', in Edwards, S. and Larrain, F., eds., *Debt, Adjustment and Recovery*, Oxford: Blackwell.

212   *References*

Calvo, Guillermo and Guidotti, Pablo (1990): 'Indexation and the Maturity of Government Bonds: An Exploratory Model', in Dornbusch, R. and Draghi, M., eds., *Public Debt Management: Theory and History*, Cambridge: Cambridge University Press.

—— and Végh Carlos (1992): 'Inflation Stabilization and Nominal Anchors', International Monetary Fund Paper on Policy Analysis and Assessment, 92/4.

—— —— (1993): 'Exchange-Rate-Based Stabilization under Imperfect Credibility', in Frisch, Helmut and Wörgötter, Andreas, eds., *Open-Economy Macroeconomics*, London: Macmillan.

Campbell, Colin and Dougan, William, eds. (1986): *Alternative Monetary Regimes*, Baltimore: Johns Hopkins University Press.

Canavese, Alfredo (1982): 'The Structuralist Explanation in the Theory of Inflation', *World Development*, 10(7), July, 523–9.

—— (1992): 'Hyperinflation and Convertibility-Based Stabilization in Argentina', in Zini, A., ed., *The Market and the State in Economic Development in the 1990s*, North Holland, forthcoming.

—— and Heymann, Daniel (1989): 'Indexación, Rezagos Fiscales e Inflación: Un Análisis de Estabilidad', in Chisari, O. and Olivera, J., eds., *Aspectos fiscales de la Inflacion*, Anales de la Academia Nacional de Ciencias Económicas de Buenos Aires.

—— —— (1991): 'Indización, rezagos fiscales e inflación', *Estudios Economicos*, 6(1), January–June, 33–46.

Canitrot, Adolfo (1975): 'La Experiencia Populista de Redistribución de Ingresos', *Desarrollo Económico*, 15 (59), 331–54.

Carciofi, Ricardo (1990: 'La Desarticulación del Pacto Fiscal. Una Interpretación sobre la Evolución del Sector Público Argentino en las Dos Ultimas Décadas', CEPAL Buenos Aires, working paper 36.

Cardoso, Eliana (1991): 'From Inertia to Megainflation: Brazil in the 1980s', in Bruno, Fisher, Helpman, Liviatan, and Meridor, eds., *Lessons of Economic Stabilization*.

Casella, Alessandro and Feinstein, Jonathan (1990): 'Inflation and the Organization of Exchange', *Journal of Political Economy*, 98, 1–27.

CEPAL (1991): 'Las Finanzas Públicas de América Latina en la Década de 1980', in *Estudio Economico de America Latina y el Caribe 1990*, 1, Santiago de Chile: CEPAL.

Clower, Robert (1967): 'A Reconsideration of the Microfoundations of Monetary Theory', in Clower, R., ed., *Monetary Theory*, Baltimore: Penguin Books.

—— and Leijonhufvud, Axel (1975): 'The Coordination of Economic Activities: A Keynesian Perspective', *American Economic Review*, May.

References 213

——— ——— (1981): 'Say's Principle: What it Means and Doesn't Mean', as reprinted in Leijonhufvud, A.: *Information and Coordination*, Oxford: Oxford University Press.

Corbo, Vittorio and Solimano, Andrés (1991): 'Chile's Experience with Stabilization Revisited', World Bank Working Paper, WPS 579.

Cortázar, Rene (1983): 'Salarios Nominales e Inflación: Chile 1974–1982', *Estudios Cieplan*, 11, 85–111.

Craver, Earlene (1986): 'The Emigration of the Austrian Economists', *History of Political Economy*, 18(1), Spring, 1–32.

Cukierman, Alex (1979): 'The Relationship between Relative Prices and the General Price Level: A Suggested Interpretation', *American Economic Review*, 69, 444–7.

——— (1980): 'The Effects of Wage Indexation on Macroeconomic Equilibrium: A Generalization', *Journal of Monetary Economics*, 6, 147–70.

——— (1982): 'Relative Price Variability, Inflation and the Allocative Efficiency of the Price System', *Journal of Monetary Economics*, 9, 131–62.

——— (1984): *Inflation, Stagflation, Relative Prices and Imperfect Information*, Cambridge: Cambridge University Press.

——— (1988): 'Rapid Inflation: Deliberate Policy or Miscalculation?', *Carnegie Rochester Conference Series on Public Policy*, 29, 11–76.

——— Edwards, Sebastian and Tabellini, Guido (1992): 'Seigniorage and Political Instability', *American Economic Review*, 82, 537–55.

Dabús, Carlos (1993): *Inflación y Precios Relativos: El Caso Argentino, 1960–1990*, doctoral dissertation, Universidad Nacional del Sur, Bahia Blanca, Argentina.

Danziger, Leif (1987): 'Inflation, Fixed Cost of Price Ajustment and the Measurement of Relative Price Variability: Theory and Evidence', *American Economic Review*, 77, 704–13.

Di Tata, Juan-Carlos (1983): 'Expectations of Others' Expectations and the Transitional Nonneutrality of Fully Believed Systematic Monetary Policy', in Frydman, R. and Phelps, Ed., eds., *Individual Forecasting and Aggregate Outcomes: Rational Expectations Examined*, New York: Cambridge University Press.

Domberger, Simon (1987): 'Relative Price Variability and Inflation: A Disaggregated Analysis', *Journal of Political Economy*, 95, 547–66.

Dornbusch, Rudiger (1976): 'Expectations and Exchange Rate Dynamics', *Journal of Political Economy*, 84, 1161–76.

——— (1980): *Open Economy Macroeconomics*, New York: Basic Books.

214   *References*

Dornbusch, Rudiger (1985): 'Freno a la Hiperinflación: Lecciones sobre la experiencia alemana de los anos 1920–1930', presented in the 3rd Convention, ADEBA, Buenos Aires, mimeo.

—— (1991): 'Credibility and Stabilization', *The Quarterly Journal of Economics*, 106(3), August, 837–50.

—— and De Pablo, Juan-Carlos (1989): 'Debt and Macroeconomic Instability in Argentina', in Sachs, J., ed., *Developing Country Debt and the World Economy*, Chicago: University of Chicago Press.

—— and Edwards, Sebastian, eds. (1991): *The Macroeconomics of Populism in Latin America*, Chicago: University of Chicago Press.

—— and Fischer, Stanley (1986): 'Stopping Hyperinflations: Past and Present', *Weltwritschaftliches Archiv*, 122, 1–46.

—— —— (1991): 'Moderate Inflation', World Bank Working Paper, WPS 807, November.

—— and Simonsen, Mario, eds. (1983): *Inflation, Debt, and Indexation*, Cambridge, Mass.: The MIT Press.

—— —— (1987): 'Inflation Stabilization with Incomes Policy Support', New York: Group of Thirty.

—— Sturzenegger, Federico, and Wolf, Holger (1990): 'Extreme Inflation: Dynamics and Stabilization', *Brooking Papers on Economic Activity*, 2, 1–84.

Dow, James and Werlang, Sergio-Ribeiro (1988): 'Uncertainty Aversion and the Optimal Choice of Portfolio', University of Pennsylvania, CARESS Working Paper, 88–104.

Drazen, Allen (1985): 'Tight Money and Inflation: Further Results', *Journal of Monetary Economics*, 15, 113–20.

Driffill, John, Mizon, Grayham, and Ulph, Alistair (1990): 'Costs of Inflation', in Friedman, B. and Hahn, F., eds., *Handbook of Monetary Economics*, ii, Amsterdam: North Holland.

Easterly, William and Schmidt-Hebbel, Klaus (1991): 'The Macro-economics of Public Sector Deficits: A Synthesis', World Bank working paper.

Edwards, Sebastian (1989): *Real Exchange Rates, Devaluation and Adjustment: Exchange Rate Policy in Developing Countries*, Cambridge, Mass.: MIT Press.

—— and Edwards, Alejandra Cox (1987): *Monetarism and Liberalization: The Chilean Experiment*, Cambridge, Mass.: Ballinger Publ. Co.

—— and Tabellini, Guido (1991): 'Explaining Fiscal Policies and Inflation in Developing Countries', *Journal of International Money and Finance*, 10, 516–48.

References 215

Eichengreen, Barry (1990): 'The Capital Levy in Theory and Practice', in Dornbusch, R. and Draghi, M., eds., *Public Debt Management: Theory and History*, Cambridge: Cambridge University Press.

Eisner, Robert (1984): 'Which Budget Deficit? Some Issues of Measurement and their Implications', *American Economic Review*, 74, 138–43.

—— and Pieper, Paul (1984): 'A New View of the Federal Debt and the Budget Deficit', *American Economic Review*, 74, December, 11–29.

Escudé, Guillermo (1989): 'Gasto Público, Rezagos Fiscales e Inflación bajo Expectativas Racionales', Serie Seminarios, Institutio Torcuato Di Tella.

Evans, Jean and Yarrow, George (1981): 'Some Implications of Alternative Expectations Hypotheses in the Monetary Dynamics of Hyperinflations', *Oxford Economic Papers*, March.

Fernandez, Raquel and Rodrik, Dani (1990): 'Why is Trade Reform so Unpopular? On Status Quo Bias in Policy Reform', NBER Working Paper 3269.

Ferris, J. Stephen (1981): 'A Transactions Theory of Trade Credit', *Quarterly Journal of Economics*, 96, May, 243–70.

Fischer, Stanley (1977): 'Wage Indexation and Macroeconomic Stability', *Journal of Monetary Economics*, Supplemental Series, 5, 107–47.

—— (1981a): 'The Cost and Consequences of Inflation', *Carnegie-Rochester Conference Series on Public Policy*, 15: 5–42.

—— (1981b): 'Relative Shocks, Relative Price Variability, and Inflation', *Brookings Papers on Economic Activity*, 2, 381–431.

—— and Summers, Lawrence (1989): 'Should Governments Learn to Live with Inflation?', *American Economic Review*, 74, 382–7.

Flood, Robert and Garber, Peter (1980): 'An Economic Theory of Monetary Reform', *Journal of Political Economy*, 88, 24–58.

—— —— (1984): 'Collapsing Exchange Rate Regimes: Some Linear Examples', *Journal of International Economics*, 1, 1–16.

—— and Isard, Peter (1989): 'Monetary Policy Strategies', *IMF Staff Papers*, 36, 612–32.

Frenkel, Roberto (1979): 'Decisiones de Precios en Alta Inflación', *Desarrollo Economico*, 19(75), 291–330.

—— (1984): 'Salarios Industriales e Inflacion', Desarrollo Económico, 24(95), 387–414.

Frenkel, Roberto (1990): 'Régimen de Alta Inflación y Nivel de Actividad', in Arellano, J., ed., *Inflación Rebelde en America Latina*, Santiago de Chile: CIEPLAN, Hachette.

Friedman, Milton (1969): *The Optimum Quantity of Money and Other Essays*, Chicago: Aldine.

Frisch, Helmut (1983): *Theories of Inflation*, Cambridge: Cambridge University Press.

Giambiagi, Fabio (1987): 'Aritmetica da Escala Movil: Uma Analise do Comportamento do Salario Real num Regime de Reajuste con Periodicidade Endogena', *Pesquisa e Planejamento Economio*, 17, 743–66.

Glejser, Herbert (1965): 'Inflation, Productivity and Relative Prices: A Statistical Study', *The Review of Economics and Statistics*, 47, 76–80.

Goodwin, Richard M. (1951): 'Iteration, Automatic Computers, and Economic Dynamics', *Metroeconomica*, III, April, 1–7.

Gordon, Robert (1981): 'Output Fluctuations and Gradual Price Adjustment', *Journal of Economic Literature*, 19, 392–528.

—— (1990): 'What is New Keynesian Economics?', *Journal of Economic Literature*, 28, 1115–71.

Gorman, William (1959): 'Separable Utility and Aggregation', *Econometrica*, 27, 469–81.

Graham, Fred (1930): *Exchange, Prices and Production in Hyperinflation: Germany, 1920–1923*, Princeton: Princeton University Press.

Gray, Jo Anna (1976): 'Wage Indexation: A Macroeconomic Approach', *Journal of Monetary Economics*, 2, 221–35.

Grossman, Herschel and van Huyck, John (1986): 'Seigniorage, Inflation and Reputation', *Journal of Monetary Economics*, 18, 21–31.

Guidotti, Pablo E. and Végh, Carlos A. (1992): 'Losing Credibility: The Stabilization Blues', International Monetary Fund Working Paper.

Hahn, Frank (1965): 'On Some Problems of Proving the Existence of Equilibrium in a Monetary Economy', in Hahn, F. and Brechling, F., eds., *The Theory of Interest Rates*, London: Macmillan.

—— (1983): *Money and Inflation*, Cambridge, Mass.: MIT Press.

Harberger, Arnold (1988): 'World Inflation Revisited', in Helpman, E., Razin, A., and Sadka, E., eds., *Economic Effects of the Government Budget*, Cambridge, Mass. and London: MIT Press.

—— and Edwards, Sebastian (1980): 'International Evidence on the Sources of Inflations', paper presented at the Conference on Inflation, Getulio Vargas Foundation, Rio de Janeiro.

Hart, Albert G. (1942): 'Risk, Uncertainty and the Unprofitability of Compounding Probabilities', in Lange, O., ed., *Studies in Mathematical Economics and Econometrics*, Chicago: Chicago University Press.

Hart, Oliver (1987): 'Incomplete Contracts', in Eatwell, J., Milgate, M., and Newman, P., eds., *New Palgrave*, ii, London: Macmillan.

Heiner, Ronald (1983): 'The Origin of Predictable Behavior', *American Economic Review*, 83, 560–95.

—— (1986): 'Uncertainty, Signal-Detection Experiments, and Modelling Behavior', in Langlois, R. N., ed., *Economics as Process: Essays in the New Institutional Economics*, Cambridge: Cambridge University Press.

Heymann, Daniel (1983): *A Study in Economic Instability: The Case of Argentina*, UCLA Ph.D. dissertation.

—— (1986): *Tres Ensayos sobre Inflacion y Políticas de Establización*, Santiago de Chile: CEPAL.

—— (1990): 'Decisiones con conocimiento limitado', *Revista de Economía*, 4, 23–38.

—— (1991): 'From Sharp Disinflation to Hyperinflation, Twice: The Argentine Experience', in Bruno, Fischer, Helpman, Liviatan, and Meridor, eds., *Lessons of Economic Stabilization*.

—— (1992): 'Notes on Very High Inflation and Stabilization', in Vercelli, A. and Dimitri, N., eds., *Microeconomics: A Survey of Research Strategies*, Oxford: Oxford University Press.

—— and Canavese, Alfredo (1989): 'Tarifas Públicas y Déficit Fiscal: Compromisos entre Inflación de Corto y Largo Plazo', *Revista de Economía*, 3, 37–52.

—— and Navajas, Fernando (1991*a*): 'Conflicto Distributivo y Déficit Fiscal: Notas sobre la Experiencia Argentina 1970–1987', *Desarrollo Económico*, 29(115), 309–30.

—— —— and Warnes, Ignacio (1991*b*): 'Conflicto Distributivo y Deficit Fiscal: Algunos Juegos Inflacionarios', *El Trimestre Económico*, 58, 101–37.

—— and Sanguinetti, Pablo (1994): 'Fiscal Inconsistencies and High Inflation', *Journal of Development Economics*, 43, 85–104.

Hicks, John Richard (1965): *Capital and Growth*, Oxford: Clarendon Press.

—— (1969): *A Theory of Economic History*, Oxford: Clarendon Press.

—— (1974): *The Crisis of Keynesian Economics*, New York: Basic Books.

Hicks, John Richard (1989): *A Market Theory of Money*, Oxford: Clarendon Press.

218 *References*

Hirsch, Fred and Goldthorpe, John, eds. (1978): *The Political Economy of Inflation*, London: Robertson.

Hirschman, Albert (1963): *Journeys Toward Progress: Studies of Economic Policy-Making in Latin America*, Cambridge: Harvard University Press.

—— (1970: *Exit, Voice and Loyalty*, Cambridge: Cambridge University Press.

—— (1980): 'La Matriz Social y Política de la Inflación: Elaboración sobre la Experiencia Latinoamericana', *El Trimestre Económico*, 187, July–September, 679–709.

Howitt, Peter (1990): 'Zero Inflation as a Long-Term Target for Monetary Policy', in Lipsey, Richard G. ed., *Zero Inflation*, Toronto: C. D. Howe Institute.

—— (1993): 'Cash in Advance, Microfoundations in Retreat', paper delivered at Conference on 'Inflation, Information, and Institutions', Montevideo, 6 September.

Huberman, Bernardo (1990): 'The Social Mind', Xerox Research Center, working paper.

Jones, Robert and Ostroy, Joseph (1984): 'Flexibility and Uncertainty', *Review of Economic Studies*, 164, January, 13–32.

Jonung, Lars (1981): 'Perceived and Expected Inflation in Sweden', *American Economic Review*, 71(5), December, 961–8.

—— (1990): *The Political Economy of Price Controls*, Aldershot: Gower.

Kaufman, Martin (1992): 'The Unit of Account Function in Hyperinflation: Argentina 1989–1990', UCLA, mimeo.

Keynes, John Maynard (1923): *A Tract on Monetary Reform*, New York: Harcourt Brace.

—— (1936): *The General Theory of Employment, Interest and Money*, New York: Harcourt Brace.

Kharas, Homi and Pinto, Brian (1989): 'Exchange Rate Rules, Black Market Premia and Fiscal Deficits: The Bolivian Hyperinflation', *Review of Economic Studies*, 56, 435–48.

Kiguel, Miguel (1989): 'Budget Deficits, Stability and the Monetary Dynamics of Hyperinflations', *Journal of Money, Credit and Banking*, 21, 148–57.

—— and Liviatan, Nissan (1988): 'Inflationary Rigidities and Orthodox Stabilization Policies: Lessons from Latin America', *The World Bank Economic Review*, 2, 273–98.

—— —— (1991): 'The Inflation-Stabilization Cycles in Argentina and Brazil', in Bruno, Fischer, Helpman, Liviatan, and Meridor, eds., *Lessons of Economic Stabilization*.

King, Robert and Plosser, Charles (1985): 'Money, Deficits, and Inflation', *Carnegie-Rochester Series on Pubic Policy*, 22, Spring, 147–95.

Kiyotaki, Nobuhiro and Wright, Randall (1989): 'On Money as a Medium of Exchange', *Journal of Political Economy*, 97, 927–54.

—— —— (1992): 'Acceptability, Means of Payment, and Media of Exchange', *Federal Reserve Bank of Minneapolis Quarterly Review*, 16, Summer, 18–21.

Klein, Benjamin (1976): 'The Social Cost of Recent Inflation: The Mirage of Steady Anticipated Inflation', *Journal of Monetary Economics*-Supplemental Series, 3, 185–212.

Kormendi, Roger and Meguire, Phillip (1985): 'Macroeconomic Determinants of Growth: Cross-country Evidence', *Journal of Monetary Economics*, 12, 141–63.

Kornai, János (1980): *The Economy of Shortage*, Volume B, Amsterdam: North Holland.

—— (1986): 'The Soft Budget Constraint', *Kyklos*, 39, 3–30.

Krasker, William (1980): 'The "Peso Problem" in Testing the Efficiency of Foreign Exchange Markets', *Journal of Monetary Economics*, 6, 269–76.

Krugman, Paul 91979): 'A Model of Balance of Payment Crises', *Journal of Money, Credit and Banking*, 11, 311–25.

Labán, Raúl and Sturzenegger, Federico (1991): 'Distributional Conflict, Financial Adaptation and Delayed Stabilization', *Economics and Politics*, forthcoming.

Lach, Saul and Tsiddon, Daniel (1992): 'The Behavior of Prices and Inflation: An Empirical Analysis of Disaggregated Price Data', *Journal of Political Economy*, 100, April, 349–89.

Laidler, David (1991): *The Golden Age of the Quantity Theory*, Princeton: Princeton University Press.

—— and Parkin, Michael (1975): 'Inflation—A Survey', *Economic Journal*, 85, December, 741–809.

League of Nations (1946): *The Course and Control of Inflation: A Review of Monetary Experience in Europe After World War I*, Geneva: League of Nations.

Leijonhufvud, Axel (1968): *On Keynesian Economics and the Economics of Keynes*, New York: Oxford University Press.

Leijonhufvud, Axel (1973): 'Effective Demand Failures', *Swedish Journal of Economics*, 75, 27–58.

—— (1974): 'Maximization and Marshall', unpublished.

Leijonhufvud, Axel (1977): 'Cost and Consequences of Inflation', in Harcourt, G., ed., *The Microeconomic Foundations of Macroeconomics*, London: Macmillan, reprinted in Leijonhufvud (1981*a*).

—— (1981*a*): *Information and Coordination: Essays in Macroeconomics*, New York: Oxford University Press.

—— (1981*b*): 'The Wicksell Connection: Variations on a Theme', in Leijonhufvud 1981*a*.

—— (1984): 'Inflation and Economic Performance', in Siegel, B., ed., *Money in Crisis*, Pacific Institute.

—— (1986*a*): 'Rules with some Discretion', in Campbell and Dougan, eds., *Alternative Monetary Regimes*.

—— (1986*b*): 'Capitalism and the Factory System', in Langlois, R. N., ed., *Economics as Process: Essays in the New Institutional Economics*, Cambridge: Cambridge University Press.

—— (1993*a*): 'Problems of Socialist Transformation: Kazakhstan 1991', in Somogyi, Lazlo, ed., *The Political Economy of the Transition Process in Eastern Europe*, Aldershot: Edward Elgar.

—— (1993*b*): 'The Nature of the Depression in the Former Soviet Union', *New Left Review*, 199, May–June 1993, 120–6.

Lewis, Alain (1985): 'On Effectively Computable Realizations of Choice Functions', *Mathematical Social Sciences*, 10, 43–80.

Lindahl, Erik (1924): *Penningpolitikens mål och medel*, Malmö: Förlagsaktiebolaget.

Lippman, Steven A. and McCall, John J. (1986): 'An Operational Measure of Liquidity', *American Economic Review*, 76, March, 43–55.

Lipsey, Richard (1981): 'The Understanding and Control of Inflation: Is there a Crisis in Macroeconomics?', *Canadian Journal of Economics*, November, 15(4), 545–76.

Lizondo, Saúl (1987): 'Exchange Rate Differentials and Balance of Payment under Dual Exchange Rate Markets', *Journal of Development Economics*, 26, 37–53.

Llach, Juan (1987): 'La Naturaleza Institucional e Internacional de las Hiperinflaciones', *Desrrollo Económico*, 26, no. 104, 527–60.

Logue, Dennis E. and Sweeney, Richard J. (1981): 'Inflation and Real Growth: Some Empirical Results', *Journal of Money, Credit and Banking*, 13, (November), 497–501.

Lohmann, Susanne (1992): 'Optimal Commitment in Monetary Policy: Credibility versus Flexibility', *American Economic Review*, 82 (December), 273–86.

Lopes, Francisco (1985): 'Inflacao inercial, hiperinflacao e desinflacao: Notas e conjeturas', *Revista de Economia Politica*, 5 (April–June), 135–51.

—— (1986): *O Choque Heterodoxo*, Rio de Janeiro: Editora Campus.

Lucas, Robert (1973): 'Some International Evidence on Output-Inflation Tradeoffs', *American Economic Review*, 68, 326–34.

—— (1981*a*): 'Tobin and Monetarism: A Review Essay', *Journal of Economic Literature*, 19(2), 567–88.

—— (1981*b*): *Studies in Business-Cycle Theory*, Cambridge, Mass.: MIT Press.

—— (1986): 'Principles of Fiscal and Monetary Policy', *Journal of Monetary Economics*, 17, 117–34.

—— and Stokey, Nancy (1983): 'Optimal Fiscal Policy and Monetary Policy in an Economy without Capital', *Journal of Monetary Economics*, 12, 55–93.

Machinea, Jose-Luis (1989): 'Stabilization Under the Alfonsin Government: A Frustrated Attempt', CEDES Working Paper.

Maier, Charles, (1975): *Recasting Bourgeois Europe: Stabilization in France, Germany and Italy after World War I*, Princeton: Princeton University Press.

Mallon, Richard and Sourrouille, Juan (1975): *Política Económica en una Sociedad Conflictiva*, Buenos Aires: Amorrortu.

Marquez, Jaime and Vining, Daniel (1984): 'Inflation and Relative Price Behavior: A Survey of the Literature', in Ballobon, M., ed., *Economic Perspective: An Annual Survey of Economics*, iii, New York: Harwood Academic Publishers.

McCallum, Bennet (1984): 'Are Bond-financed Deficits Inflationary? A Richardian Analysis', *Journal of Political Economy*, 26(1), February, 123–35.

Milgrom, Paul and Stokey, Nancy (1982): 'Information, Trade and Common Knowledge', *Journal of Economic Theory*, 26(1), February, 17–27.

Minsky, Hyman (1977): 'A Theory of Systemic Fragility', in Altman, E. and Sametz, A., eds., *Financial Crisis: Institutions and Markets in a Fragile Environment*, New York: Wiley.

Modiano, Eduardo (1988): 'The Cruzado First Attempt', in Bruno, Fischer, Helpman, Liviatan, and Meridor, eds., *Lessons of Economic Stabilization*.

Mondino, Guillermo, Sturzenegger, Federico, and Tommasi, Mariano (1994): 'Recurrent High Inflation and Stabilization: A Dynamic Game', UCLA Working Paper no. 678.

Morales, Juan-Antonio (1991): 'The Transition from Stabilization to Sustained Growth in Bolivia', in Bruno, Fischer, Helpman, Liviatan, and Meridor, eds., *Lessons of Economic Stabilization*.

Okun, Arthur (1975): 'Inflation: Its Mechanics and Welfare Costs', *Brooking Papers on Economic Activity*, 2, 351–99.

—— (1981): *Prices and Quantities*, Washington DC: The Brookings Institution.

Olivera, Julio (1964): 'On Structural Inflation and Latin American Structuralism', *Oxford Economic Papers*, 16, November, 321–32.

—— (1967): 'Money, Prices and Fiscal Lags: A Note on the Dynamics of Inflation', *Banca Nazionale del Lavoro Quarterly Review*, 20, 258–67.

—— (1970): 'On Passive Money', *Journal of Political Economy*, 78, 805–14.

Orphanids, Athanasios and Solow, Robert (1990): 'Money, inflation and Growth', in Friedman, B. and Hahn, F., eds., *Handbook of Monetary Economics*, Amsterdam: North-Holland.

Ortiz, Guillermo (1991): 'Mexico Beyond the Debt Crisis: Toward Sustainable Growth with Price Stability', in Bruno, Fischer, Helpman, Liviatan, and Meridor, eds., *Lessons of Economic Stabilization*.

Ostroy, Joseph (1973): 'The Informational Efficiency of Monetary Exchange', *American Economic Review*, 63, 597–610.

—— and Starr, Ross (1990): 'The Transactions Role of Money', in Friedman, B. and Hahn, F., eds., *Handbook of Monetary Economics*.

Pagan, Adrian, Hall, Anthony, and Trivedi, Pravin (1983): 'Assessing the Variability of Inflation', *Review of Economic Studies*, 50, 575–96.

Palerm, Angel (1990): *Price Formation and Relative Price Variability in an Inflationary Environment*, UCLA Ph.D. dissertation.

—— (1991): 'Market Structure and Price Flexibility', *Journal of Development Economics*, 36(1), July, 37–54.

Parker, Geoffrey (1974): 'The Emergence of Modern Finance in Europe, 1500–1730', in Cipolla, C., ed., *The Fontana Economic History of Europe*, ii, Glasgow: Williams Collins.

Parks, Robert (1978): 'Inflation and Relative Price Variability', *Journal of Political Economy*, 86, 79–95.

Persson, Mats, Persson, Torsten, and Svensson, Lars (1987): 'Time Consistency of Fiscal and Monetary Policy', *Econometrica*, 55, 1419–32.

Persson, Torsten and Tabellini, Guido (1990): *Macroeconomic Policy, Credibility and Politics*, Chur and London: Harwood Academic Publishers.

Phelps, Edmund (1970): *Microeconomic Foundations of Employment and Inflation Theory*, New York: Norton.

—— (1973): 'Inflation in the Theory of Public Finance', *Swedish Journal of Economics*, 75(1), March, 67–82.

—— (1983): 'The Trouble with "Rational Expectations" and the Problem of Inflation Stabilization', in Frydman, R. and Phelps, E., eds., *Individual Forecasting and Aggregate Outcomes: Rational Expectations Examined*, New York: Cambridge University Press.

Piterman, Sylvia (1988): 'The Irreversibility of the Relationship between Inflation and Real Money Balances', Bank of Israel Economic Review, 60.

Prebisch, Raul (1982): 'Crisis Inflacionaria del Capitalismo', *El Trimestre Económico*, 54, 207–34.

Ramos, Joseph (1986): *Neo-Conservative Economics in the Southern Cone of Latin America*, Baltimore: Johns Hopkins University Press.

Robinson, Joan (1938): 'Review of The Economics of Inflation by C. Bresciani-Turroni', *Economic Journal*, September.

Rodriguez, Calixto (1978): 'A Stylized Model of the Devaluation–Inflation Spiral', *IMF Staff Papers*, 25, 76–89.

—— (1979): 'El Plan Argentino del 20 de Diciembre', CEMA Working Paper.

Rodrik, Dani (1990): 'How Should Structural Adjustment Programmes be Designed?', *World Development*, 18, 933–48.

Rogoff, Kenneth (1989): 'Reputation, Coordination, and Monetary Policy', in Barro, R., ed., *Modern Business Cycle Theory*, Cambridge, Mass.: Harvard University Press.

Rustem, Berc and Velupillai, Kumaraswamy (1990): 'Rationality, Computability and Complexity', *Journal of Economic Dynamics and Control*, 14, 419–32.

Sachs, Jeffery (1987): 'The Bolivian Hyperinflation and Stabilization', *American Economic Review*, 77, 279–83.

—— ed. (1989): *Developing Country Debt and the World Economy*, Chicago: The University of Chicago Press.

Sanguinetti, Pablo (1992): *Fiscal Policy Coordination and Tax Reform in High Inflation*, UCLA Ph.D. dissertation.

Santaella, Julio (1992): *Stabilization Programs, Credibility and External Enforcement*, UCLA Ph.D. dissertation.

Sargent, Thomas (1977): 'The Demand for Money During Hyperinflation under Rational Expectations', *International Economic Review*, 18(1), February, 58–82.

Sargent, Thomas (1982): 'The Ends of Four Big Inflations', in Hall, R., ed., *Inflation: Causes and Effects*, Chicago: The University of Chicago Press.

—— (1987a): 'Inflation and the Government Budget Constraint', in Razin, A. and Sadka, E., eds., *Economic Policy Theory and Practice*, London: Macmillan.

—— (1987b): *Dynamic Macroeconomic Theory*, Cambridge Mass.: Harvard University Press.

—— (1993): *Bounded Rationality in Macroeconomics*, Oxford: Oxford University Press.

—— and Wallace, Neil (1973a): 'Rational Expectations and The Dynamics of Hyperinflation', *International Economic Review*, 14, 328–50.

—— —— (1973b): 'The Stability of Models of Money and Growth with Perfect Foresight', *Econometrica*, 41, 1043–8.

—— —— (1981): 'Some Unpleasant Monetarist Arithmetic', *Federal Reserve Bank of Minneapolis Quarterly Review*, Winter, 15–31.

Savastano, Miguel (1990): *Speculative Attacks and Currency Substitution Under Managed Exchange Rate Regimes in Developing Countries*', UCLA Ph.D. dissertation.

—— (1992): 'Collapse of a Crawling Peg Regime in the Presence of a Government Budget Constraint', *IMF Staff Papers*, 79–100.

Sheshinski, Eytan and Weiss, Yoram (1977): 'Inflation and the Cost of Price Adjustment', *Review of Economic Studies*, 44, 287–303.

—— Tishler, Asher, and Weiss, Yoram (1981): 'Inflation and Costs of Adjustment, and the Amplitude of Real Price Changes', in Flanders, J. and Razin, A. eds., *Development in an Inflationary World*, New York: Academic Press.

Shubik, Martin (1990): 'The Game Theoretic Approach to the Theory of Money and Financial Institutions', in Friedman, B. and Hahn, F., eds., *Handbook of Monetary Economics*, Amsterdam: North-Holland.

Simonsen, Mario (1983): 'Indexation: Current Theory and the Brazilian Experience', in Dornbusch, R. and Simonsen, M., eds., *Inflation, Debt and Indexation*, Cambridge, Mass.: The MIT Press.

—— (1987): 'Price Stabilization and Income Policies: Theory and the Brazilian Case Study', in Bruno, Di Tella, Dornbusch, and Fischer, eds., *Inflation Stabilization*.

Stiglitz, Joseph (1969): 'A Re-Examination of the Modigliani–Miller Theorem', *American Economic Review*, 59, 748–93.

Strotz, Robert (1957): 'The Empirical Implications of a Utility Tree', *Econometrica*, 25, 269–80.

Sturzenegger, Federico (1992*a*): 'Currency Substitution and the Regressivity of Inflationary Taxation', *Revista de Análisis Económico*, 7, 177–92.

—— (1992*b*): 'Inflation and Social Welfare in a Model with Endogenous Financial Adaptation', National Bureau of Economic Research, Working Paper no. 4103.

—— and Tommasi, Mariano (1994): 'The Distribution of Political Power, the Costs of Rent-seeking, and Economic Growth', *Economic Inquiry*, XXXII, April, 236–48.

Sunkel, Osvaldo, Maynard, Geoffrey, Sears, David, and Olivera, Julio (1973): *Inflación y Estructura Económica*, Buenos Aires: Paidos.

Tanzi, Vito (1977): 'Inflation, Lags in Collection and the Real Value of Tax Revenue', *IMF Staff Papers*, 24, 154–67.

—— Blejer, Mario, and Teijeiro, Mario (1987): 'Inflation and the Measurement of Fiscal Deficits', *IMF Staff Papers*, 34, 711–38.

Taylor, John (1980): 'Aggregate Dynamics and Staggered Contracts', *Journal of Political Economy*, 88, 1–23.

Tommasi, Mariano (1992): 'Inflation and Relative Prices: Evidence from Argentina', in Sheshinksi, E. and Weiss, Y., eds., *Optimal Pricing, Inflation and the Cost of Price Adjustment*, Cambridge, Mass.: The MIT Press.

—— (1994): 'The Consequences of Price Instability on Search Markets: Towards Understanding the Effects of Inflation', *American Economic Review*, forthcoming.

Van Hoomissen, Theresa (1988): 'Price Dispersion and Inflation: Evidence from Israel', *Journal of Political Economy*, 96, 1303–14.

Végh, Carlos A. (1992): 'Stopping High Inflation: An Analytical Overview', *IMF Staff papers*, 39:2.

Velupillai, Kumaraswamy (1986): 'Computability in Decision Processes', unpublished.

Vining, Daniel and Elwertowski, Thomas (1976): 'The Relationship between Relative Prices and the General Price Level', *American Economic Review*, 66, 699–708.

References

Waldspurger, Carl, Hogg, Tad, Huberman, Bernardo, Kephart, Jeffrey, and Stornetta, Scott (1990): 'SPAWN: A Distributed Computational Economy', Xerox Research Center, Working Paper SSL–89–18.

Weiss, Yoram (1992): 'Inflation and Price Adjustment: A Survey of Findings from Micro-Data', Sackler Institute of Economic Studies, Working Paper, 3–92.

Williamson, John, ed. (1985): *Inflation and Indexation, Argentina, Brazil and Israel*, Washington DC: Institute for International Economics.

Woodford, Michael, (1990): 'The Optimum Quantity of Money', in Friedman, B. M. and Hahn, F., eds., *Handbook of Monetary Economics*.

Yeager, Leland (1960): 'Methodenstreit over Demand Curves', *Journal of Political Economy*, 58, February.

—— (1981): *Experiences with Stopping Inflation*, Washington: American Enterprise Institute.

Name Index

Subject Index